**THE LIFE AND TIMES OF
GARRY P. WALLEN**

An Autobiography
By Garry P. Wallen

The Life and Times of Garry P. Wallen

By: Garry P. Wallen

Edited by: Deborah Brenna

Nephtali Ink Books and More LLC.

Copyright 2024—Garry Wallen

ISBN: 978-1-965046-03-6

Large Print, Archival Edition

All Rights Reserved All rights reserved. 2024

No part of this work or the images within may be reproduced, transmitted, stored or used in any form whatsoever, printed or electronic, without the prior written permission of the publisher.

All images within this book are owned by the author or used with permission.

The opinions, beliefs, and viewpoints expressed by the author in this book are solely those of the author and do not reflect the official policy, position, or opinions of Nephtali Ink. The publisher does not endorse or assume any responsibility for the views expressed by the author.

This book is true to its source and may contain statements that are a reflection of the times. It also contains some natural grammatical and spelling errors that have been left in as indicators of voice and times.

For more information or to inquire about the author, please contact:

Nephtali Ink Books and More LLC

https://www.nephtaliink.com

info@nephtaliink.com

FOREWORD

I have had the wonderful privilege of reading, editing, and publishing this, my dad's autobiography. Dad has always felt that he wasn't much for book learning and struggled with the language arts. He is also dyslexic. These things stole a lot of his confidence when he was a young person, and I think he worried about what some folks might think about this book. I personally think he did a fantastic job with it. If you listen closely, you can hear his voice. I hope that those who read this in the future, long after he is gone, will know him like I have known him, and that his voice will live on in their hearts like it always will in mine.

I would also like to point out the wonderful historical aspect that this book will provide for generations to come. It's not often we get to view the past from the perspective of an average person who lived it. Dad did a great job of capturing what it was like to grow up in the '40s and '50s in rural Michigan. It really is a neat perspective on a much simpler time in our history. Dad's account of his time in the military, during the Vietnam War, is also a unique one. So often we hear about all the horrors of war (which is important) but don't get to see any of the background and how life continued during those times. We can also get a sense of the changing times and economy from the 1940s to the 2000s. All of these things are well worth learning.

To know someone is to love them. Reading this book, you will come to know my dad, and it is my hope that you will also come to love him. For the future generations of this family, this is a rare glimpse at where you come from. I think it took a lot of bravery to tell parts of this story. Dad's life was not always easy and had its fair share of complications. Dad was brave enough to tell us all about the choices he made, some of them good, some of them bad, but all of them his own. As we all do, he did his best to navigate the complexities of life, and sometimes he made decisions that would have far-reaching consequences. But, in knowing his heart, I know he made the choices he did with the best intentions. For some of us, who are the closest to this story, there are painful reminders of choices that affected us negatively. There were a few versions of this story, as Dad tried to work through all that went on in the later parts of his first

40 years. He has left some of those things out of this final version, out of respect for those who lived through them, while still staying true to what he experienced. Every story has two sides. Big decisions in families affect everyone. And our best intentions are sometimes lacking. Having lived my own first 40 years, I can tell you that I still have a lot of "growing up," to do. And I know my dad did a lot more growing up and becoming since then, especially as he poured himself into his company and built the legacy we are all proud of. It is my sincerest wish that we all learn something from his triumphant spirit, his stubborn go get 'em attitude, his hard work, and his many successes and failures. His past is our past, his legacy our legacy.

-Deborah Brenna

INTRODUCTION

It is a wonderful thing, this thing we call memory. To go back into your life and search for all those things that have made you who you are. The deeper I go delving into my own personal story, the more I realize why I am the way I am, and who I am. I know myself better and have found a little more satisfaction in my life. Maybe by the time I am finished with my story, I will know if I like myself or not. Life has been really good for me. I grew up in the '50s with loving and caring Parents. Mom and Dad were awesome in spite of all our hardships. They taught seven of us kids the kind of love that could get you through just about anything. I see all the Wallens and the Nietlings in that light. Just a great group of people, full of love for one another. There are over 300 of us now, since my dad, Ed Wallen, and my mom, Pauline Nietling, fell in love and married back in 1935. The 300, of course, includes all the in-laws.

I would like to dedicate the years of my life from 1981 on to my wonderful wife Mary Ann. She has been the love of my life. She has been my best friend; always there as my confidant; there to keep me out of trouble; and there to spread the hugs, kisses and love in this family. She sure has taken up where Mom and Dad left off. We have shared a love for God. We have shared a great love for our children and grandchildren. All 14 of them, including the in-laws of course.

My God has stood beside me in all that I do. He held my hand when it was shaking and has pushed me along a little when I needed it. For those of you who will read this story of my life, after I have passed on, please rest assured that the good Lord has taken me to his home. I will be in a much better place when that happens. I will still be loving all of you from there.

This book will be written to the best of my recollection. I will be turning 82 years old this fall and my mind is still pretty sharp, as far as I can tell. I have been writing in segments. Once you get started it's hard to stop in the middle of a segment of your life. This, so far, has been very rewarding for me as I discover things in my life that had faded so far away. An easy example of that would be the good feelings that I had once felt for my first wife, Janet Korf.

I am trying to be true to myself in this writing and put down the feelings I experience now, as well as in the way I remember feeling them from many days gone past. I would highly recommend to anyone interested in doing a book of their life to DO IT. It is, for sure, a whole new experience of who you are. It must be written true to how you see yourself and remember things. Not as you would want others to see you.

Part of this book could be considered a history of the Edward J. Wallen Sr. family, in the early days of my life and that of my brothers and sisters.

Great Grandpa Frank Wallen
1846-1922

Great Grandma Mary Sloutman Wallen 1854-1940

Great Grandpa John Nietling
1827-1902

Grandparents Theresa and Peter Nietling

Grandpa William Wallen

1878-1971

Grandma Anna Wallen

1881-1972

Bill and Anna's Wedding–

The start of something wonderful for all of us.

Edward Wallen Sr.

1911-2006

Pauline Nietling Wallen

1912-2002

Edward and Pauline's Wedding—This wonderful union set the stage for seven loving children and many that followed after.

THE EARLY YEARS

I was born Garry Peter Wallen on October the 29th, 1942, the third son of Edward and Pauline Nietling Wallen. I am the fifth born in the family. I had two older sisters and two older brothers. I guess I was the tie breaker on the side of the boys. The boys lost out in the long run though, as I was followed by two younger sisters, making us seven strong.

I grew up in a love filled environment. We were poor folks in the matters of money by some people's standards, but so what? We sure did have a warm and wonderful family. Mom and Dad may have had two or three too many kids. I sure am glad they did, as I was number five. They displayed so much love for each other, as well as to all of us.

Mom and Dad had sort of a long-distance relationship. Mom grew up in Chesaning, and Dad was from a little town called Perrington in Gratiot County, Michigan, maybe 45 or 50 miles apart. That didn't deter their love for each other, and after a time of courting, they were married on January the 26th, 1935, at Our Lady of Perpetual Help church in Chesaning. They then moved south, to live in the same rented house with Mom's brother George Nietling and his wife Louise. That was in Gross Pointe Farms, outside of Detroit. The Nietling's lived upstairs, and the Wallen's lived downstairs. My oldest sister, Beverly Ann, and then Elaine Marie were born while they lived there. George and Louise then moved out of that house, and it left my parents with lots of room. Dad had a good job working at the US Royal Tire Factory. He was building tires.

Bev was born on January the 2nd, 1936, and Mom was soon pregnant again, as Elaine was born on the 17th of December, that same year. Wow. Go Dad!

Their thoughts soon turned to owning their own place and they bought a nice little house in Centerline, in 1938, just outside of Detroit. It's sort of funny, that little town was called Centerline due to the fact that it was the first place in Michigan to paint a center line strip down the middle of the road, to help keep the traffic apart.

That little house was great for us boys, because in 1938 my

oldest brother Edward Joseph Jr. was born, and then in 1939, brother Richard Lawrence came along on the 14th of November. Rich always liked to brag that he was the product of Saint Valentines Day, which was exactly nine months behind his birth.

So, Mom and Dad took a little break in the kid production, and I didn't get to be born until almost three years later, on the 29th of October 1942. I was born at home. Money was a little thin, and besides, Mom had to be there to take care of the four other kids. There would be no hospital for the three of us boys. The girls were all born in a hospital.

Beverly was the oldest and could help out some with the rest of us. My Aunt Agnes Wallen (Tootie) came and stayed to help out for about a month after I was born. We kids must have been a handful, with 5 of us in that cute little house.

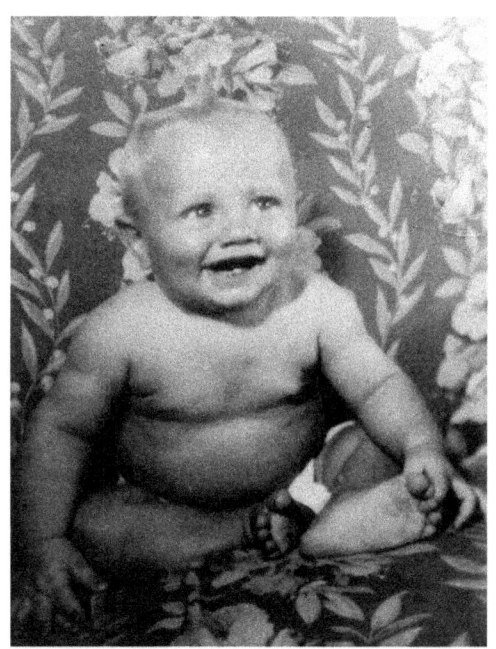
Baby Garry Peter Wallen

World War Two was in full swing at this time. I was born less than a year after the bombing of Pearl Harbor, on December 7th, 1941. A lot of guys were being drafted into the Service at that time, but Dad had not been called up yet. He decided to move us back to Chesaning, Mom's hometown. That was shortly after I was born. So it was, we moved to a farm on the corner of Peet Rd and M-47 (now M-52), just outside of Chesaning, in 1943.

Dad had quit his job in Detroit. We were on the farm for only a few months and the government came calling to Dad with a letter stating that he either had to return to working in the factory or go into the Navy to support the war effort. So, back to Detroit we went, until the end of the war. We lived in a place that Mom called the "chicken co-ops". It was some sort of military housing. She really went through it with five of us kids. To top it off, she had one more, as my beautiful, little sister, Mary, came along in 1945. Just a few months before the end of the war.

Things were looking up, as we were now six kids and two loving parents, and the war was over. We had beaten the Germans and dropped the A-bomb on the Japanese. The world was at peace. Dad moved us back to the farm in Chesaning. Grandpa Bill had worked the farm while we lived in Detroit, and he stayed on for a while after we moved back there. Grandpa Bill Wallen was a great guy, and I learned to love him greatly.

One thing that I would like to say here has a little history to it. There was a prison camp that was set up in Owosso, about 12 miles from our farm. It was mostly German prisoners that were held there during the war, and they had not been returned to Germany by the time we moved back to the farm. It was a common practice for farmers to go to Owosso and pick up four or five of these young guys each day. They would work in the fields for .50 cents a day. Dad took advantage of this and used these guys to work the farm until they were freed to return to Germany, several months after the war ended. Mom would make them lunch and would carry water to them in the fields. She spoke German and could talk with them. Up until their release from prison, they thought that the Germans were winning the war and that they would be the victors. In the end, those poor guys didn't have much to return to, as Germany had mostly been destroyed.

Cousins Carol and Garry Wallen

It was late in 1945, and it was on this farm, where I have my first real memories of my life. Mary was still a brand-new baby, and I was just three when we became farmers. Brother Richard was seven and went to school, so I was left home along with my little sister and Mom. I can remember being out at the road with Mom, holding Mary, and the other 4 kids would get on the school bus. The neighbor lady, from across the road, would be out there as well, with her kids. Why I should remember that I don't know. Maybe

Beverly, Elaine, Eddie, Dick, and Garry

because I knew that Mary and I would have Mom all to ourselves when the school bus left with the rest of us kids.

Just east, and across the street from us, was another farm owned by an older fellow by the name of Merle Cook. He became friends with Dad that fall. Dad asked if he could get milk from him until we could get our own cows. The ole boy said, "Nope, but if you come on down, I'll let you take one of my cows home and use her for the winter." That was the way it was in those days, people loved to help other people. This act of kindness cemented a relationship between us until the day Mr. Cook passed on, in 1968. Merle was a bachelor and had never been married. He became a part of our family, and we loved him.

So, we now had our own cow for our milk. The next year we got our own cows that gave us milk to sell. Dad got a half dozen or so pigs, as well as chickens, and about six very very mean Geese. I remember every one of those critters as being much bigger than I was. Except for maybe some of the chickens, of whom I could chase around.

We had a wonderful mutt dog by the name of Pat. Pat was Dad's best friend and was with him all the time. Pat got himself in trouble a few times though. He would sneak down to Merle's farm and steal a chicken. He didn't bother ours, but he would bring one home from Merle's place. Sometimes it would still be alive. Dad finally cured him of that nasty habit. One day, Dad took the dead chicken and wired it to the inside of ole Pat's mouth. That chicken was there for about two days, and it was stinking by the time he got it undone. Poor dog. Ole Pat goofed up another time, when he got tangled up with a skunk back in the woods. That was an awful smell. Dad did complain a lot about Pat smelling, as every time he would get in the car he would start to fart! We all loved him though. He was a great hunting dog for my Pop.

One day, when Dad had just finished slopping the pigs (feeding them), for some reason, I got into the pig pen. I did not know how dangerous pigs were. I was out there with Dad and somehow, I got stuck in the mud that the hogs had rooted up. I had sunk in deep, and I knew that those hogs could eat a kid rather quickly. I remember screaming as loud as I could, and Dad came a running. I thought I was in deep trouble that time, but Dad saved the day. Those hogs had me surrounded. I was one scared little four-year-old. I can still remember screaming.

Those darn geese were some of the meanest critters I ever came up against. When my brother Richard had to go to the barn, or feed the chickens, he would always carry an empty pale with him, and a stick. He was smart, as he ran, he would whack that pail with the stick and the geese would leave him alone. I got into big trouble one day though, because I had a long stick, and when the goose came after me, I whacked it in the neck and broke it. Not the stick. I broke the goose's neck. Looking back, I bet we had a goose roast that next weekend.

My first major owie happened to me on that farm. I was playing with the back half of a tricycle; the fork and handlebars were missing. I had set the front of the trike on the rear bumper of Dad's car, and it set up there like a regular tricycle. That bumper was a convex shaped piece of steel. I climbed on to the seat, and when I did, the thing slipped off the bumper, bringing my face slamming full force into the sharp edge of the bumper. "Right between the eyes," as they say. I had a major cut. I still have the scar. That is when I first found out what a butterfly bandage was. Dad put me back together, and I am sure it soon healed.

Life was really good to me in those days, because I had a lot of time with just my little sis' and Mom. Mom would work all day every day. She did a lot of ironing of school clothes, as I recall.

Our little family was doing very well, on into 1947, when a real tragedy struck us. Dad was over to my uncle, Art Wallen's, farm. He was on a tractor in a real soft, muddy area, and somehow, the tractor flipped over backwards and pinned Dad underneath. He was stuck there for a while, until Art finally got him out. He had crushed several vertebrae in his back. For a young guy with just an 8th grade education, and a strong will to work in the physical world, he was destroyed. He could not work. He recovered but was in awful pain for many years to come.

So, the farm was sold in 1947 and we moved across town to a small, little farm just south of Chesaning, on Corunna Road. We called it The Blakesley Farm. I was five years old, and to me, this was exciting. I had no concept of what had happened to my Pop. All I remember was that Grandpa Wallen was around a lot more. During the move, our cows were rounded up and driven two miles down the Peet Road and into Chesaning, down Broad Street, across the river and then south two miles, to our

Grandpa Bill Wallen

new place. We were to be there for only a short time, as Dad could not work as a farmer.

For a little five-year-old, this new place was heaven. I remember exploring all those outbuildings and the barn. I found a model airplane in one of the outbuildings, and I had a new toy for a long time. I think that one little discovery had a profound impact on my life, as I have always loved airplanes, even to the present day.

There are fond memories from that place. Grandpa was always around, and Mary and I would run to him when he came in. Grandpa was a big guy, and we would each grab him by a leg, sit on a shoe, and he would walk us around the house like that, and, of course, he had to rough house with us a lot.

One time, when we were at Grandpa's farm for a family outing, my cousin Roxy Wallen threw me into the horse water tank. I was tall enough not to drown, but Mary went screaming to Grandpa. He pulled me out, picked up Roxy, and shoved her under the water. Taught that kid a lesson!

We had a near-fatal incident happen while we lived on that farm. Mom took real sick and ended up with an extreme case of pneumonia. Everything they tried did not work. She just kept fading. The doctor came to the house every day and did not know what more he could do. The whole mood of the family was very somber. Us little kids did not know how bad it was. The doctor finally told Dad that there was one more thing he could try if he could get some. It was a new drug called penicillin. Mom's last chance for life. As soon as he started her on it, she started to improve. That was a "Thank God!" moment, for sure. She made a full recovery that spring, just in time for our next move!

I was in the side yard at the Blakesley house, one day, and had a long string which I had attached to a pop bottle. This meant doom to the big picture window on the side of the house. As I slung the bottle around and around it let go and went right through the big window. Even today, when I drive down Corunna Road, I remember that little happening. I know I was punished but I don't remember how bad it was. I guess I knew I was guilty and deserved it.

It was a neat place to live because my cousin, Chuck Nietling, lived right across the street. He was my age and we played together a lot. He would come over and we played in the outbuildings. Lots of fun for a couple of five-year-olds. One day, we were playing in Chuck's garage where his dad, Uncle Fred, kept his boat. The tongue of the boat trailer sat up on a cement block. We climbed into the back of that boat and were sailing the seven seas when with a large thud and a bounce, we had run aground. The boat fell off the block with a crash. Then we were really grounded! Uncle Freddy was such a nice guy, the family lost him at an early age. I believe he was only 46 when he died.

Just north of the Blakesley house was the house that my mom grew up in. We called it the Nietling house. She lived there until she and Dad were married on January 26th, 1935.

Then, my favorite Aunt and Uncle moved from Kansas, into a house just south of Uncle Freddy Nietling's house. Aunt Francis and Uncle Andy, though I always knew her as Aunt Curlie. A few years later, she would become like my second mom.

Dad was hurting so badly by this time that he had no choice but to sell the rest of the livestock and get into a new line of work. So, in 1948 we moved again. This time it was to Owosso, on Cass Street. We moved into a house that Dad had gotten in some sort of trade. Now, this house was straight out of the movie "A Christmas Story," right down to the window in front, the driveway location, and the front porch. Like in the movie, we even had the bullies on that street.

Dad got himself set up in a tire shop back in Chesaning. It was located downtown, at the corner of Broad Street and Chapman Street, where the soda shop is now. If I remember right, Grandpa Wallen helped Dad a lot there, as well.

So, one day, Dad brought a tire home for me to play with, rolling it around the neighborhood. That did not last long for me though, as the bully kids took it away and rolled it down the street and into the river. I believe that I was sad.

There are a lot of neat things to tell about, from those few months of living there, in Owosso.

We had our very own ice box in that house and the ice man would come every few days. The truck would stop in front of the house and this nice guy would get out and, on Mom's order, he would chip out a certain size chunk of crystal-clear ice. That was great but us kids would always try to be there to beg a little piece of ice from the guy. He was always nice and would accommodate us. We could then spend 20 minutes or so sucking on a crystal of pure cold. No yum, just cold.

We also had a milkman that came every few days with our supply of milk. With six kids, I would believe that we used a lot of milk. It would come in a wire carrier, in bottles, and there was a little cardboard plug with a pull tab in the top of each bottle. The milk was always there early in the morning, as it was cool, and we were sure to be home to bring it into the ice box. Once in a while, there would be a brown bottle of chocolate milk. This would be an extra treat and, of course, it would not last long.

The next really neat thing to come down the street was the guy pushing an ice cream buggy. He would ring a chime-sounding set of bells. I can still hear the "chingie, chingie, chingie," sound as he arrived in front of the house. For five cents you could get a Popsicle Pete popsicle or for a dime you had yourself an ice cream bar. When Mom could afford it, we would have ourselves a treat. The older kids sometimes had their own money and us little guys could just watch. Yes, life could be cruel at that age. We would also collect the popsicle sticks, and if ya got enough of them, you could send off for a special prize. Or they were just fun to play with.

We had two sets of railroad tracts at the end of the backyard, and it was very noisy when a train would rumble on by. It was also a neat place to play. We would see who could walk down the rail the farthest without falling off. And it seemed that there were always things to find along the tracks. We would also pick up coal that had fallen from a train and take it into Mom, to use in the kitchen stove. Yes, we also placed a penny on the track from time to time, but that got old.

One Day, as we were playing peacefully in the front yard, my two oldest sisters came running from the backyard screaming. There was a man laying alongside the tracks. It scared the H out of all of us. Hobos were often seen back there. We all went running to the back yard and Mom made us all stop as she approached the "dead guy." Mom turned around with a really disgusted look on her face. She then broke into her "oh so cool" laugh. Bev and Elaine had put a body together by stuffing some clothes to look like a man. Then they came running and screaming. It was a very good prank to play on the rest of us. I am sure that Dad got a kick out of it when he got home that day. He was a prankster himself.

Speaking of Dad being a prankster. When he was working at the US Royal Tire factory in Detroit, he pulled a good one. According to Dad, there was this really squeamish guy that always ate his lunch with Dad and the other guys. Dad had killed a mouse one day and when it came time for lunch, he brought the mouse. He stuck it just at the other side of his sandwich so it would stick out. He then started to eat his sandwich. Dad said the guy went running and threw up all at the same time. I bet he never ate with Dad again!

The Owosso house was a fun place for us little ones, but my older brothers, Ed and Dick, did not have it so easy. The bullies would try to chase them home and my two brothers learned to fight very well that school year. It's a good thing that I was not attending school that year. I would have been just like that little Randy guy in the "Christmas Story" movie. That would not have been fun.

One day, Mom and Dad loaded all six of us kids into the ole Chevy and we drove to Chesaning to visit our friend Merle Cook. I don't remember how long we were there that day, but I had a fascination with outbuildings. I loved to play there. I overstayed my time on that particular day though. As I emerged out into the sunlight, all was quiet. No brothers, no sisters, and no Mom, no Dad. They had gone home. Merle was nowhere to be seen. I was a five-year-old alone on this great big ole farm. Too many kids, I guess. They forgot me. I was the "quiet one." I ran to Merle's door just screaming scared.

Merle came out and there I was. I bet he got a big chuckle out of that one. So, to calm me down, he put me in his car and drove me two miles to the little town of Oakley. I got a great big ice cream cone and was very happy at that point. When Mom and Dad got home with only five of us, they made a hasty return back to Merle's farm to retrieve me. I think that I had handled it much better than my mom did.

Dad had so much trouble with his bad back, trying to run his tire shop, that he once again had to move on. He opened a gas station in Chesaning. It was located on the corner of Brady Street and North 4th St. He did auto repair and sold gas and oil. My Grandpa Bill Wallen helped Dad a lot in the station.

One day, I got myself a good talking to from Grandpa. He had opened himself a candy bar and a bottle of orange pop. He left it on the counter and went out to pump gas for someone. It was just way too much for a little kid to resist, and away I went with the candy and pop. I went around the side of the station and sat in the sun, knowing I had done wrong. Grandpa was my buddy, but not this time. I was made to dump the pop out and throw the candy away. It was no good because it was stolen. He then gave me a real good talking to. It must have done a lot of good for me as I did not steal again.

THE MERLE COOK FARM

Dad was not real happy with where we lived in Owosso as it was not a good neighborhood for us kids. We ended up moving back to Chesaning and moved in with Merle Cook. We moved onto that farm in 1949. So it was, once again, as spring turned to summer, that we were living in a different house. This time we had a big barn, a corn crib, a tool shed, a milk house, and a not too big, three bed room house to live in. Six kids, Mom and Dad, and Merle. His bedroom was downstairs and the eight of us slept upstairs. Mary and I shared a bunk bed. That was a lot of kids in just one room. When one got sick, we all got sick. Our poor Mom sure had a time of it.

The Cook Farm was just right for Mary and me. We had so much to do. Lots of exploring and fun places.

There was no bathroom in the house when we first moved in, but Dad soon got one installed. The water system was so bad that

Painting by Edward Wallen Sr. *The Cook Farm*

The Cook Farmhouse with Gratts Cook (Merle's brother) and wife, Merle's sister, and Merle.

you had to wait just to fill a water glass. Mary and I had to take our baths in a tub with water heated on a wood stove. Mom was brave to move us in there. The living room was quite small, and my only memory of it was when there was a Christmas tree in there. There was also a fireplace that was never used. There was also a narrow cellar for the furnace and the two big barrels Merle used for his annual cider storage. We learned to love that. There was also a dining room, but I don't remember ever eating in there, it was always full of stuff.

We were much closer to Dad's work, and I would try to go with him any time I had a chance. He would give me old car parts to tear apart an' see if I could put them back together again. Lots of fun, and I was learning. I even pumped gas for him sometimes. I just could not reach the car windows to wash them, as was the custom in those days.

Mary and I had much exploring to do at this new place. We had 40 or 50 acres to explore, and a water pond. Every kid should have a pond to play in. All kinds of frogs to catch. We could get a whole jar full. Once in a while, we could catch ourselves a snake to add to the collection. The pond had water in it all year and that is where the cows would go and drink. We were not allowed to go in the water though, but, well, sometimes we had to go in a little ways, especially when we were after those little water spiders and tadpoles. We could get half a pail full of those little guys. Not very many of 'em ever made it into a frog though, when we had 'em in captivity.

There was a place we came to call the three trees. Three huge Elm trees in a row at the side of the big field behind the house. Merle had dug a big hole there and so there was a large hill of dirt next to the hole. I think that maybe he had planned to bury junk and things in the hole. At any rate, we had a hill to play on with a deep hole next to it and the three big trees for some shade from the summer sun. Mary and I would go on picnics back there with our sandwiches and cookies. That was always fun for us little ones.

There was also a rock garden. There were a lot of rocks in that place, with a lot of trees. We had walnut trees. We had hickory nut trees. And we had a butternut tree that we learned to love a lot. It was so cool to go back there and pick up all the nuts. After shucking them and letting them dry for a month or so, Mom would bake hickory nut cookies and a lot of other neat things with the nuts. At the butternut tree, we picked up the nuts just for eating, as they were so darn tasty!

On the east side of the farm was the best thing of all. There were about 30 apple trees with every kind of apple you could want. Merle even did some grafting, where he would take a branch from one kind of apple tree and graft it to another tree. This allowed for different kinds of apples to grow on the same tree. How cool was that! In the fall we would all go back to the orchard and get as many apples as we could. Merle had made a cider press and we would press out a hundred or so gallons of cider. He had several big ole wood kegs in the cellar. It was cold down there and that cider would stay fresh till spring. What a treat. There was one keg always tapped and he had a little rubber hose down there that you could slip in the plug at the top of the barrel and take a drink. Ice cold and yummy. Come springtime though, the cider would turn hard. Maybe that's why Merle would stay down there with his barrels a lot.

He also had about eight or ten big ole bee hives, with thousands of bees around them in the summertime. They were so cool. If you ever got to watch a large swarm of bees overtaking a spot somewhere, like a light pole or a tree, it's scary, but wow! What a sight. Talk about some real fine honey. We had the very best. Along with lots of beeswax. It would come to the surface in the big ole pot that we heated the honey in, to get it out of the hive wax. I don't remember ever getting a honeybee sting, but those darn yellow jackets, they were always in the apple trees, and the hornets that hung around the house, they got me plenty.

The best apples that I ever ate in my life came from that field of trees. They were called snow apples. Not very big in size but they had a pure white pulp to 'em and oh so good!

Merle was such a nice guy. In the fall, he would walk through the orchard and pick out a bunch of the really best apples. He then would bottle up eight or ten jugs of cider and get out the honey. He loaded all that into his old Chevy and went around to all the neighbors and friends in the neighborhood, passing out his prized goodies. He had such fun and everyone just loved him for it.

We also had a big plot for Mom to plant a garden. We had grape vines, a pear tree, and a tree of plums.

All those outbuildings and a cellar to play in. This was heaven for a six-year-old with a little sister. By the way, the four older kids would not allow us to play with them. I think Mary and I slowed them down too much.

There were two older kids that lived down the road. They were the Adams boys. I think at times they were a little sweet on my two older sisters. Their names were Jerry and Ward Adams. They loved to pull pranks on the Wallen household, of which I will get into later. They played a lot with the older kids.

Left to Right: Mary, Elaine, Bev, Mom (Pauline), Ed, Dick, Garry

STARTING SCHOOL

I started in the first grade in the fall of 1948. I can still remember my first day of class. Either Mom or Dad took me to class that first day and there were a lot of the other mothers or dads with their kids too. I think I remember that day because of Richard Nietling. He cried for at least the first two hours. Richard and I had become good friends before that first day of school. He was my cousin. Actually, he was my double cousin. His mom and my dad were sister and brother, and his dad and my mom were brother and sister. I had gotten to know him from family visits, and we always had great times together. His parents were Aunt Curly and Uncle Andy. They lived on a farm just south of where Uncle Freddy lived. They had a large farm with a big woods, back by the Shiawassee River. So, Richard cried real hard the first day of school and that is probably why I remember that day. He was my best friend at that time. Leon Kulhanek was my other best friend, but he wouldn't be starting school until the next year.

I was now a school kid and my sister, Mary, had to stay home. Except for now she had mom all to herself. I don't remember much about that. I was in school now and learning how to be sociable. I had lots of people to make friends with. Those kids are all still in my memory banks, and I think I still love them all in some sort of way. I was going to a Catholic School and that meant going to Mass every morning before school. We also had nuns for teachers. As I look back, I think that they used all the nice nuns for the grade school kids and put all the mean ones in charge of the older kids. Going back to that classroom I have only a few memories there. The little Dick and Jane books, or maybe that was second grade. The lunch pails and the warm milk that sat in the room until lunchtime, in glass bottles with the little cardboard lids. Yuck! You could not beat our home-grown milk. Especially before it had gone through the separator.

Then there was drawing stuff, which I just loved to do, and we made really neat things to take home for Christmas. I remember the prettiest blue paper that we used for a background in a manger scene. We made pretty stuff and got to hang it in the hall for all to see. Then we could take it home for Mom and Dad. Recess was really great, as we got to play with the other kids and get to know them. Richard Nietling and I were together a lot in those early days of school, and I had some sleepovers at his house which were a lot of fun.

We also got to go spend time at Uncle Art Wallen's Farm. Carol, Marilyn, and Don, our cousins, were Mary and my best friends. We spent a lot of nights at their farm. That was always a hoot for us. There were a million things to do. They had a huge hay mow. The milk house had a tower above it, and we would climb that baby every time we went there. Art had no indoor plumbing. So, we had to carry water for the kitchen, and they had a two-holer toilet out by the milk house.

Those first years in school held my interest a lot and I did pretty well with my grades. I think I learned a lot of the good basics during that time. I also think I learned a lot of people skills at that young age, as that was taught to us in a big way. We had religion classes every day and soon I was ready for my First Holy Communion. I learned about God and Confession and lots of neat songs to sing in church. I would have been in good standings in school if I could have just kept the learning going for myself.

Many years later I learned that I was dyslexic. Sometimes I saw things backward, I guess. As I advanced from one grade to the next, my learning became harder and harder, so I shied away from it. When it came to my schooling, I turned out to be a loser. My self-confidence in school dropped to zero and the nuns were just plain annoyed with me. I don't blame them though. I just would not learn.

As reading became more advanced, I fell further a further behind. Math became almost impossible for me. I learned the basics but that was as far as I got. By the 4th and 5th grades I was a dunce. My people skills were good but academically I was not advancing at all. Life in school was bad for me. Tests were terrifying! I just would not study. With six kids in school, Mom and Dad had little time for me and I think they just accepted that I was not very bright.

Looking back, from my older days, I think that if I had been taught how to study and learn, and why I should learn, I would have done just fine. I proved that to myself later in life. Once I fell behind, my interest was gone and there was no catching up. One year was compounded by the year before and so on it went, until the 7th grade. I will pick it up there a little later.

HOLIDAYS

One Thanksgiving, Dad created a real lively, once in a lifetime event. Pop was always coming up with something fun. It was Thanksgiving Eve and Dad got home just a little after dark. He came in and Mom wanted to know where the turkey that he was supposed to pick up was. So, Dad goes back outside and returns in a few minutes with this gunny bag and that bag was thrashing around. Mary and I were standing there in the kitchen when Dad opened the bag. Out rushed this big, tall, live turkey and it began running around the kitchen. When we tried to catch it, it ran into the living room, hitting every place that might be an escape route. I think we felt bad for the bird, but he was going to be tomorrow's dinner. As I recall, we all tried to catch the darn thing. I think we were all a little afraid of it, if we got it down, as soon as it would squirm, we would let it go. Dad finally tackled the critter and stuffed it back into the bag. A little later, it was dispatched with the drop of an ax. I bet we had a fine turkey dinner that next day. I know it was a fresh bird. Dad never brought home a live one again. As far as I can recall.

In grade school, we always had really neat Christmas times. There were all really good songs of the time. We had all the good drawings and crafts to make and then there were the school plays. We would practice for weeks and then on the big night, each class would have a play to present to our parents. What a joy that was. I was a shepherd one time, and Dad made me a really neat cane to carry. I broke the curved part off just before we were to leave for the play that day. Good ol' Dad, he put black tape on it and it was as good as new. That part of school at Christmas time was always really special. I have such good feelings from that time. Easter was also exciting but not near as good as Christmas.

Mom and Dad always saw to it that our holiday was always over the top. The homemade fudges and cookies and pies. Sugar cookies made in Christmas forms. Cookies made from walnuts and hickory nuts. Way yummy. The tree was always set up a week or so before Christmas.

Sometimes when we got the tree, it looked really skinny and bare. There were times that we could not afford much, so Dad would always bring home extra branches. That would allow him to drill holes in the tree trunk and insert branches as needed, we always had a great tree that way.

One of the joys was making the tree garland. Mom would have us make popcorn and we would make plenty of it. We always had lots of popcorn, as we grew our own. So, with a large tub of the stuff, we would take needles and thread and put together popcorn garland. It looked so good on the tree. We always took the extra and made popcorn balls with Mom's special caramel or maple mix. Dad would decorate with those bubble lights and also the large tree lights. They proved to be a bad thing one year as they would get hot and one time the tree actually caught fire. It was quickly put out and the holiday went on. Those branches that were drilled into the tree always dried out early and were a fire hazard. Two main decorations I remember most about that tree after all these years are, for one, a little Santa that was just a sticker with Santa's picture stuck on large pipe cleaners. For some reason, we always fought over who got to place it on the tree. The other thing I remember is the Star that Dad always placed on top of the tree. That star had a light bulb in the middle of it so the star would light up. Before Mom passed away, she gave me that old star from the 1930s. It still had its box. Both the star and the box were smushed flat, but I pushed and pulled and got it looking quite nice again. We used it here at home with our kids for a number of years until I passed it on to our daughter Debbie. I think she now uses it. It would be over 80 years old by now.

Most of the kids slept in the one big bedroom upstairs. I can still remember, Mom and Dad would go to Midnight Mass, or maybe we would all go on Christmas Eve, anyway, when church was over, it was time to wait for Santa, in bed of course, except that we very rarely ever slept. So, at about 3:00 AM, we would try to sneak downstairs for a quick peek at the goodies. Most years it would be a booming voice stating, you kids get back to bed, Santa has not been here yet. Too late, because we had already seen the toys, but back to bed we would go. How could a kid sleep after that?

Bev. and Elaine got to stay up and help when Santa came. That never was fair. I think I was eight years old when I finally found out about Santa. And then it was Mary that told me the truth. She had gotten it from the older ones.

One Christmas, I remember getting a gas station with all the trimmings. I think I was about six years old then. There were even four or five cars that went with it. It had an elevator to the roof for car parking and there was a car hoist so you could work on the cars. What fun! Dad had a gas station so it was only right that I should have one. Then one year I hit it big. I got an electric train. "JACK POT!" The one Rich had gotten earlier was just a wind-up one. I built all kinds of fancy things to go with my train. It had a light and smoke would come out of it.

One year though, I wasn't so lucky. I had wanted a real carpenter set. That year Mom ordered everything from the Sears and Roebuck wish book. I was to get a carpenter tool set. It was sad because the stuff came a week late and when it did arrive, there was no tool set. It had been backordered. Dad jumped right in there for me though and built a nice toolbox, long enough to put a hand saw in it and then he rounded up a bunch of his old tools and surprised me with a complete set of tools. (Maybe a little rusty but they worked, and I was a happy kid). I think I built stuff with that set.

One Christmas after we had moved into the green house, I got a bunch of model airplanes to put together. That was wonderful for me as I loved airplanes. When I was about 11 or 12, I saw the movie called *The McConnell Story*. It was about an Air Force test pilot who wound up being killed in a plane crash at the end of the movie. I was in love with June Allison and airplanes forever after that. I even joined the Air Force when I got older. So, Mom got me five or six airplanes to put together that Christmas. I loved it.

One year, I had saved up about six dollars, or so, and I bought Mom a nice step stool for the kitchen. She used it for many years.

We had a lot of close times in the old Cook house. Dad had a little saying every time we would get a little out of hand. He would be roughhousing with all the boys, and we would start to get the best of him. That was when he would stop us and proclaim, "FUN IS FUN and TOO MUCH IS NONE." That was his way of calling time out on us. I could only rough house when Mom was not around. She always said that I would get hurt.

Garry, Dad, Ed, and Dick

MEALTIME

Mealtime was always special. We had a large table in the kitchen and Mom would cook up some really neat meals. The big thing though, was, whatever she cooked, that was it for that feedin' time. If you did not like what she served, like liver or boiled cabbage, or mush, or a big pot of beans, you could not ask for anything else, because there was nothing else. Eat or starve except, that is, for in the fall. We could always go to the garden for fresh veggies or fruit.

I remember one time we had this big ole snappin' turtle back in the pond. Merle tried for weeks until he finally caught it. I believe we kids were all around when he killed that thing and cut it up. He gave the meat to Mom so she could make some turtle soup. That mean ole turtle from that muddy ole pond. I bet I ate in the garden that day. I mainly remember Merle trying to kill the thing. He couldn't get it to keep its head out so he could cut it off. In today's terms, it was gross.

I do remember only good feelings though, at mealtime. In those early years, my Dad was not around for many meals. He worked a lot of hours in that gas station as I recall. Merle was there a lot with us. He always made his own breakfast though, and it was almost always yucky poached eggs. I still don't like them. He would never get them completely cooked.

FARMING

The workings of the farm were always exciting to us kids. In the first few years I wasn't old enough to take part in the work, but as I got to be eight or nine I had to carry my own part of the farming. We had a John Deer tractor and I got to drive sometimes when we were hayin'. I was cool then. We had a belt driven conveyor to hoist the hay into the hey mow. The wagon would be brought in from the field, unhooked at the conveyor and then the tractor would be turned around, and the belt would be hooked to it to drive the conveyor. Working in the hay mow was awful. It was always hot, humid and sweaty up there. We put up all the hay that would be needed for the winter months for the cows and then Merle would sell the rest. Merle had his own hay baler that we would use. One of us kids would have to ride on the side of the baler, sitting in a steel seat, and feed baler wire through the bails every so far. Then someone else had to sit on the other side to accept the wires and tie them off. That kept the hay held together until it was used.

For several years while we lived on the Cook Farm, us kids would hire out to a guy that farmed Pickles. I believe his name was Louie Waldo. His farm was south of us on M-47 somewhere around Oakley. We became pickle pickers. It was really hard work. You would stand straddle of the row and then bend over and pick up one side of the bush, pick what was there and then throw the bush the other way and pick what was there. There were always lots of honeybees on the new pickle flowers. As I recall, we had sort of tall, tapered baskets to drag along and put the pickles in. That was a hard day's work for us smaller guys, but we kept up. When we would go home in the afternoon, our hands would be black from all those little picker things on the pickles, but those little hands would have some money in them, and we could go buy stuff. We learned a lot about work at an early age.

We helped Merle clear a part of the rock garden so we could expand the veggie garden. Some of the rocks were bolder size. We had to dig holes alongside of them. Then Merle would place the right amount of dynamite in the hole. We would all get way back and he would set it off. Some of those pieces would go 50 feet in the air. Then the work started as we had to pick up all the rock. We put the rock in a thing called a stone boat and hauled them out of the field. Of course, we then had to unload all those stones. It took several seasons before we really had the field cleared of the stones. Merle had a double bottom plow that was just about the right size for that John Deer Tractor. We had maybe an acre and a half cleared of stones, and he would plow and disk it up for us to plant potatoes and pickles.

We had some amazing potato crops for a few years. We all worked with dad to plant them and then in the fall it was digging time. Dad came up with his invention to dig potatoes. He made a rig that was pulled behind the tractor. It would dig the potatoes out of the ground and then us kids would go behind and pick 'em all up and bag them. Hard work but I bet we had fun. We were working with Dad. The potatoes were fun, but the pickle patch was a "beaner." Even at a young age it was a back breaker.

Mom did a lot of canning in those days. She canned beef, chicken, pheasant, some squirrel and all sorts of veggies, and fruits. She canned apples and made apple sauce. We had lots of tomatoes and made tomato juice. We crushed grapes and made lots of grape juice. There were purple and white grapes. Mom had a rig that looked like a pot with a perforated bottom. A large leaf rotated in the bottom as you would turn a crank and the juice would squeeze out the bottom into another pan. That is how we made juice.

We went out and picked up every hickory nut we could find and stored them in a gunny sack to dry. We stored the potatoes in the cellar in the potato bin and would go to the apple orchard and find the best apples just to store in the cellar. The pears were usually gone by the first snow as were the plums. The bees would provide us with a winter's supply of honey, and we kept some fresh in their honeycomb. Some we would heat. The honey would flow, and all the wax would melt and flow to the surface of the pot. That wax made good chewing gum. There were also plenty of jellies and jams that Mom made. It was put in jars and sealed with wax. When the cold really set in for the winter, we were always ready and would eat well. Mom would see to that.

We had fresh cows milk to go along with all the rest of the goodies. The milk would be separated from the cream with what was called a separator. The fresh milk was poured into the five-gallon tub at the top and as it would run down into the separator it would be spun out and the cream ran into one milk can with the milk running into the other. What a treat to get all that cream. We had a churn and would churn all of our own butter. Talk about work, our arms would fall off just as the cream changed into butter. We also had a churn to make ice cream, usually it was vanilla flavored ice cream. Great family fun, and a real treat for us kids. We did not mind that sort of work. I also remember that cream with a little sugar was super with fresh strawberries in the springtime. We had buttermilk also, but I did not care for it.

Several times a week when we came home from school, the house would be filled with the smell of fresh bread baking as well as a large supply of cookies. Sometimes those were filled with the nuts we had picked up. Mom usually had us crack the hickory nuts for her and then she would make the cookies. She was awesome with oatmeal cookies as I recall.

Mom loved to bake pies. We had lots of eggs from our chickens and so there were lots of custard pies. A lot of those nice apples that were stored were sacrificed for apple pie.

Fried chicken with mashed potatoes, gravy, peas or corn, and apple pie. What a Sunday dinner! All home grown. The poor folks were eating well. What a mother we had. I have no idea as to how that great woman ever kept up with all the washing, ironing, cooking, gardening, canning, churching, teaching and loving us all as she did.

The older us kids got the more work was put on us. Lots of things were fun, like pickin' apples or other fruits as well as gathering nuts. It was cool to go out and get two or three chickens to kill for dinner. These sort of things were fun but when it came time to clean the gutter of cow poop in the barn with a pitch fork and wheel it out back, no fun. It was also not much fun to climb up into the hay mow and throw down the bails. The bails had to be spread out to all the cows, in their trough.

The girls had lots to do with helping Mom in the house. Dishes was a big one. Setting the table and making ready for breakfast or dinner was another. Setting the table was fun at times as the two bigger girls would con Mary into setting the silverware by hopping around the table like a rabbit and setting the places. Seeing to it that us smaller ones were ready for school had to be done. Laundry and folding were another thing for the girls. We all learned a good work ethic.

I loved working the garden with Mom in the spring and summer time. She taught me a lot about planting and hoeing and weeding and the harvest.

OUTDOOR MOVIES

Merle was such a nice guy. In the summertime, on Saturday nights he would load us kids into his old Chevy and take us to Oakley. There was this old two-story building with a large block wall on the west side of it. Between that wall and the railroad tracks, there was a lot about a half-acre in size and it was set in wild grass. We would get to sit on that grass and watch an outdoor movie. Lots of shoot 'em ups and kid stuff to see. Merle would sometimes give us a nickel or even a dime. Then when the movie reel would run out, it took a few minutes to change to a new full reel. That would give us a minute to run to the little store that was in that same building with the block wall. We could get a little candy or gum. Great fun for us little guys.

How many people can ever say that they had a long driveway? Ours was full of potholes, and every time we would have a nice summer rain, we had maybe 200 feet of mud puddles to run through. Mary and I sure would take advantage of it. We would be a real dirty mess from it. I can still feel the splashes as we ran full tilt up one side and down the other, just covered in chocolate colored water. Then we had added fun cleaning up, as we would hose each other down. I remember mom getting such a big kick out of it. It would be laughs, laughs and more laughs. When you are a kid, it is amazing what you can find to have fun with.

We never dared come to our mother and say we were bored. We always were told the same thing. Well then, sit down and look at a book. That was always her answer. We had no in-house babysitter such as a TV.

PRANKS

One time Merle came to us and told us of a tree that he had grafted in the apple orchard. It just so happened that that little tree, about 8 foot tall, had only one apple on it that year. We were to let it ripen without disturbing it and absolutely not pick it. The fall came on and that single apple became ripe. My two older brothers, Rich and Ed became overwhelmed with desire to eat that apple. Well, when Merle went back to get it, the apple was still hanging on the tree, but someone had eaten the thing! Leaving only the core hanging there. It had not been picked though, just eaten. Merle could not stop laughing so the boys were not punished.

One summer night, when I was about eight years old, we were all in the house when we heard a real loud noise coming from the outside corner of the house. It had the sound of someone cutting the corner of the house with a saw. Very distinct and very loud. The older people all filed outside to see what was going on. Nothing was found. It was very strange, and we all went back inside only to hear it again. This went on for three or four times. And it was a big mystery. We finally caught the culprits. It was Jerry and Ward Adams, the older kids from down the road. They had hooked up a string line to a nail of which they had shoved up under a piece of siding at the corner of our house. They had put a weight about four foot back from the nail so that when they dropped the string, the weight would take the string to the ground and people could walk over it without finding it, very clever. So, they would get back from the house about 40 feet and pull the string tight. They then would rub the string with some violin rosin until it became sticky, and it would resonate down the string and throughout the house, sounding like a saw.

The Adams boys liked to play tricks all the time. I remember one time when they were running through the apple orchard covered in white sheets. It scared the heck out of Mary and me. The big kids sort of laughed at us about that one as they did not believe us. Until one night they seen them and chased the boys down. Caught 'em.

There was a little trick that we liked to play on some of the farmers during harvest time. It was a nighttime prank. I was a little young at the time so I didn't get to go along as often as I would have liked. It was called "pull the bag" and it was done at night. We would tie several hundred feet of bailing twine from the barn all together so we had one very long line. Then we would take a gunny bag and fill it full of straw. It would be real lite. So off to the highway we would go with the bag, the string and a few ears of corn. The "bag of corn" would be placed along the side of the road with a few ears of corn scattered around it as if it had fallen off someone's load. The string was hooked to it so it could be pulled back into the field when someone stopped to get their free bag of corn. It was so funny when someone going 60 miles an hour would slam on the brakes to get that bag of corn. We would have our sucker and we grabbed the string and ran like crazy pulling that bag way out into the field. The sucker would then back up for a long ways until he figured out that he had been had. Once in a while some guy would be so mad that he would chase us. The longer he would run the madder he would get and yelling crazy stuff at us. How do you catch several kids laying in a stubble field at 10 o-clock at night in the pitch dark. Several times though, they would find our bag or our string and take it with them. Wrecking our fun for the evening. That little prank was always lots of fun. We also did the string and rosin trick on some folks that lived a mile or so from our place.

MAKING MERLE MAD

One time when Merle had broken the marking pole on the corn planter, I watched him intently. The marking rod was used to leave a track in the dirt as a row of corn was planted, then when he was on his way back up the field he would drive by the mark in the dirt so as to make even rows, spaced just right. He had a new and long wood pole about eight foot long. The pole was carved just right, for size and length. Merle was very fussy about the way he did things. He even put a nice coat of varnish on that pole. So, the pole was ready and there was a string hooked to it that ran back to the machine and then up to the tractor. This allowed for him to raise and lower the marker as he drove the tractor. That day as he started out to the field to do some planting with his new rig complete, I ran to the side of the tractor for some reason and poor ole Merle had his new stick too low. It struck me in my shoulder and snapped completely in two. That may have been one of the only times I ever heard him cuss like that.

There was another time when he was really mad. This time it was because of all of us kids. Mom and Dad were away one night and Beverly was in charge of all of us. She was the leader of that evening's doings and had us all in Merle's bedroom. Merle had this big thick feather tic on his bed and we were, all six of us, jumping up and down on his bed. He came in from milking the cows and when he seen us all in there, he was really mad. It didn't seem like a very big deal to us, but wow! Look out for Merle! Mary and I were sent upstairs to bed while the rest of the kids were made to sit on the stairs and wait till Mom and Dad came home. He gave them all quite a lecture.

One day when Mom was In Merle's bedroom doing some cleaning, we heard her scream. She came out of his room with getting sick on her mind. It seems that Merle was using his boot to go pee at night instead of going into the bathroom. When Mom picked the boot up the pee ran everywhere and it smelled! I think she, as well as us kids, had learned not to go into that bedroom ever again.

One really funny thing I remember about ole Merle was something he did to the inside of his car. He had an old Chevy. I think it was a 1949. He had done a repaint on it and used a paint brush to do the job. The car was painted light blue with red fenders. A lot of Merle's taste was in his mouth. It was quite a car. He had caught himself a good-sized fox, and he kept it on a chain. One day he had it in a gunny bag and had put it in his car, in the back seat. Well, the darn thing ate its way out of the bag and commenced to tear up the whole inside of his car. He was afraid to open the door to get it out for it would escape. I do not remember to this day, how he got it out. That old Chevy was given to Bev some years later I believe.

Mary and I spent a lot of time playing in all the outbuildings, sometimes making mud pies and cakes. Mary would go into the granary with me and we would play in the old wood bins but when it came to the corn crib, it was "no dice". You had to climb up the side wall slats to get up into the top of which there was some floorboards. This was great fun and I had built my own little hideout up there. So Mary was chicken to go up there even when I told her how cool it was. She tried several times but as you climbed up you could see out through the slats. Finally, I convinced her that I had candy up there and she made the climb. That was cool, but I did not have any candy. She got really mad at me and then, she would not make the climb back down. She was scared and I think Mom had to help us out of that one. We just always had so much fun playing together. The hay mow was a favorite. We stacked bales of hay to make a hide out or a fort. Even the big kids couldn't find us. We played back in the field a lot. Ed and Rich had made themselves a tree house and we would frequent that place a lot. It was built in one of the three trees.

I can still hear in my mind, the sound of the milking machine when Merle was milking. We would have to go ahead of him and wipe off the cow poop and mud from the utters, so we would be there with him. That ole machine would go, "grama, grama, grama" as it sucked the milk out. It was old but did the job. The cats would hang out in there and sometimes we would grab a teet and give em a squirt in the face. Sometimes the "grama, grama" sound was not there. It would be broken and that was when some of us kids and dad would have to do the milking by hand. Then it was just squirt, squirt, squirt and the cats loved it.

Merle had a little dog by the name of Legsy that was there on the farm. It was not much of a dog, but to him, He loved that little guy. Legsy was with Merle all the time except when he was on the tractor. I guess that's about all about Merle for now.

SPOOKY TIMES

We didn't have a TV set until I was about 12 years old and one move later. Our neighbors did though. (The Kelly family about a half mile east of us toward town). There were certain nights that we were allowed to go to their house and watch a show. It was always dark outside when we went and very dark when we came home. There was this really old two-story spooky house that was about halfway between the Kelly's house and ours. No one had lived there for years and it had fallen in disarray. Mary and I would not even go near it in the bright sunlight. We would go down to the neighbors to watch some spooky shows, "Lights Out" and the "Inner Sanctum" (Very scary, especially for a seven and a five-year-old.) That would be little sister Mary and Me. The bigger kids would also be scared but could handle it better. Those shows would be so spooky that we would sit there on the floor with our eyes closed and just hold onto each other. Of course, after the shows were over, the big kids would scatter and Mary and I were always left to walk home down that lonely ole gravel road by ourselves, over the creek bridge where a nasty Troll lived, and then on past that big, looming, two story, old spook house. We would sneak up to the bridge but then run like crazy the last quarter mile into the safety of our own yard. We watched that big ole house every step of the way. The front door was always wide open and we just knew a zombie was gonna come out and get us. I guess we outran that monster every time as we always seem to have made it home to tell Mom about the movies we had seen.

The little hall at home was also a scary place. I can still remember trying to get Mary to go turn on the bathroom light before I would go down that little hall to use the potty. For some reason that was a scary place for me. Mary was always sweet and would go do it for me. There was a deep dark closet at the end of the hall. I believe that is what had me scared.

BAD DREAMS

This is about the time I started having a recurring nightmare. I guess I was seven or eight years old. My dream was very scary for me. I think most people as they look back to childhood, had those bad dreams. There was this creature that chased me. It looked like a very large wolf that had been crushed on its right side and as its body was low and long to that side, there was something like the teeth of a hay mower attached and a little wheel was out there on the end to keep it up off the dirt. It had the head and face of something like a bat. The head was a little small for its body and there was some sort of growth coming out of the top of it. I can still see it clearly to this day. The second I would see that thing in my dream, it would chase me, and it was very fast. Sometimes I could run like crazy and out run it. Sometimes it would be gaining on me and sometimes I could not run. As hard as I tried, I just could not run. Well, I guess I must have always got away because I am still here. I think I had that dream well into my mid-teens. It was always scary, and I would always wake up. My Mom was always there to comfort me. Several years ago, I found an old chunk of wood on the beach by our current day lake house that looked just like the head of that creature. I have saved it. I even put two dull red stones on it as the eyes. No, I do not have that dream anymore. I look back on it with chuckles.

THE MOVE TO THE GREEN HOUSE

Merle's house was great for us younger guys but for the older ones, especially Bev and Elaine, it was not good at all. All of us trying to stay in one bedroom and that little bathroom. It was rough. The girls were starting to have dates and our place was a bit of an embarrassment for them. I think we all did not want to leave Merle but it was really important to have more room.

Dad came up with a house just a mile down the road from the Cook farm. It was a big ole sort of a rambling place on two and a half acres with five bedrooms. This place was lovingly called the green house as the siding was green. As it turned out, it was the most beloved place for all of us. We just all have so many wonderful memories there. It was at 11854 Peet Road.

There was a rather large tool shed out back and it had a storage area over the ceiling in it. It had a barn type opening with a large sliding door on it that didn't work very well. I don't think we ever parked a car in there.

In front of that building was a 30 or so foot long chicken coop. It had a door at each end and was set up for a long perch area for chickens. That building didn't last long and was soon torn down. Then there was a shed maybe 16 by 20 foot with one door going into it. This was the building that I would learn to hate, as we would soon get one single cow and I had the job of taking care of and milking it.

There was a rather large box elder tree in the back yard which always had box elder bugs on it and there was a hefty branch coming out of the back of it that we used when we had to pull motors and such from our autos. I think we called it the hanging tree. There was always a chain hoist hanging from it.

**The Green House— 11854 Peet Rd. Chesaning, MI.
We spent our teenage years here.**

LARGE GARDEN

The property was laid out so there was an area of approximately a full acre that could be put to gardening. The soil was soft sandy black and rich dirt. Just right for gardening. It also had a creek running across one corner of it. We always had a really large garden there and I learned a lot about gardening. It was always great fun doing it with Mom and Mary.

Dad had gotten us a large rototiller. It was an old thing and I was the one chosen to do the tilling. That was done against Moms wishes. She thought it was just too big for me. I got the job done though. Mary and I had to pick all the clunkers out of the fresh till. A clunker was a chunk of dirt which was not broken up by the tiller and usually contained a lot of crabgrass roots. It had to be knocked apart and the roots thrown into a bushel basket that we would drag behind us. After several years we had almost all of the crabgrass gone. So the soil was soft and black when we started to do the planting. Perfect for all the veggies that we planted.

We planted a lot of everything, even Kohlrabi plants. A lot of potatoes and tomatoes. We got a huge strawberry patch going as well. It was great. I remember times when we got home from school we would head straight to the garden for snacks. It was always so cool to pick the first ears of sweet corn of the season.

Mom was so fun to do gardening with. One year her and I were digging up the sweet potatoes and we came across a huge one. It measured over 22 inches around it. We were so excited, but it turned out the potato was no good. It was all like wood inside. I learned a lot about gardening in those years with her. It was always a treat to sit and talk with her as we hulled the peas or cut up the green beans. She was always there to help dig the potatoes or pick the strawberries in the spring. Tomatoes were sorted so that the good clean ones could be stored for several months. There were times when we would go to the blueberry farm and pick berries for canning as we did with cherries. We also had a large pickle patch and we had enough to sell. So, when I picked several bushels full I could make a buck or two.

NASTY COW

Dad had gotten us a cow and it was a real pain for me. I was in charge of the darn thing. I had to keep it watered and fed. The pen had to be cleaned regularly and worst of all I had to milk that critter, by hand of course. That cow hated me as much as I hated it. It would wait till I would have a half a pail of milk and then it kicked the pail over. She loved swatting her tail at my head when I was milking. It was always breaking out and I would have to fetch it back in. Talk about stubborn. It wanted to go be with the neighbor's cows. I would whack it with a board, and it would not budge. One day though, when I came home from school. The cow was gone. We would be getting lots of meat for the freezer. I was never so happy. No more going to school smelling like cow poop.

OUR CREEK

We had a creek that was just the thing for Mary and me. We played there all the time. Sometimes when the water was a little high, we could go swimming in there. We were always catching frogs and tadpoles.

In the winter my two brothers would go trapping for muskrats and sometimes catch a mink. They had a dozen or so steal traps and made a few bucks every year by selling the pelts. Come springtime each year we got to go spear fishing in the creek. The water would be up a little and there would be suckers and pike to catch. What a treat that was. We were sorta living off the land. Rich was the best spear chucker of all of us. He got us the most fish. Mom would always tell us to pray to Saint Anthony as we fished as he was the patron Saint of the lost. Mom just loved it when we kids would get the fish.

That creek served another purpose for us small time farmers. After last frost we would set out the tomato plants and Mary and I would have to carry buckets of water every day to water those plants...All that work would pay off though, every fall when the tomatoes would set fruit, we would have one of mom's favorites, BLTs.

THE WALNUT TREE

Several years after we had moved into the green house, we were on really hard times. Dad could be laid up for weeks at a time.

We had this huge black walnut tree in the front yard and the trunk was tall and straight. One day there was a knock on the front door and this guy was from some sawmill. He was out buying walnut trees for his mill. He was offering Mom $200 for the tree and would not be cutting it down for a while. We were in bad shape financially and she took the money. That much money in those days would go a long, long way. When they finally came and cut it down though, we were all sad. We loved the walnuts and the tree.

Mary and I were the ones who had to shuck all those nuts. We had to knock the large hulls off the nut and then set them out to dry. Our hands would be stained for days after the hulling. Dad got us a big ole truck tire rim one time and with the big lug holes in it, Mary would set a nut on the rim, and I would whack it with a hammer, pushing the nut through and leaving the hull. Still a rather dirty job. Ya but those walnut cookies! We could always tell by the stained hands, which other kids were also gonna eat walnut cookies.

MAPLE SYRUP

There was a big ole sugar maple tree at the side of the house and it should be noted that every spring, it would be my job to drill and tap that tree just as the sap started to come up. Wow what a treat that was! We would boil and add and boil and add until we had a nice big pot full of maple syrup. Mom always liked it real dark which meant it would be extra sweet. Sometimes we would boil it right down into maple candy. You could also take a drink right out of the fresh maple water as it came from the tree. Ice cold and sweet.

ART'S FIREWOOD

Art had sold off a lot of his woods for lumber and he had a huge pile of left over slab wood that could be cut up for firewood. We went out there in the winter when we could not afford coal at home. We cut firewood from that pile and took it to be burned at home. We used a big ole buzz saw to cut it into usable pieces. Art had an old tractor that had to be hand cranked to start and the tractor had a pulley wheel to turn the buzz saw. When it was 10 above zero and that tractor had to be hand cranked to start, we were glad for the big size of Uncle Art. They would bring out a pail full of hot water and pour it into the radiator to heat the engine just enough for Art to crank up the ole girl. Then we hooked a wide belt from the tractor to the saw. We would then be in business. That big ole blade would be making a wherrr sound and we would be cutting wood. Rich and I would be there to pick up the pieces and load the trailer. We had to work our butts off to load that trailer. We also had to cut wood for Art's use. That was just the half of it because when we got home, we had to unload the trailer and stack the wood in the basement by the furnace.

WRECKING JERRY'S TRUCK

We could not afford for us kids to have bikes. Rich and Ed were a little older and had jobs at different places so they could get bikes. I walked everywhere I went, or hitch hiked to town.

I learned to drive when I was thirteen and I had an accident that year. Jerry Kubica (sister Elaine's husband) was over with his truck, and we loaded it with junk to go to the dump. Jerry allowed me to take the trash to the dump if I would unload it. All went okay until I started for home. It was only a mile, but it was a very rutted road. The back tires stuck in a rut and swung the back of the truck over. As I went to apply the brakes, I hit the gas pedal instead and shot right into the ditch. The bumper was bent a little as well as both of the fenders. My head hit the windshield and broke it. I was scared stiff. But Jerry forgave me, I think.

FIRST JOB

A year earlier when I had just turned 12 years old, I got a job. Rich and Ed had gotten a job setting pins in our local four lane bowling alley and they were ready to move on to bigger things, so I got hired on, four nights a week. For that first season I had to walk from home, to and from the bowling alley. I made ten bucks a week and gave some of the money to Mom. Some I would save and some I would use to shoot pool with at our local pool hall next to the bowling alley. I saved all I could with the thoughts of a car in mind. I also became very good at shooting pool.

This proved to be really hard on my schooling. I just did not have time for such things. 6th grade had become awful for me. I had also discovered GIRLS. How fun was that! I made it on into the 7th grade. I believe that I was 13 then.

FAILING SEVENTH GRADE

I really messed up that year in school and the big blow came that next spring when it was decided that I should take that grade all over again. I think there were three of us in that class of 22 kids that had to be set back. My buddy Richard Nietling was sent forward and I was sent back to my other cousin, Leon Kulhanek's class. It was totally embarrassing for me. It did not help me study any better though. This was my first major failure in life, and it started me down a road of looking at myself as a dunce, a dumb person, a failure at doing smart things. I just did not like to have to study. I always learned good whenever I was working around Mom or Dad. I just could not get reading and book learning. I was always scared in class. Working with either of my parents, I learned a lot on how to do things. That was much more important to me. I just didn't get book learning. The second seventh grade went a little better but not much. I was just too far behind. And the nuns did not like me very well.

ODD JOBS

So, I had my little job going for me and I did other jobs as well. I helped the Adams folks do their hayin' and all of us kids got into pickin' pickles at a pickle farm. We all made a few bucks here and there. One time I was helping a farmer clear rocks from their field. There were four or five of us and I wound up hitting one of the older guys in the side of the head while throwing a rock onto the stone boat. He had walked into my way, I guess. I was not asked back the next day even though I gave them a good day's work.

I got tangled up forking beans one time for a farmer. That happens to be one job that really kicked my butt. I was so tired at the end of the day. I did not go back to that job again. I had done it with hay but that was much easier for some reason.

That reminds me of one time I was hay bailing with the Adams gang. We worked for several months bailing and stacking this huge stack of hay. Now, when you're stacking bales, you have to keep them fairly tight as I recall or they could catch fire with spontaneous combustion. This haystack was maybe 60 feet long, about six bails wide and stacked 8 or so bails high. It was big. One night there came a red glow in the sky from down Harry Adams way and I knew what it was. That stack was on fire. It burned for days, until it was all burned up. I felt so bad for those guys.

FIRST CAR

The spring after my 14th birthday, which would have been 1957. I had saved up about $60. That was a lot of money for a kid. I had also been giving some of my earnings to Mom to help out with home. I also had bought all my own school clothes from the time I was 12 years old.

I now had enough money to get a car. Jerry Kubica had a friend in Owosso that had a '50 dodge in an old barn, and they said it would run. So, Jerry took me over there to look at it. It was maroon colored, and had almost all the windows broken out and the seats were rough. Chickens had been in it. The motor ran good and the trany seemed fine. The guy wanted $50. That was great because I would then have ten bucks left for insurance. We closed the deal and I had my first car heading on down the road. I drove straight home and went to cleaning it all out and washing it. A lot of the paint had faded off and it was rather dull looking. The radio worked but only on AM. The tires were just okay. I managed to pilfer the windows I needed from Onley's Junk Yard. We will leave that at that. My Grandfather had taught me better.

So now at the age of 14 I had a lethal weapon in my care. I had a car. Dad went into town and got a hold of our Chief of Police, Brooks Gerding. He was the uncle of one of my best friends Dick Gerding. Dad told Brooks that I would be driving some as I had a job and needed to drive. Brooks said that that would be okay. But just for school and my job.

A few months later I got another job stocking shelves and doing carryout at the local IGA store. Working for ole Harvey Cottonham. That job was fun, I got to meet lots of people working there. I still set pins on some nights, but the main thing now was the IGA. I was pulling in about 25 dollars a week by then and that was big money for a kid my age. I didn't save much of it and I did still help out at home.

With my little jobs and working in the garden with Mom and the discovery of girls, and helping out neighbors on the farms, I was busy and did not have much time for school. I was growing up too fast for my own good.

FUN WITH COUSINS

I had spent a lot of time in my earlier years over at Leon Kulhanek's or Richard Nietling's house. Rich had chores to do as well and sometimes I would help him get done so we could go play. One time back when we were about 8 years old, Rich and I both climbed to the top of their silo. It was up an enclosed shaft maybe 30 feet in the air. For some reason we took off all of our clothes and threw them down the shoot. I guess we were cool. Little did we know, my dear Aunt Curly was down at the bottom and seen the clothes come flying down. She just picked 'em up and away she went. I don't know why kids do such silly things. I believe that she just gave us a scolding and it could be that we had to run 2 or 3 hundred feet back to the house to get dressed again. That might have been punishment enough.

Aunt Frances (Curly) and Andy Nietling

Aunt Curly was like a second mom to me. I was at their house a lot. She even cut my hair. I spent a lot of nights over there.

My first ever camp out was with Richard Nietling. We packed all the provisions and that must have taken a half a day. We were going to go deep into Andy's woods and build a fire and stay the night. We had eggs, and bacon, and soup, and good stuff. We had pots, and pans, and water. We also each had our BB guns just in case. We were 12 years old and really brave. Off we went on that warm afternoon down the lane and soon we were at the woods, carrying all that stuff. So, that was the reason we reasoned, that we would NOT go deep into the woods down by the river as we had planned. (Too much stuff to carry). So, we camped just into the woods, just to the point at which we could still see the farmhouse, or home as it was. We spent the evening getting in a little firewood and set up our makeshift tent. It took a pack of matches but we got a fire going and that was comforting on that hot summer evening. I think we had hotdogs for dinner, and maybe some soup. As darkness set in we huddled to the little fire and started hearing all the noise of the woods at night. Everyone knows that raccoons have to come around camp sites and beg. Well, they sure did that night. We were brave and used our BB guns on 'em but I don't think we hit anything, maybe some trees. We stayed up most of the night and a few years later we both admitted that we were scared to death that night. So many strange noises for little kids. Everything goes running around at night in the woods. We made ourselves some bacon and eggs that morning. I remember that we could not get the bacon to cook and the eggs were pretty runny, but again we were brave and ate the stuff.

There were a lot of times that Rich and I would meet back in the woods that our parents did not know about. This was at about 11, 12, or 13 years old. I would tell Mom that I was going back to the woods and Rich would do the same. I would then go across the road and back to the woods to the south of us. Then under the cover of the woods I would go a mile or so east to the river. I would wade across the river and into Andy Nietling's woods. There was so much to do back there. There was a place we call the big cliff. It was a sharp drop off of about 25 feet and straight into the river. We played there a lot. I remember shooting the water with the BB guns. We thought that we were getting away with something but at times Mom or Curly would call each other and say, he is on the way. So, I guess they knew what we were doing.

We stole a pack of Andy's cigarettes once, when we were about 12, and hid them in an old overturned out house back behind the outbuildings. We hid them and finally after a month or so, we got up the courage to try one. That was not a good experience for us. We had to keep trying though until we had them all smoked up. The longer they sat in their hiding place, the stronger and dryer they got. That was stupid.

Curly and Andy had a nice TV set. Mom and Dad, and Mary and I would go over there a lot on Sundays and us kids would get to watch the TV. I think Lassie was the one show we never missed if we were there.

FIRST TV AND PIANO

We got our first TV in 1954. I was 12 years old and the TV looked like it was 12 years old. Dad put up the antenna and we were soon watching our own TV in our own house. The Mickey Mouse Club turned out to be a regular for my little sis and me. We no longer had to sit around that big old radio and watch the dials as we listened to the Lone Ranger and such. I think dad had taken the TV in on some sort of trade.

Dad also brought us home a player piano from some sort of a trade. That ole Piano was really something for us kids. We could just pump away and listen to the music, or we would hammer some song out that we had learned to sort of play. We wrote numbers on the keys and then sounded out a song until we could play it. Writing down the numbers as they corresponded to the music. 1-1-3-5-8-7, equaled "On Top of Old Smokey," a favorite old song of ours.

RICHARD, AND I, AND THE EXPLOSION

Richard and I got some of Andy's shot gun shells one time and of course we dug the powder out of them. Probably three or four of 'em. We had set out on a plan to make a big flash bomb. We had a soup can and put the powder in it. Then we broke up a bunch of wood match heads and added in some sparklers. It was ready to go. The plan was to drop a lit sparkler in the can and jump back. We waited till it got a little darker and we went at it. Our parents were in the living room right next to where we were doing it. Richard lit the sparkler and here it went. He bent over the can and stuck the lit sparkler in it. He was looking down into it when it went off. It blew him right backwards, burning his eyes and eye lids. All his brow hairs were gone. And he could not see. Our parents came running out there to our screams and the big bang and flash. Richard was taken to Owosso to the hospital, and I was busted for a long time. Rich was burned but it turned out okay. We never did that again. I bet it was Richard's idea.

That farm was really great. We had so much to do. So many outbuildings to always explore. Aunt Curly always had some really good pies baked and fresh baked bread. She was such a good cook. She was my best friend right up until she passed, much later in life.

OVER THE ROOF

There was one thing that all of us kids would do from time to time, and I think that little sis Mary and I would do it the most. There were two windows in the upstairs bedrooms that opened out onto the porch roof. When all else were asleep, we would slip out that window, climb up onto the main roof, go over it and down the back side where we could step over onto the home heating oil barrels and drop to the ground. This most often occurred when there was a nice warm summer night and a clear sky with a full moon. We could see better that way. I don't remember a lot about what we did once we were out of the house. I guess, just the excitement of getting out was enough that I don't remember what we did. I know at times we would catch a lot of fireflies and put them in a jar. They were always dead by the next day though. We never really did have to sneak out of the house. If we told Mom or Dad where we were going, they didn't mind. We did it just to get away with something. It was my sister Mary's idea and her fault!

BEDROOM MOVES

It was special times when someone got married or moved out. There was always a big shake-up upstairs. The vacated room was usually taken by the oldest kid if they wanted it. I wound up in the front bedroom with a closet. I had the bunk beds, from when we were little guys, in my room. It always gave me a place to throw stuff. I had gotten into electric stuff at a young age and learned the basics by trial and error. I got so much stuff in that room that Mom would not even go in there. I had radios taken out of their cabinets and I made strange antennas that I would hook to the different radios. Sometimes I would get foreign countries on the things. I had speakers all over, even under the mattress on my bed. There was even a small one under my pillow. I think my room was special. Once I got really settled in it, I didn't move to any other rooms.

SNEAKY BROTHER

Rich had the room just over the oil barrels and it was at the top of the stairs. One Sunday afternoon as I came home, I pulled in the drive and there was this girl hanging on Dick's second story windowsill over the oil barrels. It turned out to be his steady girl, Janet Stempfle. She looked at me in total embarrassment. Mom and Dad had company over. When I went into the house, I ask why was Janet hanging on Dick's windowsill. Everybody ran outside just as he finished pulling her up into his room. It proved out that that boy was trying to be sneaky. He did not want anyone to know that he had his girl in his room. I bet he was upset with me!

WINTER STRAWBERRIES

This may be a good spot to interject something that I had shared with my Mom when I was about age 16. One Saturday morning in about January or February, there was snow on the ground, when I showed up for work at the IGA store. My boss Harvey Cottonham, the store owner, was really upset. One of his coolers had gone out overnight and he lost all his frozen strawberries. There were maybe six or seven cases that had thawed out and could not be sold. Ole Harvey instructed me to dump all of them and clean out the cooler. "Yes Sir Mr. Harvey" I said, and I went right to work on the cleanup. Those berries were still partly frozen, so into the trunk of my car they went. All of them. I finished my clean up and at lunch time I headed straight home with those berries. Mom was so darn happy. She went right to work on some short cake for dinner and from there she began making strawberry jam. She was thrilled. We had jam well into the coming Spring's strawberry season. Good ole Harvey's loss was sure a blessing for our family!

HIGH SCHOOL DAYS

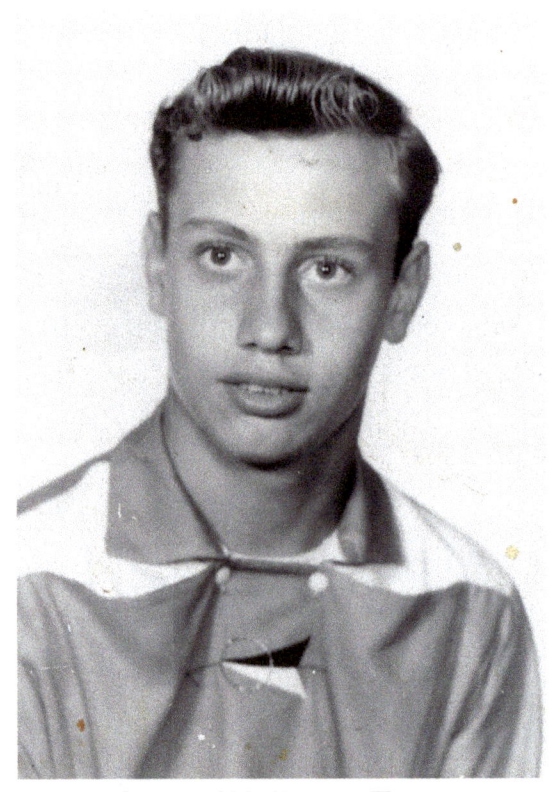

Garry Wallen—Teen

Going back to my high school days, I remember making it through the seventh grade the second time with probably the best grades I had ever gotten. That is not saying much though. As even those marks were not good. I did pass but when I got into the 9th and 10th grades it was really bad again. I passed those grades, but just barely. I made it through with things like typing and glee club (singing) and I was interested in history but all the other stuff I just could not do. I was too stubborn I guess. I had a really hard time learning things. Heck, I could hardly read. I don't think that my 24 classmates looked down on me. Socially I was doing good. I loved people and was good friends with most of them. Jack Schultz was a grade ahead of me and he was the only one that tried to take me under his wing and help me study. He was class president of the class ahead of me. Jack is still my friend to this very day.

We had a nun that was Principle when I was in high school. She was only 26 years old when she came to our school. She came from a family of nine kids, of which she was the only girl. She hated boys and that sealed my fate. I did not like her, and I showed it. She in turn did not like me. Now, since I have forgiven her, I will not mention Sister Peter's name!

Going into my eleventh year of school, we had a home room teacher that was really old. They had brought her to us from some sort of a retirement home for nuns that had some little mental problems. We all had problems with her and that is where my final downfall happened in school. I had gotten into it with her, and it got out of hand. Sister Peter got hold of me and that was really bad. She said nasty things and then I said nasty things, all the while she was whacking me with her ruler. When the dust settled, I had been expelled from school for good. The same thing happened to Fox Gross that year. We were OUT. I was so far behind by that time that it was no use to try and get into the public school system. I would get myself a good job and go to night school. I was seventeen.

BEING AFRAID OF THE GIRLS

Back in the days of my eighth grade, I had my first real true Love. I had had crushes all the way back to my second grade. But this one was special. Elaine Agnew lived only a half mile down the road. We went to several class parties together. Or at least we met there. And we went to the movies several times. When I would ride the school bus she was always there, and we would sit together. We even went ice skating together, that was awesome because I was a good ice skater. The big problem I had was that I was scared to death to be around her. I acted funny and I knew it. I did not know what to say or what to do. All I knew was that I was in love. I learned much later that kids were not in love with each other, they were really only in love with being in love. What a grand feeling to be in love.

One day my Dad had set up an appointment with the Agnew's to demonstrate the Kerby vacuum cleaner he was selling and he asked me to go along with him as he knew I was sweet on sweet Miss Elaine. I went with him. There sat her Mother and Dad. I froze in my chair. They brought me a soft drink and set it beside me on the stand. I sat there for an hour and was too scared to take a drink. It was by far my most horrible night ever. I did not recover from that one for a long time. Shortly after that, I was given the pink slip. Sweet Elaine sent me a note stating that we were to break up due to me being conceited. I did not know what that meant until I looked it up in the dictionary. Yes, I was heartbroken, for maybe two or three days until someone else came along. That was really the learning age of romance.

Fred Gwertz and I double dated for the junior prom and that was another tough one to get through. There was a girl that went to Chesaning Union School that I was sort of sweet on. Her name was Barbara Burnett. I was 16 at the time and Fred was even younger than I was. We did the flowers and all that stuff with the white sport coats. When it was my turn to pick up Barbara, I was again really scared. I hardly knew her let alone having to meet her parents; say the right things; pin her flowers on just right; get my flower on just right; and let the parents know that I had good intentions for the evening.

How could a kid, dressed like that, pull this thing off just right. I was petrified. Fred was already shaken from his date pick up and now I was as well. The whole night was sort of a flop. We sat there at the dance and hardly spoke to each other. Fred was the same. Fred and I always had laughs together but not that night. We may have danced a time or two with these chicks but not much. Then still dressed like that in those white suits, we went to Owosso for Pizza. Another silent ride and we were all too scared to eat the pizza we had ordered. Well, we finally said our good nights, saying what a great time we had. I think we all just had a big sigh of relief when that one was over with. I never dared to ask sweet Barbara out ever again.

One of the best places to find girls was at our little local movie theater. They did all the first run movies and us guys went often. The plan was always to go in just a little late. Once we got inside, we would walk up and down the aisle until we found the right spot. It would have to be right behind some girls. Niel Birchmeier, Leon Kulhanek, Dick Gerding, Fred Gerwartz and I, usually two or three at a time. We would sit down and get a little disruptive. Pull their hair.

Our Local Movie House

Put our feet way under their seat or just start talking to them. Before long we would be sitting with them and start making out. We met a lot of Chesaning High School girls that way as well as some of the Grover Chicks. Grover Chicks were girls that went to a Catholic High School about eight miles east of town. They called it Maple Grove. They did have some good-looking gals over there.

One day we were sitting behind these gals and two other guys came in and sat behind us. We did not know it but one of our gals to the front of us had just broken up with one of the guys behind us. Words were exchanged and an invite to go outside was issued. So out we went, leaving these gals to someone else. When we got outside, we all decided to just talk it out and then we drove off with the two guys heading to Saginaw for a steak sandwich. That was a common thing to do in those days. The two guys became really good friends of ours and we still are even now. Fred Tomcula and Kenny Houghton were their names. Soon they were part of our gang looking for chicks on a Saturday night.

It might be mentioned here that we all had to go to confession at church every other Friday or more often if need be. So, the trick was to sit and watch for the girls who had the longest penance from the Priest. They were always the most fun and would go just a little farther than the other ones. Sally Johnson was our class president and she started going steady with Jack Schultz early on. She never dated anyone else. Those two are still married to each other and doing very well. Sister Peter, our wonderful high school principal, tried to break them up at one point. She told Sally that Jack would go far in life and she had to break up with him and leave him alone. She was no good for him. They did not listen to her very well. I think Sister Peter may have had a bit of a crush on Jack herself.

We also done a lot of cruising through town. Sunday afternoons was always a good time for that as well as Saturday nights. It was a good way to meet girls. There was a little restaurant at the west end of town and that was the meeting place for all the guys after they took their gals home. It was called the Cottage Inn. We would pool our money for gas and head to Saginaw to a place called Tony's for a steak sandwich. Those were great. They were huge with too much steak sauce on them. Our buddy Dick Gerding could eat two and top it off with a large banana split.

BAD COP

We had this one cop in town that did not like teenagers. He had decided at one point that he was going to stop our cruising on main street. He had a no-u-turn sign put up at our normal turn around point. I know of at least three times our little gang pulled it up and threw it into the river. Dick Gerding was our fastest runner and he would always be the one who would get out, pull the sign up and run maybe 400 feet to the river. We would pick him back up at that point. They stopped putting them up after four or five signs were lost. So, at that point, they just painted a big white sign right on the road. It lasted only a few days until someone late at night took black paint and painted it over. I think Brooks, our chief of police, put an end to stopping the no-U-turns.

IN TROUBLE AND FUN

These guys that I usually hung out with were pretty neat and clean-cut guys. The Haughton boys, Wayne and Kenny however were hell raiser kids though. Wayne drove like a maniac. Sometimes he even scared me! Those guys were always around, we visited his dad's gas barrels a time or two, in the middle of the night.

Fred Tomcula, the Haughton boys, Mike Koviack and myself one night were up to no good. One of the farmers who lived close to Wayne would shock their corn. That is to say that they would bundle it and stack it standing up. These bundles would be sometimes 4 feet thick. So it was, one nice fall night. The four of us like a small army hit that field. We dragged bundle after bundle from the field to make a large barricade across the road from middle of the ditch to the middle of the other ditch. We went home satisfied that we did a good trick on someone. What a fun night we all had. That is until the next morning when a milk truck tried to get around it, got stuck and almost tipped over with a load of milk on board. We were in the clear until Kenny Haughton who lived only a mile from the corn field, got on his phone and started bragging to one of his other buddies about our roadblock.

Kenny's phone, like all phones in the country at that time, was a party line with about six people on it. One of those people was the county sheriff. Kenny soon had a knock on his door. The cop had heard everything on the party line. All four of us were summoned to the scene. I was lucky because Mom and Dad were up north at the time. All we had to do is put it all back and clean it up like new. That took most of the day. The funny thing about it was that without knowing it, that farmer's son was destined to be one of my very best friends and marry my sister Mary, my other very best friend. His name was Ed Dick.

Leon Kulhanek and Dick Gerding

One night when we were cruising around town just looking for something to get into, we came upon a neat plan. I believe that Leon, Fred, Dick Gerding and I were the culprits. I was driving my blue 1956 ford at the time (now, this was about 2:30 in the morning). We went over to the Chesaning Body Shop. With very little effort, we uprooted their sign of about six foot by four foot. We loaded it onto the roof of my car and proceeded down the back streets holding onto it out the windows of the car. We were brave because the town cops usually went home at one or so. Stopping at an alley close to the Walker Martin Funeral Home. We ran the sign across the parking lot and placed it in front of the Funeral Home. We then of course had to drive by it several times to get a good laugh. There was a picture of it in the local paper soon after that. Chesaning Body Shop sign placed in front of Funeral Home. We did not get caught and had many laughs about it in years to come.

Somebody built a fire out of tires under our only stop light in town one night. I believe that that must have been the Haughton boys. Nobody liked this one cop that we had, and funny things always happened on his shift. The chief of police, Brooks Gerding, was very well liked and we never teased him much.

The Good Guy– Chief of Police, Officer Brooks Gerding in his 1949 cop car.

MY TEENAGE CARS

I started out with that 1950 dodge as my first car. It did not last long for me as maybe I was a little rough on the old girl. So, the following year I got myself another car. It was a '53 Chevy, sort of plain Jane, but it ran really well. It had the famous six-cylinder blue streak engine in it and was fairly fast. I could smoke um in two gears if I did a double clutchin'. Double clutching happened when you let the clutch out with full motor rev and got a slight start. Then you pushed the clutch all the way in and let er rev again, just for a second, and then pop the clutch out again. It was fun, and also dumb. I think I replaced the transmission in that car three times in the two years that I had it, as well as two pressure plates. I learned to do auto repair work very fast and very well. I had a wonderful teacher, my dad. We always bought used parts. Maybe that is why they went out so fast.

Dad taught me the limits of frustration working on cars. One day I was changing the transmission in that '53 Chevy and had spent over an hour trying to get the pilot shaft lined up so it would all go in together. That was the big trick in replacing the trany. You had to hold the back of it up with one hand and rock it in with the other. I could not get it in. So, I called Dad out there, but with his bad back he could not get under the car with me. There was a big box elder tree in the back yard that we all did our car work under. Even the dirt was all oily. So, Dad comes out and sets himself down beside the tree. After another 10 minutes under there he had me come back out. Set down next to him and just smoke a cigarette and relax. We talked a little bit and I felt myself calm right down. Pop was fun to talk to. So, he says, now go put it in there. I was totally surprised. I slipped it right in there. I learned something big that day. How to slow down and make it work. I would use that lesson for many years to come. I think Dad knew that I would never be good at book learnin' and so he gave me more attention in the field. Grandpa was the same with me, even when I was younger. I blew the engine in that '53 as well and did just fine changing it out. Dad had to reset the distributor for me but I soon caught on to that job as well.

I got just plain tired of that '53 Chevy and switched to a 1956 Ford. I still could not afford a fancy car but that one was nice. My buddies and I had a lot of fun in those old cars.

When I turned 16, I took a driver's training class and got my driver's license. This was the very first year that it was required to take that class to get a license. Would you believe I aced that course. My car was even used when we all had to go to the parking lot and look under the hood so the teacher could show us different things.

'56 Ford

Well, I drove that Ford until the spring of my 17th year. One Sunday I got up early and was gonna go to the eight o'clock Mass. I got my Sunday clothes on and out the door I went. The steering on that ford always pulled a little to the right, and with that in mind as I pulled out of the drive, I opened up a package of gum. It slipped and fell down between the seat and the door. I looked down as I fumbled for it. I had hardly accelerated the car, but when I looked up, the side of the bridge was just going under the front of the car. I had just enough speed to drive up on the low abutment and slowly tip off into the creek. Bottoms up. I had been in the water of that creek many times before, but never with my Sunday go to meetin' clothes on. With a big crunch, I landed in the water, pushing the roof in. The car filled halfway with water. That was it for that car. It was a total loss. Mom and Dad were in total shock when I walked back into the house all wet. What a mess I had made out of that one. Those nice new white walled tires and the new exhaust system were very well exposed. I did not like that car anyway.

I got sorta booted out of high school. I sorta lied about my age and got a job building trailer houses at the Roy Craft Trailer Company. I was 17 years old working in a factory. Knowing how to work hard paid off well for me. I was making fairly good money at that time, so I went looking for a good car this time. No more badly used junk for me. I found a beautiful 1957 Chevy, two door, hard top, with a 283 engine, and a 350 automatic transmission. It had about 18,000 miles on it and they wanted $1,800 for it. This was a fast car for that time in history and a fast time for me. It was salmon colored but that was alright with me. I wanted it. I got about $400 from the insurance company from the '56 Ford and that was a good down payment with enough left for insurance. I went down to the Chesaning State Bank and bingo! I got my car. I was on top of the world at that point.

The car had dual baby spotlights on it and I put duel exhaust pipes under it. Wow did it sound great. I then added lake pipes. These were exhaust pipes that tied into the exhaust system close to the engine and before the mufflers. The chrome pipes ran down

'57 Chevy

the side of the car below the doors and had chrome caps at the ends. With one turn of the wing nuts the cap would rotate down and open the pipes strait off the engine. It was like not having any exhaust system at all. Very very loud. I was cool and even though Louie Rads, the cop that hated all us kids, tried to catch me with the caps down, he never did. He would be coming through town one way, and I would be going the other, with a load of kids in my car. We would watch as he would turn onto a side street and he would try to double back. We would drop those caps and the car would sound like an airplane as we headed out of town. The poor guy would get so mad that when we drove back into town all quiet, he would get right on my bumper behind me and follow real close just wanting me to make one wrong move. I am not the only one he did that to. Ole Louie just did not like kids. Also, he was just not very bright.

DUI

He did get me one time though. When I had the '56 ford. I had conned a guy into getting me a case of beer. Drewry's beer it was. That's what all the kids drank as I recall. So, Dick Gerding had a cooler, I had the car. It was a bright sunny Sunday afternoon and Dick, Leon, Neil Birchmeier and I went cruising with our beer. We did the right thing though as we drove out the Peet road, past my house and on out to the gravel pit where we at times would go swimming. We each drank a few beers and sat around shooting the bull. We then drove out into the country further and had a few more beers. Just slow and easy so as not to draw attention to ourselves.

Getting later into the afternoon and somewhat under the influence, we headed back into town still slow and easy, each drinking our last beer. With all the windows open and the music blaring, Neil Birchmeier flung his beer bottle out the window, right in front of a guy's house as the guy was standing in his yard. That guy called the cops right away and by the time we got another two miles into town, Louie was already on to us. He was heading out to meet us as we came into town. As soon as I seen him, I headed down a side street, Dick and Neil jumped out with the cooler and ran around a house and I got nailed. "Not so bright Louie" got me. There was water all over the seat. He just had me follow him over to Brooks Gerding's house and I stayed there with Leon until he rounded up the other two of us. I got a DUI and a minor in possession. The other three just got a possession ticket. It cost me $45 and Brooks called my Dad. Leon's Mom, which happened to be my Aunt, forbid Leon from hanging out with me anymore. I guess I was the bad guy in this mess. Only because I had the car. Dad told me if I wanted to drink beer, to get it and come on home. Do it there and not on the roads. I never did bring any home though. Ole Louie had finally won one but not on his own.

CHESANING

I guess it should be noted that Chesaning was a small town at that time with about 3,000 people living there. It was a wonderful little town where everyone knew everyone else. There was the Our Lady Schools and the Chesaning Union public school system. Most of the classes at the Catholic School held about 22 to 25 kids each. Unions classes were 500 or so kids each class each year.

It was about two miles through town, and we had one red light on the east end of the business district. From the west end of our three-block business section, a boulevard started which divided east and west traffic. At the east end of the business section was the crossing of the Shiawassee River. There was a dam just north of the bridge. By Christmas we always had enough ice on the river, behind the dam, for good ice skating. The kids all hung out at the Cottage Inn or Schultz Drug Store. We also had a soda shop called Doc's place. We had a community center just off Main Street which held most of the town activities. It was called Peets Community Center.

ANIMALS AT THE GREEN HOUSE

Backing up again to the time that we moved into the green house on Peet Road, I would like to talk about animals. We had left Merle with all the cows except for one, which was moved into a small barn with a little fenced in area. We had a black and white dog we called Prince and no cats.

The following spring, we sent for 100 baby chicks. They were delivered by the mail man. They always sent 105 in the box and that was because you would usually lose five or so before they started to grow up. We had a hatchery in town which also sold the chicken feed. Mom would put a warming lamp on them as soon as they arrived, and they had to be really babied for the first three weeks or so. Then they could be placed in the hen house to grow up. We always kept about twenty or so that would winter over so we would have eggs. As soon as the new flock started laying, the old ones would become Sunday dinner. We had a lot of Sunday chicken dinners from those hundred chicks. Come fall, it would be Richs and my job to go kill twenty or so chickens on a Saturday morning. Ring their necks, in what was a bloody mess in the back yard. Mom would have the water on to boil and Mary and I would get to pluck feathers till we were blue in the face. Mom would be canning chicken. The older kids would help with the cutting up and us younger ones would pluck, yuck. That would go on for a few weekends till we had 60 or so chickens canned.

Mom would always plan the chicken slaughter so as not to interfere with peasant hunting. That started on October the 20th every year. The guys, Dad, Rich, Ed and I would be up early with lots of excitement at hand. We would eat a good breakfast, get everything ready, and wait for 10 o-clock to come up. That was the legal shooting time. Every year we would start out in the back of our lot and almost always get three or so pheasants on our own property before we crossed onto the neighbor's fields. Everyone always hunted wherever they wanted. That was just a given. There were so many birds to go around. Dad would always have me run the first three birds back to Mom. She would have them ready to eat when we came in for lunch. I always had to use the little 4-10 shot gun to hunt with as we did not have that many guns to go around and I was the smallest guy. My Brother Rich was called, "Dead Eye Dick". He used a single shot ,16 gage, 36-inch barrel Long Tom". The kid was a good shot and brought back a lot of birds during the season. That kid could shoot. He was not as good as Dad though.

We were only allowed two cock pheasants per day, and no hens. So, one day Dad came back from Willing's woods and he had two cocks and two hens. He claimed that he got all four birds with one shot. He was in the woods and all four jumped up together. One shot and all went down. I believed him. I do believe it was luck though.

When I first started hunting, I was an awful shot and to this point I had not gotten a single bird. I took our dog prince one afternoon after school and the 4-10. I headed down the road and was gonna hunt a corn field when ole Prince put a nice cock up out of the road ditch. The dog made a magnificent leap into the air and snagged the bird to the ground. What luck. I wrung its neck, and I got way back and shot it with the 4-10. I ran home with it. I had gotten my first bird. Well sort of. But I never let on that I got it sort of second hand. Good boy Prince. I did a little later on, develop into a "crack shot" myself. When I was in the military I scored as an expert marksman.

Mom would can some pheasant as well and sometimes we would bring enough squirrel home and she would can some of that as well. Those hunting days were always awesome for us guys.

Come springtime there was always much ado. We had spear fishing in the creek. The two older brothers would get into trapping for muskrat and mink. The garden had to get readied to plant. The barn had to be shoveled out and the manure from the cow was spread on the garden areas and around the fruit trees. Then there was the chicken poo that had to be wheeled out and spread on the garden. Lots of things were being born back in the woods. The starlings, nasty, nasty birds, would always lay eggs in a hollow tree on the east fence row. We would in turn drop cherry bombs down there. Those birds were awful to have around.

About the second spring living there, Ed and Rich came back

from the woods with a little baby raccoon in tow. It was named Huey and was made into a house pet. The things that my Mom put up with! Anyway, that little coon made one heck of a nice pet. It had the run of the house. It always had to cut up when we either started to eat or were kneeling down saying the Rosary. It would take to running full tilt around the house in need of attention. It would run across the back of the sofa and if you were bent over kneeling down, Huey would be there pulling your hair. He would go outside and just hang out. He loved his family and I believe he was house broke as well. I don't remember any messes. One cold winter night he got into the basement of the house. That is where we stored all the labors of the canning and jamming season. He tipped a jar of jam over onto the floor and it smashed all over. Huey ate his fill of the jam, glass and all. We lost him the next day. We were all very sad.

The next spring, Rich and Ed got us another one. His name was Dewey and he was just about the same as the first one. Just a whole lot of fun. Naturally the household was disrupted with him as it was with the first one. We all loved him. The following year there came a problem with him though. The State Game and Fish people had found out about him and learned that he was a house pet. Mom was shocked when she found out that we had him illegally. She went into the bedroom and got him off the foot of the bed and surrendered him to the officer. Dewey was gone and once again we were all very sad.

The next wild pet that the brothers brought home was a baby crow. We had him for about two and a half years. This turned out to be Mom's all-time favorite pet. We named him Cornelius. He followed Mom around like a little puppy. She used to love to tell the tale about him of when she would be in the garden planting peas. The crow would be there waiting for Mom to dig the trench with the hoe and start to plant the seed in the trench. She would chase him away, but he would hop down to the beginning of the row, dig out the seed peas and eat them. She would be mad but laughing so hard that the crow would get its way. He stayed outside a lot but also spent a good bit of time inside with Mom. He was always underfoot for her. I think ole Cornelius came to us with a broken wing. He was brought back to health but never could fly very well. He just hung out with Mom and that bird always had her laughing as he was such a clown. Sadly though, on a blistery, snowy, gloomy, cold January day, Mom got a call from the neighbor lady. She thought she had seen the crow hopping down the lane beside her house. Cornie had a special hop and walked almost everywhere he went. He just did not fly well. Mom got all bundled up and down the road she went and up the neighbor's lane. Sure enough, ole Cornie had stopped hopping and was just sitting there. He had gotten himself disoriented and was heading for the wrong house. It was just too far for him. Mom bundled him up real warm, but it was too late. Mom figured he had gotten pneumonia. He did not make it through the night. Once again, we were all very sad.

Rich also robbed a hawk nest and brought home a chicken hawk. This guy was called Link, and I don't remember him getting real close to the family members. That was Dick's pet. It ate a lot, and all the neighbor kids would catch all kinds of birds and mice. They would bring their catch to the house and feed the big bird. It was a sight to see, watching him eat. Link made it through the first winter, but the cold got him the next. He was never allowed in as a house pet, that I recall. He was out in the tool garage when he passed away.

We had lots of other pets as I recall. Things like pigeons, frogs, snakes, barn cats, and I had my own special cat. He was a black and white cat that I called Felix after the cartoon cat. That guy met his fate on the road as I recall.

I also had a squirrel that I tried to tame. He was a little too old to tame though. After getting bit a few times I finally let that critter go. I am sure I filled that cage up with something else.

Having all those chickens and that cow to take care of, taught me some responsibility, as did the pets and watering the garden and of course the little jobs I had in town.

MOM EXPECTING

Early on in the year 1958, my poor overworked Mom was not feeling well. She had been sick almost every day from Christmas on. Just out of sorts and throwing up a lot. She thought it had a lot to do with her change of life as she was now 45 years old and a little worn out. This woman had invested her whole life into our family. It could never be said that a woman ever worked much harder than she did bringing up her family. She was awesome. Well, about some time in February of '58 she had had enough and went in to see her doctor. The Doc ran some tests and said he would get back to her in a few days. She came home from that next doctor's appointment really shook up. She now knew why she was so sick. She was in denial but had to face the facts. Mom was going to have a baby. That news spread throughout the clan and there were a lot of mixed-up emotions.

My new little sis Charlene, oh, and my '53 Chevy.

I was 15 and going to have a little sister. I loved kids, and there were already a bunch of nieces and nephews around. This one though would be living with us. I was excited and happy. Mom finally accepted her plight and life was moving on.

My brother Edward was in the Air Force living in New Mexico and he and Janet were PG at the same time as Mom and Dad. Things were popping all around us. It Seemed as though everyone was having babies, Elaine and Bev., and now Eddy and Mom and Dad). Mom was a petite woman, always such a beautiful lady. I think Dad must have been proud of Mom and himself. PG at their age was rare but not unheard of.

The months rolled on and Mom was doing fine. What she thought was totally impossible was now very evident to all. I can just imagine what all her brothers and sisters were saying or thinking. But no matter because our little Charlene was born in August of that year, on the 14th. What a joy she turned out to be! Mom and Dad were thrilled as well as all the rest of us. I believe she took the spotlight. Ed and Janet also had their baby in New Mexico on the same day. That was pretty cool! Char became the apple of Dads eye. That may have just knocked my younger sister Mary out of that spot. They always called Char their little bonus. I believe that to be true and that little lady kept both Mom and Dad on the go, thus keeping them young. She was just such a joy to all of us.

Top, Left to Right: Ed, Dick, Dad holding Char, Garry

Bottom, Left to Right: Bev, Elaine, Mom, Mary

THE TRAILER FACTORY AND SIGN PAINTING

My first two jobs were gone. I had sort of outgrown them and then I had the big Roy Craft job. I was very responsible with that job. There were guys feeding their family's from working there. I knew how lucky I was to have that work.

Even though I was way ahead of my classmates in just being out in the world, I had a very empty feeling inside for I had been such a failure in all my schooling. That at times seemed so important to me. I was done with the nuns, but I had failed myself and I knew it. I had this job but that was not much security. I had car payments a little over my head. Without a diploma how far could I go in this real world. I made contact with the school system in Saginaw and got started in night school. I took my two worst subjects to start out with and again, I was making a mistake. Those two courses were so hard for me because I was so far behind in any of the basics for those classes. I knew I had really messed up. No matter how hard I tried, I just did not get it. I think I received a D and a C in those two classes. I felt really bad but tried again in more classes.

The overtime and the bonus' stopped coming at the Roy Craft. Soon we were down working only four days a week. This was not looking good, I knew I could be in a jamb. There were times when I did some work for Jerry Kubica doing basements. Setting up those 120-pound basement panels was a real killer. I worked for him off and on to fill in from the Roy Craft. Then in early 1961 the trailer company had to lay me and about 30 guys off. I kept my car payments up with unemployment checks. It sure slowed me down.

Beverly had gotten married to Tony Dobos and he was a bill board painter with a Sign Company out of Owosso. There was an opening for a job there and I applied. I had to show them that I could handle a paint brush during the interview. I guess I did alright because they put me on. This was now my fourth job already in my young life. I was now a sign painter working for a company that sent you all over the state. They paired me up with this butch haired, really grumpy guy that got really drunk every night. We had to stay in hotels every night. Sharing a room with a guy like that was awful. He did not like me because I was too young to drink with him and hang out at the bars. It was not going well with this job either.

Most nights, I hung out at the local pool halls in the towns we stayed in. I had learned to shoot pool very well and could hold a table almost as long as I liked. I knew a lot about the hustlers in pool shooting and could spot them easily. That made it fun for me. I made decent money in those places.

About six months after hiring on and working with this jerk, it came to a head one day when I forgot to close the paint truck door and we had walked about 200 yards to the sign from the side road carrying all the paint stuff. He chewed me out so bad that I just could not take it anymore. We almost went to fisticuffs, so I walked out to the highway and hitch hiked home. I was once again on unemployment. That was going into the winter of 1961. I had to drop out of night school because I was on the road all the time with that job. So that winter I started back at night school and was drawing my little assistance checks every week. Not a very good shape to be in for an 18-year-old.

TEENAGE FUN

Socially I think I came up through the ranks rather nicely. I had dated a lot of girls and got over being afraid around them. I think that most kids go through what I did as a young guy. I learned from each encounter a little more about girls.

One time when I was maybe 15, I went roller skating in Saginaw with a bunch of guys. I met a girl that night that was a perfect 10. She was beautiful, and I skated with her most of that night. We had a great time laughing and joking around. I came away from that night with a huge crush on this beautiful long-haired blondie. I was in love, and we had made a date for two weeks later at the skating rink.

I felt that I just could not wait that long. The longer I waited the more I became fearful of how I would handle another night with her. I had worked myself up so much in those two weeks that when the night finally came, I really blew it. I was so uptight with this chick that I had had so much fun with. I couldn't skate, I couldn't talk to her or joke with her. I was a big dud. She was just so beautiful for a 15-year-old. That ended that right there. No more dates with that young lady.

I did meet a real cool little gal that worked in a convenience store in Saginaw after that time. I dated her for a while. She was very nice. We did movies and ice skating at Hoyt Park in Saginaw. She was not the knockout that the blond was, but she was a really cute kid. We had a lot of fun, and this was a good learning experience for me. She wound up going to school with my sister Mary in Saginaw for a while. I don't remember why we stopped seeing each other. It was probably because I had started dating a gal from Chesaning and another one from Owosso. I think I had a crush on all three of them at one time. That is what being in love with being in love was all about. And it was so fun for a 15 - 16-year-old.

The gal from Chesaning was Carol Gross. She was my classmate in grade school and just a super nice kid. She was also a very pretty one. We dated off and on for four or five months. Carol was best friends with Dick Gerding's steady at that time and her name was Hazel May Birch. Hazel was a lot of fun, as was Carol. Now this might sound like a tall story and I am bragging but it is true, I had lots of girlfriends once I got movin' on things.

LEON AND THE TWINS

I was dating this cute little 15-year-old county girl that lived about 12 miles outside of town. One Sunday as I was heading out of town on M-57, with this cute little gal tucked under my arm, I could see in the rear-view mirror lights a flashing and a car coming up on me fast. I pulled over and found out it was my best buddy Leon. He had to talk to me right away. I went back to his car, and he told me about these two cool looking little blond chicks (twins) that he met the night before at a wedding dance. He had a date to go to their house that afternoon. He had one that he was sweet on and needed someone to go be with the other one. "Please Ole Buddy" is the way he put it. Leon was the type of a guy that would do just about anything for ya, even back then. So, here I am with this cute little gal sitting in my car all ready to go to the country and park for a while and I have to take her home because of my friend's emergency. It didn't make sense to me but Leon was my best friend. So, I disappointed this little gal and myself and took her home. I came back to town and met with Leon. Off we go to Owosso and meet these little blondies.

This was the start of a relationship that, over the next 18 years, would take me to the top and also to the very bottom of what a relationship should be. I met Janet and Jane Korf that day. They were twins, looked a lot alike, and very cute. They were also only 14, just getting ready to turn 15 years old. We spent the afternoon with them.

Janet played the piano and so did I, so we had something in common. Leon set another date up with them and I believe that was to do a movie. I think Leon dated Jane maybe three or four times and dropped out. I dated Janet maybe one or two times longer than Leon and I dropped out.

I was having lots of fun around home. Carol Gross, a real cutie in Chesaning and a real sweetheart of a gal was fun to go out with, I liked her a lot. We double dated with Dick Gerding and Hazel Mae Birch a few times. Things were just too busy for me at times, I guess. I still dated the gal from Saginaw some and that one finally dropped off.

We got some guys together once in a while and would go to Saginaw and go ice skating at Hoyt Park. There was always lots of chicks to pick up over there and it was always loads of fun. Sometimes we just drove around town to see how many dates we could get for the next Friday night. That was goofy, but fun. We went to that city a lot; I remember when the first McDonalds opened there.

The next summer a few of us guys were over in Owosso for some reason and as we were walking down the sidewalk, this cute little blondie came out of one of the stores. I recognized her and stopped to talk. It was Janet Korf, the gal I dated for a short time the year before. She was going with a guy by the name of Ray at the time. I wasn't going with anyone at that time, so I asked her out. I believe she said to call her and I did. We started dating that summer of 1960. It became rather regular and soon I was dating her once a week, every Friday night. We got to see each other sometimes on Sundays as well, although I did like to have my Sundays to spend with my buds. We built a relationship that fall and were having fun. It was a little funny as her name, Janet, was the same as the names of my two brother's girlfriends.

GOING STEADY

Janet still had two and a half years of school to go, and we were not allowed to see each other much. That Christmas Eve of 1960 we were setting out in my car in her driveway, and we decided to start going steady. I had given her my class ring. I don't know what that all meant to me, but I was learning. I was going to be true and blue to this pretty little thing, that is what it meant. I knew one thing for sure though. She was a very good kisser. Is that silly to say?

I started to get involved a little with the Korf family, Uncles, Aunts and such. One of the first things that happened to me though, was not good at all. I was accused of breaking into one of Janet's Aunt's house and stealing their money. I was totally embarrassed by such an accusation, and I could only deny it. They did not know the lesson that my Grandpa had taught me as a little kid. I was not a thief. That went on for a few weeks until they found out it was their own son that did the deed. I was never forgiven though, by parts of that family. I was always looked down on. They also did not approve of me because I came from such a poor family, to them. I was a high school dropout and couldn't hold a job. Owosso was a very clicky town and word got around how the Korf families saw me. Coming from a poor family and not much of an account. I felt bad because my Mom got word of it. It really hurt her and she cried for my sake.

Because of some of the rigid standards of the 50s and early 60s, as well as the Korf family, there was little chance to really get to know Janet. There were things you didn't do and things you didn't talk about. I was going steady and from that time on I dated only Janet. We were allowed to date one night a week; pick her up at seven and home by eleven. That was it, "or else." We had some Sunday afternoons that we spent at the Korf house, or once in a while we could go out. After the first year, we could stay out till midnight.

Her Mom broke us up at one point, because Janet had missed her period and she had found a note to Jane from Jane's boyfriend Phil talking about them making love. She thought I had gotten her daughter pregnant. I think it was Janet's doctor that ended that little mess by inspecting Janet and finding out she was not PG. We were allowed to see each other again with no apologies. She gave us a "just be careful" talking to.

That is how things were in those days with the Korfs, very rigid. I did not feel real welcome in that family, and I guess I never did, except for ole Marv, Janet's Dad. He really liked me and I him. I just didn't understand.

Anyhow, I knew very little about Janet. We only had a little petting and no real talk about life and what it held for us. As it turned out, Janet sort of had a tiger by the tail. I knew that about me. I was sort of wild but also very dumb and gullible. I was 18 years old. I still had a lot of party time left in me.

THE AIR FORCE DAYS

Airman Garry Wallen

My class from high school had graduated and were scattering to the four winds. I had nothing going for me, so I decided to sign up to the United States Air Force. They were taking dropouts at that time. I was lucky. Leon had joined the Air Force and was doing very well.

Janet and I had talked it over and decided it would be best for me. I could finish schooling in the service. Maybe learn a trade. If we tried, we could hold on to what we had going for us. She still had half her junior and all her senior year to go through.

It was February. I would enter the service at the end of May. It was 1962. I had a few months before I went in, so Jerry Kubica let me work for him for a while. As it turned out, it put me in really good shape to be joining the military. I was 19 years old and in really good physical shape.

I left home for the first time in my life that May. It will be 62 years ago this coming May. I had joined the Air Force and wound up at Lackland Air force Base in Texas.

The first 6 weeks were in basic training. It was total hard labor. They knocked all forms of being a kid out of me and instilled an adult, ready to do and to learn. I had finally woken up to life. That Drill Sargent was one mean dude. I wondered, "What the hell did I get myself into." Up early and run our butts off all day. I had done some work with Jerry Kubica and also was a light weight in the flight. Working for Jerry built up my body stamina and it really showed in basic training. I was strong. I think that even made that drill instructor mad at me.

I did have a major problem though. I was dyslexic and often mixed up my left from my right. I didn't know why at the time. So, the D.I. would make me carry a stone in my right hand. When he said, by the right flank, I should think about the rock being RIGHT. That worked some and there were a few other guys in my flight that had to do the same thing. No one knew what dyslexia was in those days. Well, when the day came for our flight to march on parade, there was three of us that were cut from the troop and left at the barracks to clean. We just could not march. Even with a rock in our hand. That time was really rough. We had one, one day pass. A bunch of us guys took a bus into town and just looked around. I think we were all too stunned too have much of a party.

Airforce Days

After those six weeks I was transported by bus to Amarillo, Texas for schooling. My orders said that I was to attend a school called hydraulics. That included air pressure on the aircraft as well. I knew that I had one and only one talent in life, that was mechanical. I got that from my Dad. So, for the very first time in my young life, I wanted to LEARN, to study and to be the VERY BEST that I could be. For the first time I was proud of ME, and I went from all F s and D s in high school, to all A s. I found out that I really wasn't so dumb after all. I could make it in life. During those months of schooling and basic training I had very little time to think about home or to be homesick. I wrote Janet when I could, but I was very busy learning about myself, learning about life and learning about my airplanes.

It was a wonderful school, full of gadgets and gismos of many types and I got to learn about all of it. I learned about pressures and all sorts of components. There were valves and regulators, restrictors and accumulators. Just all kinds of stuff. I had died and went to heaven! I really could learn and a lot of self-doubt began to fall away. Maybe I could make certain people happy with me. Dad was very excited for me. I believe he even felt a little success on his own part.

We were allowed weekends off at that Air Base, so I got to see a little of the surrounding area. I took a small plane ride around the base and got to fly the plane. It was a demo in case I would want to get my pilot's license. A bunch of us guys traveled out to a place called Palo Duro Canyon. I had never been in any place like that before. I was a flat lander. The canyon was gorgeous and very enjoyable. We had a very large swimming pool real close to the barracks and I used it a lot. They also had a nice Airman's Club that we would go to. On weekends we could have a beer at that place. Those four months, or so, of schooling went very fast for me. I was ready to be in the Air Force for real.

FIRST 30 DAY LEAVE

After graduating that Tech School with honors, I had a 30 day leave to go back home. There was a much better gait in my step as I was proud of myself for the first time in my life. Janet was still in high school, so we were still kept on a ridged time frame together. I believe we saw each other six or so times in that 30-day leave. It was a little hard being with her, after not seeing her for six months. I didn't know her much anymore and there was not that much to talk about. I got to see all of my family members and they threw a little party for me. A few of my old buds were still around. Mom and Dad were happy for me. I think they would have liked to see me make a career out of the service.

So, I partied with some of my old friends a few times. I think we went to Saginaw a time or two and that was about it for that leave. I was excited to get to my new station. I was so much wanting to get to work on real airplanes. Janet and Mom and Dad were at the Bus Station when I boarded that big ol' Grey Hound Bus. Once again it was hard to say goodbye to Janet. I knew that I would be missing her a lot, but I was ready to get to my new base and get settled in.

TRAVIS AIR FORCE BASE

On my return back to the military, I was transported by bus to Fairfield California, Travis Air Force Base. That was a long bus ride. I had fallen asleep and when I woke up, we were heading through the mountains of Colorado. I could not believe my excitement at seeing real mountains. I had always wanted to see them.

When we hit California, we also hit fog. It was like pea soup. Thick. We made it into Sacramento and the driver would not go on until it cleared. As I recall, I was 12 hours late checking into my squadron which made me AWOL. I called the day Sargent "Sir" and he quickly told me to go take a shower and wash off all that basic training and ONLY call officers Sir. I was okay at that point, nothing about the awol was mentioned and I settled in with great anticipation of working on aircraft. I loved it more than anything in life. I was a hydraulic technician!

The next day I cleared into base. That meant checking in at squadron command, getting my tools issued, and reporting to the Hydraulic shop. What excitement that was! I had never been close to a real jet before. I checked my tools in and met some of the guys that I would be working with. Then I was sent back to settle into my room.

I had two roommates, that I met that afternoon. Jeff Whit and Terry Cato. Those boys were sure a "hoot.". We would have just loads of fun in our future days together. As third man in the room, it made it a little crowded, but we did just fine. I hit it off with them very well right from the start.

My first real day of working on a real plane came the next day. I think I started out with doing a bleed job on a primary Hydraulic system. It was so cool. You had to wear ear plugs in your ears and then put the mickey mouse head set over that. It was so loud! The aircraft was chained down at the run-up pad and the jet engine started. We had to hook up bleeder hoses and have the run-up guy move all the flight controls. This caused the trapped air to come out of the bleeder hose. The engine would be run up to full military power, as it was called. Then several times he would throw it into afterburner. I have never felt anything like that. It was pure power. If that plane was flying at level flight right then, it would be going about 840 miles an hour. The tools in your toolbox would actually be floating from the noise of that jet. I knew most of those procedures from my Tech schooling and it was so cool to see them in action.

A lot of what I learned to do, and I became very good at, was to troubleshoot. That involved checking things out in a tech book and tracing down the problem. We had a lot of air injection problems, and I was good at them. I soon fit in and was doing my job, always with a rather large smile on my face. Sorta like a hunting dog sitting there looking at you and ready to fetch. Give me a job to do on an airplane.

I soon had a lot of Air Force buddies. I started going out with them and having a good time. They all knew that I had a steady girl back home so some of the pressures of going out were not put on me by the guys. We could drink at the bars on base. There were a lot of girls around whenever we went out. I stayed true and blue to the gal back home.

I worked my butt off at my work, loving every minute of it. I was very good and worked the night shift. The day shift guys would often leave the big problem jobs for me, and I loved it.

The months rolled on into a year and it had been almost two years since I had left home. The letters home were getting fewer and all those little feelings I had when I joined the service were about gone. I was having a lot of fun with my new friends and home seemed so far away. Then I got a letter telling me that Janet had gone to the high school prom with another guy, I think his name was

Blankenship. At that point I was actually hoping that they would get together, and I would be on my own. It had been so long since I had been with Janet that it didn't matter much anymore. I had been having good times and partying a lot with my buds.

WEDDING BELLS

I decided to tell Janet that I wanted to be free until I got out of the service and if we still felt close when I got out, which would be a four-year separation by then, then we could pick it up again at that time. I guess you could say that I sent her a "Dear John" letter. Boy did that ever not work!

My feelings of freedom were cut short because I started receiving letters from her aunts, her Mom, her sister and from her. The very same people I felt were condemning me when I was home were now telling me how rotten I was for leaving that poor girl in such a mess. Then came the tape recording from Janet, a newly released song, "The End Of the World" by Skeeter Davis played in the back ground through most of the tape as she talked, over and over again. You should google Skeeter Davis and listen to it, it is a very sad song.

Even one of my buddies wrote Janet a letter trying to tell her that this would be best. I wanted the freedom to really experience what life was all about. I didn't know about that part of me, and I did not want to feel guilty if those experiences should go too far.

So, I wound up calling home in an attempt to make her feel better and let her know that we could pick it up when I got out of the military. I could not keep it going on two or so letters a week. I was done and wanted to drop it there. I had been true and blue. So, we talked and we cried and we set a WEDDING DATE, ON THE PHONE. I did not want to do that because nothing had changed. I did not know her, and she did not know me. So now we were going to get married. I really was very mad at myself for doing that, but it was too late now. Plans were made over the next four months or so and I went home on leave. It was two years almost to the day that I had joined the Air Force.

Everything had changed at home. Mom and Dad had moved,

and all of my old buddies were gone. The night before the wedding, Mom and Dad tried to talk me out of it because they could now see where I really was in life, and they knew I was doing the wrong thing. Mom cried as she felt this was all wrong for me.

I found myself married to my old high school steady. Mom was right. That was the start of my really messing up Janet's as well as my life. I think I even knew it then. I had almost two years left away from her, and I had only seen her a few times since I had left two years earlier. All I knew is that she was a very pretty girl. I did not want to hurt her. Janet was too sweet for me, and I knew it. I had gotten to know myself some by then. I should have backed out!

We had a 10 day or so honeymoon in Niagara Falls, Washington DC and Gettysburg PA. I thought we had a really fun time. We went to see the fresh grave of John F. Kennedy, all the battle fields of Gettysburg, plus just a lot of fun stuff.

I had gotten orders for a permanent change of station just before I came home to get married. I had called and told her about it. We were both very sad, but she still wanted to go through with the wedding. And we did. My new orders stated that I was to be transferred to the Philippine Islands.

Garry and Janet Korf Wallen

June 20, 1964

Tony and Beverly Wallen Dobos

Jerry and Elaine Wallen Kubica

Edward and Janet Bishop Wallen

Richard and Janet Stempfle Wallen

Edward and Mary Wallen Dick

Eric and Charlene Wallen Castillo

Paul and Beverly Wallen Williams

CHANGES AT HOME

Gary McEldowney & Garry Wallen USAF

I flew back to Travis Air Base for that last month and right away put in for another month back in Michigan. That month went fairly fast as I had to clear base and get ready for the permanent move. I found out when I got back there that my new best buddy Gary McEldowney was also being sent to the Philippines. He and I had worked really well together and it would be great to have him with me in the P.I. I cleared Base, said my goodbyes with all the folks I knew at Travis and flew back home with all my worldly possessions. It's strange but I don't remember much about that 30-day furlough back home. Janet was working then, and I think I may have worked for Jerry Kubica for a week or two at that time.

The old Merle Cook farm was completely different now. Elaine and Jerry had moved into the old farmhouse and it had caught fire and burned completely down. Merle and I had torn down the big ol' barn years earlier and Merle rebuilt on the stone foundation. He built a really nice house. Jerry and Elaine had in turn built a house on the sight of the old farmhouse.

Mom and Dad had sold the Green House where I had grown up. They moved in with Merle, in what was now called the Stone House, so everything was different for me. I know that Janet and I spent a week or so staying with my folks in the Stone House. Being married and staying with family was rather hard for us. The time did go quickly though, and I was off again on another adventure, somewhere in this big world. I would be close to Vietnam. Mom was worried.

I flew back to Travis and checked in for my flight overseas. I had a lot of excitement going on in my head. I knew that I was about to experience a whole new chapter in my life. I was heading to a foreign county, a place I knew nothing about but wanted to learn. My best buddy Gary McEldowney would be there with me in just two short months.

OFF TO THE PHILIPPINES

It was a very long flight over there, close to 12,000 miles from home. It was a 24-hour trip. I'll never forget getting off that plane in the P.I. It was like getting hit in the face with a blow torch. Really hot. I got used to it rather quickly though.

It did not take long to settle into a routine. I was put up in an open bay barracks. One big room with about 40 guys in there. I guess I have to say, it was a lot of fun. We had house boys that took care of just about everything, even shining our shoes. There was a day room downstairs and beer was .15 cents a bottle. It was also within walking distance from my workstation. I met all the Hydraulic Shop guys and got right into my work.

Shortly after I got there, I got a letter from Janet that really crashed me. She was telling me about our honeymoon trip and she let me know that it would have been a great trip, if only I would have left her alone. That letter destroyed a lot of what I had felt about myself as well as a lot of what I felt for her. I had so many mixed up feelings that I didn't know where to turn. So, I just worked really hard and I got into the bottle way more that I should have.

If I may brag a little, I was very good at what I did and I got right into the work. Soon I had been noticed for my work and within 30 days of being at Clark Field, I was sent to Bangkok, Thailand as the Hydraulic Tech on the base, on temporary duty. It was such a wonderful time. There was just way too much to see in that country. It was a very beautiful city and the people there were just about as nice as I had ever met. We had only six F102s on base and we flew only once a day. If nothing was broke on the planes when they returned from flight, I could go back to the hotel and do whatever I wanted to do for the rest of the day. That is why I have so many pictures of

Bangkok.

We stayed at The Royal Dutch Airlines hotel. It was a little old, but beautiful. There must have been 10 acres of grass around there and a bunch of ponds with swans all over the place. It was also full of palm Trees. There was not a blade of grass out of place there. It was awesome. I stayed there for 70 fun filled days. I returned back to the Philippines and found Gary Mac had gotten there.

The two of us got to working in that shop and before long we were really turning out the repair parts. When we got started, they were returning 85% of the parts to the states for repair. That was parts coming out of Vietnam and they were repairing only 15%. By the time Mac and I left the Islands, we were repairing 85% and returning only 15%. We were very proud of that. We had an attitude about the same as the guys on the TV show, "MASH". We had a bad attitude towards the Air Force but did our job and did it well. Our NCOIC called Mac and I his "GOLD DUST TWINS." We had kept him out of trouble a lot.

A lot of the repairs that we made were illegal to do as they were supposed to be made only at the proper depot level state side repair shop. We had one Sargent who did not like us and spent a lot of his day trying to prove we were doing things we were forbidden to do. Mac and I were very good at fixing the paperwork so our work would be legal and we caused that poor guy more grief than anyone should ever have to put up with from a couple of really young punks. Mac always liked to tell the story about the afternoon that we were taking off from work and Sargent Tarman was rummaging through a waste basket to find some of our paperwork that we would have altered and as we walked by, I kicked the can out from under him and told him to get out of the trash can. We were well protected by the guys over him that really liked us though and there was nothing he could do.

One day they even sent the military police to town to retrieve us from our favorite bar, to fix an F-105 that we knew very little about. Nobody from our shop knew what to do. We were a little bit, "too many beers" at the time but we fixed that plane in about an hour, repaired a valve. The plane took off for Vietnam and they took us back to the bar. I still have the thank you letter sent to me from the pilot who was stranded at our base because his plane was broken.

Mac and I even took a temporary duty to Vietnam for 60 days as there were eight of our F-102s there in Danang. We were swimming in the South China Sea," absolutely beautiful beach, the day the Marines landed about a mile south of where we were partying. That was cool, we now felt safe.

We did a lot of things there that we should not have done. We would rent bikes and go all over town to areas we were forbidden to go in. Mac even had a few drinks one day with some Viet Cong. He slipped out when he found out how much danger he was in. That kid was always slippery. We actually had a lot of fun there. We were indestructible, too young, and too crazy. Mac use to say, years later, that if we had known ourselves back then, we probably would not have liked ourselves very much! It was all in the attitude, I guess. We were happy to leave Vietnam and get back to the P.I.

THE PINK ELEPHANT BAR

We had a favorite bar in the Philippines called the Pink Elephant and we could be found in there most nights. It was in a section of Angeles City just outside of the base, several miles from the gate. It had 12 rather dirty little bars on one street and most of the field maintenance guys would hang out there. What a fun place. A lot of very young drunk mechanics all wanting to party. Some of the guys who were either afraid to go or did not want to go to town wound up going nuts, for real, as they had no release in life from being away from their moms and dads.

There were fights. I never got hurt very bad, but I did put one engine shop guy in the hospital for a few days, he had hurt his back (bragging again). There were about six or eight of us guys that hung out regularly and there were times that we would go to some other bar just to pick a fight. There were no knives or guns, just fun, or dumb, however you would call it. I was a 145-pound wiry little shit as were most of us back then. We were rather cocky.

We got together one night and about six of us went to another part of the city to a bar that was frequented by the medics. We went in and all got our beers and that is when the fun started. This one crazy kid by the name of Miller grabbed this one medic guy by the arm and loudly ask "Are you a Medic?" The guy answered, "Yes I am." Miller then proceeded to put his lit cigarette out on the guy's arm and announce rather loudly, "Well fix it". Of course, we all got into a really big, but fun, fight. One of our guys caught a beer bottle upside the head but we got out of there before the Air Police got there and made it back safely to our bar, The Pink Elephant. We had to stay on guard at our place for a week or so after that in case of an attack by the medics. They were not much of a lot to be worried about though.

Mac and I tried to break up a fight just outside of the gate one night. There were these three sergeants that just happened to be passing through our base on their way to Bangkok. They were drunk and complaining loudly about our San Miguel beer. These other guys behind us in the line for the bus started a fight with them. It turned into a bit of a brawl, so Mac and I thought we better break it up before the Air Police came. Well about the time the cops got there, Mac and I were right in the middle of it, not doing real well and we got arrested with the rest of 'em. I remember that, because that was the only time we got to ride in the paddy wagon. After we explained our position, we were let go from the brig.

Talking about the line to get on the bus… There was this group of black guys that liked to walk to the front of the line. You had to be careful with them because some of them carried knives. So, one night, they cut in line and I sort of had had enough. I started giving this one guy some crap and he hit me upside the head with his umbrella. They all liked to wear these real thin silk slacks. I just reached down grabbed him by his privates and picked him up off the ground. His scream was deafening and when I dropped him he rolled down the hill into the ditch. He was still screaming. His buddies ran to him thinking I had stabbed him. Of course he wasn't hurt… much.

THE DIRTY DOZEN

There were always quite a few young ladies in those bars every night. Some were hookers; some were just after drinks; and some just worked as waitresses. I became friends with some of them in the Pink Elephant but stayed away from most of them.

There was a 17-year-old that worked only behind the bar and I became good friends with her. Her name was Terrie. We talked a lot, and she knew that I was married. I guess she knew a lot about me. My buddy Mac started dating a gal that I believe was a few years older than we were. Her name was Angie, the best friend of Terrie. She had a little baby girl about 2 years old and she used to bring her to work every so often. Angie was always high on drugs and quite a crazy girl.

There was an older guy that managed the Pink Elephant, and he took a liking to Mac and me. His name was Ming. A very fine fellow indeed as he always took good care of Mac, and Tom and me.

Sometimes we would go bar hoping just because we would know that different bars had different songs on their Juke boxes. There was a bottle of booze you could buy called Boon Coon, awful stuff. Sometimes it would be 10 proof and sometimes 200 proof. Some said it could make you go blind. There were times that we would eat from the vendors in the street. You never knew what you got for meat. I know we ate wild monkey and a few times, and what we called "dog on a log." I think it really was some poor dog. We ate a lot of peanuts roasted with garlic and that was really good.

There was an open ditch running through the city and it crossed the street in the dirty dozen about mid-way. All the garbage was dumped in there from the bridge and the stink was really bad. Every time we had a big rain though, it was like flushing the toilet. It turned into a raging river, and everything was flushed away, even the smell.

The dirty dozen area was like a scene out of the old west. A lot of bars, close to each other, a lot of drunk people all over the street. The hookers. And all night, every night, there was music flowing from every bar. What a place. No guns, no knives. So that set the stage for a lot of rather crazy days and nights in the dirty dozen. Weekends were always a "hoot."

By this time, it had been over three years since I had left home, it seemed so far into another world, almost an unreal world. Maybe even a softer place. We always worked hard, and we always played hard. As I said, we were indestructible and bullet proof. That is the way it was at that age. The Air Force highly recommended that all G.I.'s stay away from that area. A place like no other in the world.

Even though Mac and I woke up in some strange places a time or two, I stayed true to my vows up to that point.

I had gotten rather close to Terry in that we would go out and eat or go to another bar for a drink once in a while. It was still just friends and I think we both felt safe being with each other. Mac and Angie were an item and they often stayed at Angie and Terry's place. Sometimes I would stay over there as well. It was a pretty rough place. Lots of bats and a zillion cockroaches lived there. It was by a railroad station as I recall.

TRIP TO THE OCEAN

Then, in late October of 65, a bunch of us guys and a group of the gals all got together and took a bus trip to a beach on the ocean about six hours north of base. The bus ride was a real experience, no sides on the bus, very bumpy roads and we stopped about every two miles to pick up or let somebody out. What a ride, there were even goats at times, put on the roof. Yes it had a roof.

We arrived at the ocean about two in the morning, dirty, hungry, and very tired. Terry had rode beside me all the way there and we stuck together at the beach. There was a little "Sari-Sari store" open and they had a big pot of something like spaghetti for sale. We all ate our fill and yuk, it was bad. The rest of the night we had more beer and slept on the beach, dead tired. It was October the 29th, my 23rd birthday.

The next morning, we all rented some nepa huts on the beach for the next few nights. The days were just one big party, we even went for a boat ride with some Filipino guy. I still have a movie of that boat ride. That evening, I remember swimming in the ocean with a trail of glowing light in the water about 20 feet lone behind me, it was awesome. There was phosphorous in the water, really cool.

Later that night with the partying dyeing down, Mac and Angie and Terry and I shared a nepa hut together. Terry and I had drank too much and decided to sleep together, something that we had talked about not doing in the months we knew each other. We were no longer safe with each other. It was her first time, and I did not know a whole lot more than she did. She was 18 and I had turned 23 that day. We did not talk about it after that. There was however, a song that she would play on the Juke Box when I would come into the bar. It was called "The Mansion you Stole", by Johnny Horton.

About six weeks after that beach trip, I stopped going to town. I had to clear paperwork on base, turn in things, ship stuff home and get ready for the return to the States. Yes, I felt bad for what Terry and I had done, and was sorry it had happened. A lot of things in life you just can't take back.

CLEARING BASE AND BACK TO THE STATES

Mac went temporary duty to Bangkok in the middle of December of '65, I stayed on base that last month or so and left Clark Field on the 18th of January 1966. I was on my flight home.

Mac shipped back to the states in March of '66. He never knew it, but his friend Angie took an overdose of drugs in June and she died. Her little daughter was adopted by the owner of the Pink Elephant. She would be about 65 years old by now. Terry left the city then and went to her mom in the central Islands.

I mustered out of the Air Force on the 22nd of January 1966. It really hit me on the way home. I was married to someone I had seen for only a few days in the last four years. I felt I hardly knew Janet. No job. No money. No place to live and my education was 10th grade. I knew hydraulic systems but that was about it. How far could that go in Owosso, Michigan? I was scared to death, but in hopes of forming a good bond with my wife. I would build a house myself if I had to and I'd find work. Those were my thoughts as I got off the plane in freezing cold Michigan. Yes, I was scared to get off that plane. I was 23 years old. I had just completed an education that would help me along for the rest of my life. I had become such a different person by that day, from the kid that got on that bus in May of 1962, four long years before. I had changed from a rather cocky and stubborn dumb kid that could not learn a darn thing, into someone with a goal in mind. All I knew was hard work. I just needed a chance in life. I really was scared to death.

TIME TO GET SERIOUS

Many opportunities lay ahead for me. I just had to make it happen. Janet was waiting outside the plane that day. We were in a new mode in our lives now. We had to start by learning about each other. That would be hard living in the Korf house, but Janet and I vowed to make it work for each other. I really missed my old buds, and I missed my airplanes a lot but this was a real life I was entering, far from all the hullabaloo. Janet and I both embraced our new life together as we started making plans. This may sound funny but there were times I would look at Janet or find her looking at me sort of in wonderment as if to say, who is that person. We were learning.

LOTS OF WORK AHEAD

I had planned to take a few weeks off before I got to looking for work and spend some time just getting to know my wife, but the following Monday, I thought I would run over to Flint to the Buick factory and put in a work application, just in case they were hiring. Little did I know but with the war going on and the draft in place, 23-year-olds were in high demand if they had their service over with. That was me and I hit it just at the right time. I called Janet and told her that I would not be home until after midnight. I started second shift that very day, not much break. Lots of work with overtime every night.

My first job was to install the front and rear tires on the Buick Riviera's driver side. The cars came by my job site at chest high so the tires had to be picked up, set on the drum and the lug nuts installed. They had a lug nut gun that would install all five nuts at once. Then I had to grab the third tire and throw it up into the open trunk. I had 60 seconds to do that job. That included the time for that car to move out and the next one to move in. Damn, that was hard, and long and boring work. I could set my body in motion and my mind could go anywhere it wanted to.

I was on the assembly line at a major auto factory and, holy cow, they paid me $126 a week without including overtime. Gas was $0.35 a gallon and a carton of cigarettes was $3. Tall cotton right there.

When I arrived home that first night after work, I was overjoyed. Janet had already been to bed for a few hours by that time as she had to work the next day. I think though, that I woke everybody up in my excitement. I could not believe that I already got a permanent job. One down and lots of things to get done. A house, yes, I will build a house. Dad and my brother Ed had built a few houses, and I knew I could as well. I felt that I was on my way to becoming a real person in life. Maybe if I worked hard enough, I could be recognized by the family as a success in this world. A lot of things that haunted me as a teenager were still with me. This was a different world than the one I had just left in the Air force, in which I was sort of top dog. I vowed to work really hard. I would make it.

BUILDING OUR FIRST HOUSE

After a few weeks Janet and I went to Dad Wallen and told him that we wanted to build a brand-new house and I was going to do the work. We had saved $1,000 over my service time. Dad said he was expecting this to happen and had the lot already waiting for us if we did not mind living in the Flint area. It was on Dye Road in Flint township. It was a full acre, worth about $3,500 and Dad said he would sell it to us for the $1,000 we had saved up. Wow, a real job and now we actually owned land. Our little dreams were coming true, life was good!

Janet and I were having a fine time in life, and we had already gotten some good success in our first month or so together. It was rather rough living where we were though. That little, tiny bedroom of Janet's from her childhood still had two single beds in it as I recall, one for Jane and one for Janet. So now it was one for her and one for me. Right next door slept, the mother-in-law. Lots of fun for a 23-year-old! I must have felt like a predator in that house.

Janet was working in the blueprint room of a local Owosso factory. We were making good money together and saving it. Janet's mother had taken her furniture shopping before I had gotten out of the service and a lot of stuff had already been picked out by her and put on lay-away. We were saving to pay it all off and with no house payment, we were doing fairly good. We were doing so well together, and success was at hand, we just had to keep it going. We were still too young to be married but we were making a go of it! We were happy!

I think it was at this time that Janet and I, maybe even for the first time in our young lives, started to feel love for each other. I mean real love. It seemed to me that the six years of the past, we were doing something that we were just supposed to be doing. I felt like I could make a future for us at that point. I had become a much more confident person about our lives together.

There were still thoughts of my old gang of buddies from the military. I sure did like to party with them. I missed McEldowney a lot, we were very close. He would be getting out soon and I would make plans the next year to go down to West Virginia and visit him. He had carried a picture of his old high school sweetheart through most of our years together and she had gotten married after he left for the service. He was heartbroken for a while, he was in hopes that they could still get together some day. He would be coming home in the middle of March.

So, things were looking up for a poor kid from Chesaning. I was starting to get a hold on what I called "Life". Janet and I agreed on a floor plan that Dad had, and it was decided that brother Edward would be building a house of the same type, right beside ours. They would put it up fairly fast and live there just long enough for them to build a much bigger house behind where we were building.

None of that mattered to me. I just wanted to get started on ours. The plans were readied and the lots staked for digging. Jerry Kubica would be loaning us his basement forms and we had a TON of work to do. I knew enough about those basement panels, from days as a kid when I used to help Jerry, to get them set up. We were under way.

This was way cool! Janet and I knew that during the next six or so months we would not have much time together. I was working 9+ hours a day, sometimes six days a week at the shop and building a house on the side lines. My job was really hard work. I had to handle about 180 tires an hour for 9 hours running. I was dead tired most of the time. My goal was within reach though. I just had to push the hell out of that thin 145-pound body of mine.

Eddie's house took off much faster than ours, as he knew what he was doing and he hired most of it done. I spent enough time watching him on his house that I learned most of how to do it and I did it. The house was a whopping 940 square feet but with the basement it was fine.

Janet and her mother would come over sometimes on Saturdays, and if they come on Sundays, Marv would come along and that was when I was most proud. He loved to watch my progress. A bit of a riff started at that time with Janet's mother and me as at times she made me feel like I was working for her, and she would tell me what she wanted done or how to do it. I was not happy with that, but she was my wife's mother. I knew to respect my elders, as it were. I had planned to be ready to move in by July and life would be good again.

I remember when I started building the furnace chimney. I was totally surprised when all my measurements came together and from the footing as I built the cement blocks straight up through the hole that happened to be in the right place and right on through the roof hole. The darn thing all lined up. I had a chimney. I don't know why I should remember that now, but I think it gave me reason to trust my measurements from then on.

On a real cold day in early April, we had the cement delivered to pour the basement floor. I say we because there was Dad and Ed Dick there to help me pour it. This was all new to me and all I learned is that cement is really heavy. We got the cement all poured and started to do the troweling. It was so cold that we just could not get it to set up. It set but the topping stayed mushy. When it rolled around to 3 o'clock that day, Ed Dick and I both had to take off for work as we both worked at the Buick and second shift started at 4:00 pm. My poor father was left there, to his surprise, to finish the floor topping on his own. It was such a cold afternoon, and it just would not set up. After working my shift of all those tires, I went back to the house and Dad was still there with some temporary lighting he had hooked up from the neighbor's house. The floor was rough, but we left it and went on home. I would tile it later. The next morning, we smoothed it out a little more as it was about set up and we could get on it. I knew then that the next weekend Janet and her Mom would be commenting on it. We just were not cement people, but we could not afford to have it done.

We had borrowed $13,000 from Michigan National Bank for the house mortgage, and that is all I had to work with. In those days, that much money went a long way.

So it went, I spent every minute I could working on that house. It got to a point where I would spend a few nights a week at my parent's house in Flint so I would not have to make that trip back and forth to Owosso every day. I was bone tired most of the time, but we were getting there.

There were a few more problems with Janet's Mom, with drywall and paint, a broken window. She picked out all of our paint colors and I was not happy, but it would not be long and it would be done. I had some trouble installing the siding as I did not have the right tools but when I got it done it looked pretty good. I think it is still on that house. We did white siding and a charcoal-colored roof. I was really proud of my roof job although it took me forever to install it. There were no leaks either.

There was one thing though, that really kicked my butt. That darn garage door was just too many parts and to much that had to be just right. I had gotten it from Sears and after two days of working on it, I gave up! It never did work right. I hated garage doors for a long time after that. Still, when I have to adjust a garage door, or work on one. I always think back to trying to install that one on my very first house.

So, the painting was done and I think I did a good job on it. Then Janet and Jane came, and they cleaned and cleaned until the place was ready for carpet. They found out that I was a slob. That was a really big day, getting the carpet installed. I felt success at last, there were things left to do, doors to hang back or install and a good clean up outside the house but we finally moved into our very own place.

2233 S. Dye Rd. Flint, MI.—My first building job.

MOVING IN TO OUR FIRST HOME

By this time, my Air Force days were getting farther and farther behind me. My buddies were getting pretty well forgotten, though I would always hold onto a great love for flying and for Airplanes. Janet and I were doing just great, we could now learn about life together, just the two of us. Life could be really good.

Jane and Phil were always fun to be around. He could be a real cut up. Everyone always thought those two were a perfect couple. Little did we know how they were really doing.

I came from a large family. Family always meant a lot to me, and I tried to get into being a part of the Korf gang, but it never seemed quite right for me. Ole Grandma Flouse was a great ole gal though, she really liked me and made me feel comfortable. She used to whack me on my behind with her purse when she saw me at a family get together. I liked her. Janet had several aunts and uncles though that always made me feel uncomfortable. The one that told everyone that I had broken into her house was always real cold to me as was her husband. One of Janet's Aunts worked at a bar just outside of Owosso and I stopped in there several times just to talk to her about the Korf family and how they felt about me. She was a good ole gal and liked me. She was reassuring. Tonie is the name that comes to mind for her.

Janet and I were growing a relationship and we worked at it. We had learned a lot about each other during those six months living at her parent's house and building a house. We got into it a few times, but her Mom was always there to solve the problem.

All the furniture was finally delivered, and I could finally see, at that point, what we had bought. It was okay, but the table and chairs for the kitchen were strait out of the early '50s. The living room sofa was sort of concave. It had a rather rough embossed fabric on, it sort of like sandpaper. I didn't care a lot for it and I don't think Janet did ether. I never said a word, it was okay.

I was just so happy to be in that house and settling into a married life. Janet and I were very happy in our own little home. Talk of children was in the air but I believe we had decided to wait a year or so before we tried.

That first year, I did a lot on the house. Tons of yard work was at hand and making the basement into a rec room was one of my big projects. I finally got the basement floor tiled, and we added some paneling down there. It was pretty nice. We soon had several Korf get togethers there. Life was good. After all the happenings over the past years, we were settled in.

I was gaining a lot of confidence in myself, much needed at this point. I was an employee with a permanent job. I was a homeowner of a house built with my own two hands. I was the husband of a very pretty girl that I was getting to know and learning to love. What more could a 23-year-old ask for.

MOVING ALONG

Over the next year things settled down very well. I was learning though, that Janet was not as affectionate as I would have loved her to be. I came from a very affectionate family. Also, it seemed that there were two sides to our family instead of one big family. The Wallen side always seemed to be on the back burner when it came to events and family things. So, I accepted it as that's the way it was to be. Janet's Mom and I had a little butting of the heads once in a while. That wasn't pleasant but we seemed to work it out. I was always excited to see her dad though. He always made me feel so welcome, something I needed from that family.

Janet was sick an awful lot and our intimate times grew farther and farther apart. I learned that she was not a hugie person. I was one that needed a lot of affection in my life. I guess that stemmed from my childhood. I often told her that and she tried hard to be what I needed. It was a struggle for her. I think it could have been a security thing for me in some way. If that's the case, I guess I am still needing my security.

In August of 1967, Janet and I drove down to West Virginia to visit with my ole Air Force buddy, Gary McEldowney. What a joy I had, seeing him again after 18 months apart and he introduced me to his beloved Jeanie. Jeanie was about as cute as a little mountain girl could be. She had gotten married while Mac was in the service and had a son. She was still married when I first met her, but she was having a real problem in life. She had a son by her husband, but I knew right away that she was still in love with Mac. She soon divorced and a little later Mac and she were married. He was one happy guy at that time. We had a very pleasant visit with Mac and his family. What a great family they were.

It was on this trip to visit Mac, that he told me that Terrie had been pregnant, back in the Philippines, when I had shipped back to the states. Mac and I both doubted that it was true, but it was something that would haunt me for many years to come. I did not even know Terrie's last name, let alone a way to get a hold of her.

STARTING OUR LITTLE FAMILY

Janet and I decided it was time to start a family of our own. She stopped taking the "pill" and after several months we were allowed to try, for real, to get pregnant. We tried for a full year and no luck. We were checked out at the doctor and were told just to keep trying. My Aunt Curly (Francis Nietling) told us one time jokingly that you really can't plant a seed and turn around and hoe it right back out again.

I guess I have to say I really enjoyed all that time of trying. Actually, as a 25 - 26-year-old it was an important part of married life. It seemed like we were having fun. Then one month, it was July of 1968, we were pregnant. We found out for sure in September. Our whole world changed forever. The fun times trying to get P.G. pretty well stopped and it was time for all the preparations.

Janet and I were separated on that point as Janet, Jane and their mother took over. I had no say. Janet and I could have had a really great time setting up the nursery, but the Korf thing took over again. The room was readied, and it was really cool. The months passed by that winter very slowly. We were excited and could not wait till our little one really came along.

Janet had a job working for a Dentist in Flushing at that time. I believe she was quite sick most of the pregnancy. I had taken up doing construction work for some of the local builders doing things like roofing and framing just to make extra money. I was still working nine or so hours a day in the Buick. Sometimes six days a week.

At this time in our lives together, we were doing okay. Responsibility was about to wash over us, and we were ready to take it on.

Things were not real peachy with mother Korf though. I think that I was building a bit of resentment toward her. She had made so many decisions for us at this point, things that I was either left out of or overlooked in. It became very touchy to me. I was not happy with her. One Sunday, it came sort of to a head and I let my feelings out. She left, going home crying.

JULIE IS HERE—YIPPIE

My Best Little Buddie

Our little world came together the next year on March the 20th of 1969. Our little Julie came along. It all happened a little different than I expected. I had taken Janet into her doctor's appointment and after a quick exam, we were directed to go across the street, right now, to the hospital. The baby was on the way. I thought we were supposed to get up in the middle of the night in a panic and rush to the hospital.

I was not allowed to watch the birth but when I first got to see my little girl, she had me around her little finger right away. I didn't understand the pointed head but was told it would be normal in a day or so. I just had so much love for that little one I couldn't stand to be away from her. She was a perfect little lady and totally healthy.

Janet and I did very good. All those baby bottles and formula and diapers that we stocked up on were put to good use in a few days when we brought her home. We were now a family.

A lot of things happened in 1969. I was still very busy working at the Buick, working nine hours most of the time and sometimes it was six days a week. By this time, I had worked my way up to a real easy job. There were nights that I only had to do about 45 minutes of actual work. That made it easy on me, but I actually felt guilty and resented the fact that a guy could get a full day's pay and not have to do much. I learned to resent the Union, but I had to be a member of it to work there. I was not brought up that way and it just wasn't right. I had been learning a lot about home building and I was doing a lot

Julie Jane

on the side. We were getting ahead nicely but it cost me a lot of long hours. Janet was sick a lot from being pregnant and all, and we decided to build another new house and sell the one at 2233 South Dye Road.

OUR SECOND HOME

We found a nice lot in Swartz Creek, only a few miles from where we were. It was a half-acre and wide enough to put a nice long house on. I drew the plans for that house and learned a lot about drawing plans at that time. I did everything on that house except for things like drywall and I did not pour the cement. I learned how to lay bricks and do Formica tops in the kitchen and baths. I had been around home construction about three years by that time and had learned a lot.

I was really enjoying home building and hated going into the shop to work. It was like being a captive for those long hours. I did not like it. I knew that at some point, I was going to quit and probably go into homebuilding. It was a dream to me at that time but reachable.

MOM AND DAD MOVE TO ARIZONA

Also in 1969, my Mom and Dad, and Brother Eddy sold out everything in Michigan and moved out to Arizona. They would be deeply missed by those of us that stayed behind. It left a big hole in our lives. On the upside though, it gave us someplace to go visit in years to come.

Dad and Mom had talked about moving west for quite some time. They loved the mountains and hated the snow and cold of Michigan.

Merle Cook, the wonderful old guy that had been like a family member since I can remember, and was living with Mom and Dad, passed away in 1968, so Mom and Dad were a little more free to move. I couldn't believe that they actually moved. They missed all of us a lot but were very happy in their decision. We just wanted for them to be happy in what they were doing. They were experiencing a whole new life with coyotes, wild pigs, road runners and a wonderfully beautiful desert. Dad and Ed needed to find work, plus they were going to build themselves some houses. They had a lot to do.

Dad was a big part of our deer hunting trip every year until he moved. The next fall when we were up in the U.P. of Michigan, I was sitting in camp one afternoon and thinking about Dad, so I decided to write him a letter from camp. I went outside and found a pure white birch tree. With my knife I cut a nice letter size section of bark from the tree which was like a sheet of paper. I sat down and wrote Dad a letter on it, telling him how much we all missed him and what the camp was like that year.

Mom said that letter ruined him for a week. He stumbled around talking to himself. He really would have loved to have been with us. That letter even smelled like the woods, fresh birch bark. Poor Dad, but he really liked his letter, and he saved it for many years to come.

MAC SCOTT COURT HOUSE

Julie– My Little Helper. (Second House)

That year, 1969 was very busy for me. I was doing a lot of work on the side. I was working in the shop, and I was building our house. I believe it was late fall when we finally moved into that house on Mac Scott Ct. in Swartz Creek. It was a much bigger place with a family room and a living room. I finished off the basement right away and built myself a little office down there so I could do bids and paperwork for my side line job. We also had a large laundry room and a big toy room for Julie to play in. It was down a flight of stairs, but she learned quickly to climb up and down them. There was no bathroom down there, unless you considered the sump pump which, by the way, ran all the time. The water table was high there.

By this time, my sister Mary and her husband, Ed Dick, and I had become real close friends and I thought that Janet was part of it. Later in our relationship, my friendship with Ed and Mary would become part of our undoing. Until now, most of our free time was spent with the Korfs and I was wanting to spend some time with my family.

Janet and I didn't get to see Sister Elaine and her husband Jerry very much, mainly because of something that Elaine had said the first time she and Jerry came to our house on Dye Road. I think it was something about who picked everything out in that house. Janet never liked Elaine after that. Ed and Mary were different, we got to see them, but there was a real division between our families as to who we saw and when. For a while I liked going to visit with Jane and Phil, they were fun most of the time.

So, In the fall of 1969, I bought my first snowmobile. I had an absolute ball on that thing. This created a little more riff between the families as I wanted to go out to Ed Dick's as much as I could in the winter months to ride in the country. We could run those gravel roads and the open fields, down the rivers, through the woods. We would chase deer and go bar hopping to those old county bars where all the snowmobilers would go.

It was a guy thing, but it was not really a good thing as it was hard on Janet. I guess I didn't realize it then, but all the long hours of work and then sometimes long hours of play caused us to drift apart a bit. Janet turned more to her family. This could have been the start of something really bad for us. Our really close times that meant so much to me were becoming fewer. Between family and friends and too much to do, it was taking its toll on us.

By Christmas time of that year, we had fairly well settled into the new house. It was time to slow down a bunch and spend some time with just the three of us. Little miss Julie was getting around all over the house by that time. As I look back, I could have predicted that little Missy was bound to be a very independent person as she grew in life. I couldn't wait for her to walk and to talk, boy could she ever jabber!

The year 1970 was a fast year with mostly a lot of hard work as I was doing more and more roofing, siding and framing jobs on the side from my work at the Buick. I think that might have been the year that I built a garage on Jane and Phil's house for them.

There was still an ever-widening gap between the Korf side of the family and I, as well as Janet from my side of the family. I think we both talked about it a few times, but we did not work on it, that was not good. I think that Janet liked for us to go out with Mary and Ed once in a while, and we as well with Jane and Phil but that was about it for the families. I think that if we had moved to another state, or somewhere else, we would have had a much better chance of making it together.

FISHING TRIP TO CANADA

Dad came up to Michigan that summer to go on a fishing trip to Canada with Ed Dick and me. We would camp on an Island in this lake and fish for four or five days.

One day we were cruising the shoreline. It was common to stay close to shore and cast into the bank and then real back into the boat. Those northern pike would lay right along shore and that's how we caught them. So, one day we were cruising along and had not had a single bite for several hours. All of a sudden, Dad stood up in the boat and hollered out, the Lord said for us to take dominion over the fishes of the sea, and I take dominion over the fishes in this lake. Ed and I thought we were going to get a sermon but that wasn't it.

Ed made his next cast into the shore line and as soon as the lure hit the water, a fish took it. As Ed tried to reel it in, that fish got up on its tail on the water, walked its way over to the boat and flopped itself up into the boat. It spit the lure out and as it flopped around it knocked itself out and just lay there. True story.

Ed and I looked at each other and then at Dad. He just sort of shrugged with this big smile on his face. Dad loved to fish but he never really did catch that great big one that he always talked about.

FUN IN THE YARD

Julie and I developed a very close relationship. She was by my side most of the time when I was home, either inside the house or out. She was my side kick. She went to the hardware store, the grocery store, and the lumber yard. Whenever I could take her she was ready to go.

I built us a little shed out back and for little "Missy," she got a sand box with the good kind of sand in it, and a swing set that had a nice slide, and all the other goodies. I planted trees in the yard and got grass to grow all the way around the house. I built a planter alongside the front porch. I even planted flowers in there. In the following years to come, we would plant a veggie garden out back. It never did very well but Julie and I had fun planting it.

One year, I went out back in early spring to clear last year's garden plants off so I could get ready to till up the ground. I could have been in a hurry because I had decided to just burn it off and be done with it. Well, the fire was going, and the wind picked up and soon I had the whole field on fire. I tried putting it out until I heard the fire truck coming. It could have been a big fine. Burning without a permit and letting it get out of control. I ran back to my little garage and got my lawn mower out. I put the mower where the fire had started. When, after the fire department got the fire out, they asked how it started, I just pointed at my lawn mower and said it must have sparked. I think I got that idea from thinking what my little miss Julie would do, point at someone else and say, "he did it". Well Julie, it worked, and I didn't have to pay a fine.

We had the nicest neighbors that lived next door. Jim and Chris Campbell. They had two little ones five or six years older than Julie. Jim and I built a real nice covered patio on the back of his house and quite often we would set out on the patio, drink a beer and talk hunting or other cool topics. He was a shop rat like me except he was in skilled trades. And I was just labor.

One day, Julie and their little girl, Janie, picked a good armful of flowers from Jim's wife's front yard flower garden. They just had a ball. When they got busted though, the tears really started to flow. They were just having fun and I would bet that my little Julie was the instigator. She had a mind of her own.

SNOWMOBILE WRECK

That year, I believe, was the first year that I got a deer on our hunting trip to the Huron Mountains in northern Michigan. We all had our snowmobiles with us on that trip and had a really great time playing in the snow.

New Years Day of 1971 was a cold, cloudy, brisk day. Janet, Julie and I went to the Korfs for the day, and we took my truck with the snowmobile on the back. Sometime during the day I took a ride from the Korf house and found other guys across the road climbing some hills just north of the Korf house. I joined in and it was a lot of fun. I remember getting back, dirty and all wet.

That night would be fateful for me, we arrived home just after dark maybe around 6:00 pm. Shortly after we got home the phone rang and a neighbor friend of mine, Jack Fick, was on the line. He and another friend of his were going out for a snowmobile ride and they wanted me to go along. I was really tired but never wanted to miss a time to ride, so, off we went into the night. It was cold, damp and snowing, just perfect.

We rode east, down the power lines by our place, and in towards Flint. On the return trip we came up to Dye Road just about where Janet and I use to live. For safety reasons, when you came upon a road, the lead guy would always stop, get off and waive the others on through as traffic would permit. I was in the lead and waived the other two on through. We then started on down the path at about 45 miles an hour. At that point, I remembered a creek with a bridge crossing our path and as the other two guys did not know about it, I felt someone would hit the creek. It was snowing rather heavily, so I sped up to take the lead and show them the bridge. As I took the lead at about 65 miles an hour, I was at the bridge. I missed it by about 10 feet. Off I flew across the creek and into the other side, a frozen ditch bank, at over 60 miles an hour.

I woke up 2 weeks later, still in the hospital. I had lost all of my front teeth, broke both upper and lower jaws, mouth wired completely shut. The side of my face was all burnt and I had lost my right knee cap. The leg cast went from my toes all the way up to my hip. I had really messed up this time. Janet was by my side most of the time when I was in the hospital. I do remember when I woke up, I wanted to see my little miss Julie and that wish was granted.

I was in and out of my bed for a few more days after I came home. I spent another week or so on the sofa until I could get around. My thoughts before the accident were to leave the Buick and go head long into construction. I was so lucky that I had not done that yet. All of my medical was paid for, and I got a good check every week for about 5 months from the time of the wreck.

Mom and Dad were really worried about me out there in Arizona and so all my brothers and sisters took up a collection for us and flew us out to Tucson for a visit for several weeks. That was my first time going there and we had a really nice time with Mom and Dad. That would have been in February of 1971. They took us around Arizona, and we saw some really neat things. That also was Julie's first time to meet her Grandma and Grandpa Wallen. Naturally they fell in love with her right away, and she with them.

BAD KNEE

The cast on my leg was removed after six long itchy weeks. I was very disappointed as I could only move my leg at my knee about 15 degrees. So off to the therapy people I went. That was awful and very painful, they strapped me in a chair and my leg would stand straight out because It would not bend, they then would hang a five pound weight on my foot. Total pain and I would have to sit there for about 15 minutes like that. It hurt so bad that I would try to hold it up instead of letting it bend my knee, but I would soon be tired and let it down to hurt, hurt, hurt.

After about three weeks of that, they decided my knee had grown together. It was called adhesions. Back to the hospital I went for a second operation. Then another month with a cast and I could now move it 45 degrees; more therapy and more pain. Once again, I could only get my leg up about half way.

At the time all this was going on, I was trying to build a house in Chesaning for my sister Bev. My knee was still sort of grown together and I could only bend it halfway. I was doing the electrical wiring one day and I was up on a step ladder. That was hard to do when I couldn't bend my knee very much. I slipped from part way up and fell down through the ladder, with my bad leg hanging up there. My knee sounded like Rice Crispies, snap, crackle and POP. I thought I was gonna die from the pain. After I got untangled and laid on the floor for a short time the pain went completely away. When I got up, I could kick myself in the butt. It had all broken loose and my leg moved normal for me. I think the Lord had gotten impatient with me and my prayers, so he just threw me down off that ladder.

My jaw had healed nicely during all this commotion. I had spent a lot of time at the dentist office and had a denture and a bridge planted in place, it all worked very well. I had lost almost all of my upper teeth and five of my lower front teeth.

BACK TO THE BUICK AND QUITTING

I then got a clearance from my doctors and went back to work at the Buick. They gave me my old softy job back and I picked up framing jobs and roofing jobs for my day work. I got so busy that I missed a lot of work at the Buick. They were not very happy with me. They knew that I had a lot of work on the outside of the shop, but they did not want to lose me. They called me up to the main office one day and I met with the plant manager. He told me all I had to do was to take my G.E.D. test and they would give me a Foreman position in the final assembly plant, which would make for a very good raise for me, and I would not be working for the union. Either take that or quit the shop.

I felt bad because I had just had almost six months off with pay and all my medical was paid at that time. They gave me a few days to talk to my wife and think it over. After talking it over with Janet, I went in and gave them two weeks' notice. There were a lot of guys that I worked with that told me that I was totally nuts. I was wondering about myself as well. That was good job security with dental and health insurance all paid for. Yup, I was crazy. It gave some of the in-laws plenty to talk about, I know that.

JANET WAS AN ANGEL

Janet was an angel during that year. She took very good care of me when I was so sick. When I had my mouth wired shut, I could only eat anything through a straw. That was bad. I had already lost a lot of weight. Down to about 130 pounds. Janet devised a way to feed me turkey and chicken through a straw. She kept the ole blender going on overtime. I hated it but she kept me fed real well and I started to recover. With out her I would have been in trouble. She kept me alive. Even after the wires were removed, she had to prepare foods that were very soft, so I could eat it. My mouth was healing but I had to be very careful. It took years after that before I could eat chicken and turkey again and I don't think that Janet ever wanted to cook it again after that.

All of this brought Janet and I, again, close to each other. That accident was quite a price to pay for bringing us back close together. Our interactions were just us and her family pretty well stayed out of our affairs at that time.

We decided it was time again to have another child and we once again were making love on a regular basis trying to get pregnant. It didn't take long and bingo we had our second child on the way. Going through all the happenings of 1971 and into 1972, our lives had gone very well together. I now had a lot more time at home. I did not have to go into the Buick anymore and so I was home in the evenings. That was awesome for little miss Julie and me. We were having great times together.

She had a very good Christmas that year and she and I had a lot of cool things to play with. Three year olds are so fun. I remember pasting large decals of zoo type animals on a wall in her playroom and she was thrilled.

JEFF IS ON THE WAY

I believe it was in March that we found out for sure that we were actually pregnant. It was once again an exciting time. Janet informed me soon after that though, that this was it. She would have her tubes tied when this one was born. It didn't matter if it was a boy or a girl, there would be no more kids. I prayed a lot for a little boy and I wanted to name him Garry. That would have meant a lot to me. I was not even consulted on the decision to have her tubes tied. I think her Mom or sister may have had a little say in that. I don't know for sure. It was only a feeling I had. Jane had gotten pregnant just a few months after we did, and I believe she was also to have her tubes tied. I was sad but had nowhere to turn. No more kids. However, I was very excited to get this one.

LOTS OF WORK AFTER BUICK

My work really picked up as I was doing a lot of framing and started building whole houses. Dad had a subdivision started when he moved west and had left 12 or so lots when he moved. That summer, Dad and Mom came back to Michigan for a few months and Dad helped me get some loans set up to do my very first spec houses, to place on those lots. I was off and running with my business. I was feeling success in my life as a businessman. I had to work really hard though to ensure that I would make it.

The economy was going okay. Not hot, but okay. I would find out over those years that home sales would run along with the General Motors labor contracts. You could not sell a house for months before the contract, and then as soon as the contracts were signed, everyone wanted their house built, right now.

I just wanted to be able to work. I was making us a good living. I was proud of myself for getting out of the shop and getting my feet on the ground with a chance to make it. I just was not the kind of personality to be a shop employee. I needed to see the sun light, and to be outside, and not have to answer to a foreman or a Sergeant in the Military. After all the jobs I had had in my life, I had gotten my teeth into something I knew and could do. I hated punching a time clock. It just was not me.

PERSONAL TROUBLES

During this pregnancy we did try to stay close to each other. We both wanted it to be that way. We were two rather strong personalities. Maybe in the end, I was wanting lots of lovin' and Janet, I felt, just did not need it that way. I think that one of the worst things that I felt was the rejection in those times when we did not have intimacy for a while.

One night I was not sleeping. It was about midnight and so I got up, dressed, and still being bare foot, I went outside into the street for a walk. The moon was bright, and I found the path back to the woods, behind our subdivision. It was less than a quarter mile back there. I was feeling really low and as I walked, I stepped onto a roll of old barbed wire at the edge of the woods. My feet were on fire as I got quite a few puncture holes from the rusty wire. I thought that I had stepped into a nest of bees. I was so upset that I just sat down and cried. I felt, somehow, I had to make changes in our lives. Being a 29-year-old I did have needs. I often wondered if I had more hormones than the average guy. I did not know what was wrong. I did know though that I had to fix it somehow. This took place in midsummer and it was not long until we hit the time that we couldn't be "close" because the baby would be due. I would not feel that darn rejection anymore. This was maybe my fault, but it was the way I felt, I had nowhere to turn.

JEFF IS HERE

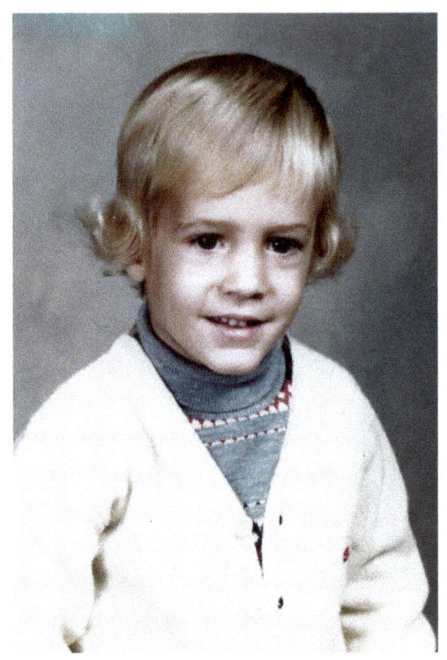

My second little buddy, my son– Jeffry Allen

Our son was born on October the 14th. He was a healthy little guy. Once again, I was not allowed in the delivery room, but Janet was good to me and I didn't have to wait long. I was so proud to have a little son. I would have to explain to Julie though, as she wanted a little sister. This little guy had a pointed head at first just like his older sister did when she was born. Just like with Julie, it was love at first sight.

Janet went ahead and had her tubes tied and I had my little boy. I, in the worst way, wanted to call him Garry but I lost that one. He would be called Jeff. She wanted the Korf thing again. There was Jane, Janet, Jimmy, Julie, and Jeff. All of 'em J's, keeping it in her family, I had no choice in the matter. I was not happy.

I turned 30 years old a few days after Jeff was born. I had missed a promise to myself. I had wanted to have a house all paid for by that date in my life. That would have been a real success for me.

That little son of mine turned out to be a really cute little kid (in spite of him having the wrong name). I was a very happy father. Julie accepted the fact that she was not going to have a little sister as she had planned.

She was very excited about having a new member in the family. I believe she was really secure in our little family. She was a motherly little gal when it came to her brother, as time moved along for us. Jeff was such a happy little guy as I recall.

My work was a little slow into the 72 – 73 time frame and it was a little hard making ends meet for a while. I was still building on the lots that dad had left for me, but it was slow. It actually gave me more time to spend with the kids and I did just that. Julie still went with me everywhere I went, if I could take her along. Janet at times would bring me lunch to a framing sight and Julie would always want to stay on the job site with me. I believe I could have made her into a carpenter if I tried. She just loved to be around. She spent a lot of time with me in my little office downstairs and drew pictures of houses. She was just a neat little girl.

As Jeff got a little older, Julie would just love to tease him in any way she could. The two of them had fallen in love. I have great memories of the two of them playing together in the basement in the house on Mac Scott Court.

Jeff had a real special way of getting around before he could walk. He would tuck one leg under so as to sort of sit on it and then his right leg would be straight out. With his right arm all the way down to his foot, he would "drive" himself around on that basement floor in a sort of scoot, scoot fashion, sitting on his butt. I think I even have a movie yet of him doing that. It was so cool!

We had a little scooter that was called a wiggle wagon that he could drive. Even before he could walk, he was good at making it go. I had bought this little red electric car that the kids could set on and drive. It had a steering wheel and a gas peddle. One time I had put Jeff on it, and he had it set to go round and round and around. He had the steering wheel full right. So, after about 5 minutes as he sat there, Jeff fell sound asleep! Round and round until he got close to the wall, and he had an accident. He hit the wall and rolled off. I believe he was shocked and did a little crying, but we had a lot of fun playing down there in the basement.

The Teenie-bopper.

JOHN GROVES AND RENTALS

As time got into 1973 and the Oil Embargo came into effect, everything slowed down in the Flint area. It was hard to sell a house and get work. I had joined the Home Builders Association of Metro Flint. This was a good move for me as I met a real estate guy by the name of John Groves. We had become good friends. John had several hundred rental houses in the Flint area, and he needed a guy to take care of repairs on them. Nobody was selling any houses at the time, so I went to work for him. I had no houses to frame or to build. This move got me through that really rough time when there was no work. Even the auto industry was laying off. So, I made it through that bad time and kept food on the table as it were.

MARRIAGE ENCOUNTER

I just loved coming home, because I had two great kids to greet me. But things seem to be turning colder between Janet and I again. She did not like my work and she showed it a lot. I had a hard time with that.

Including service time, we had been married for almost ten years and we had lived together for almost eight. At one point, she told me that I basically needed to grow up. People our age did not do all the lovey stuff that I wanted in my life. It was one of those things that I just did not know how to handle. For reasons that I maybe yet do not understand, I needed that closeness more than anything. I was hurting. My family were all that way. Janet and her family just were not.

I built a house for a guy out by the Maple Grove Church. They were a very nice couple and I got to know them fairly well. Somehow one day we got to talking about marriage and I found out that they were real involved in a thing with the Catholic Church called Marriage Encounter. It sounded like just the thing Janet and I could get involved with and it could really enhance our life together. I was feeling totally frustrated. I wanted in the worst way to get some help. I knew that married life should not be the way that we were living it. She did not like my work and did not like it when someone would come over for a paycheck or a work order. She also did not care a lot for most of the people in the Home Builders Association. We had lots to work on!

Janet agreed to try this marriage encounter with me, and we set it up. It turned out that we were to stay the weekend at a nunnery in Flint. We went through a series of lectures and skits with question and answer times throughout the weekend. We both felt a closeness from all the people involved as well as each other. It was so good. We had to write love letters to each other on different topics and then discuss them. It opened up a lot of good communication for us. When we were through with the weekend, we were walking on air.

There were so many things that we needed to talk about, and we had hit on some of the main ones over that weekend. That was step one of the program. Step two was for us to join a group of people that would meet every week and work on our marriage. We stayed with it for several months. One of the things that we all did at the beginning of each session was to give each other a big hug. It made me feel like these people really cared about us. They were great caring people. Janet and I were making real headway in our relationship.

As really nice as these people were to us, Janet could not take the hugging. We started missing meetings and before long, she announced that we were quitting the group. I really did feel bad, and maybe she did too, as we were making some progress in our relationship.

Before we had started the marriage encounter, there was a person that I had become fairly close to. We were not involved physically but had spent a lot of time talking. She was also in a rough marriage and looking for answers as was I. These conversations made me realize how well a good marriage could really be. I wanted that more than anything. That of course was the hopes I had with this group we were now quitting. Things then returned to where they were before the encounter and our lives went on. It seemed as though there was a big chill over us. That thing with the barbed wire still hung over me, and I was scared.

NOT GOING TOO WELL

I spent as much time with my little guys as I could. We spent a lot of time in the basement and a lot of time in the yard. Evenings we would spend time in the family room watching TV or just playing with stuff. Janet was always busy around the house and would not be in there with us. When I spent time in my little office, Julie was always there with me and sometimes Jeff as well. Janet and I had reached a point where we would almost avoid each other. At least it seemed that way to me.

Going through 1974 and into 1975 was rather rough between us. Our little house there was just not what I intended it to be. To top it off, I felt even more distant from the Korf side of the family. Janet's mother and I just sort of had bad vibes. At this point, I did not know what Janet had been talking to her about as far as her and I. It is hard to write down the happenings and feelings of this time in my life. I think I have buried a lot of it deep in my mind. I am sure that Janet would have her own thoughts and feelings on this time in our lives together and she sure has a right to that. I only know my feelings.

GETTING INVOLVED WITH THE HBA

By 1975, I had gotten fairly involved in the Home Builders' Association. I was elected to sit on their Board of Directors, and I accepted that position. At that time, I did not know what that would entail. We had a lot of meetings of the evenings and sometimes they would run late. I was learning a lot about my industry, but I was away from my little guys more than I wanted to be.

It was great for my business though, as I got to know a lot of the bankers, suppliers and contractors. There were other builders I could discuss things with that helped me on my own building jobs. I even picked up a lot of framing work. It helped me very much with my bidding on houses and getting things done.

I met a guy by the name of Francis Butts. He was building a series of town houses in Flint. I got the contract on his framing work, and we made some really good money. We had to frame them up, including the basement walls, and I had built up a really good framing crew. We were quick and did a really good job for Francis. I think we were there working on his project for well over a year. It was good pay for us, and it gave me a good push in my business.

There was another guy in the Association that I got to be good friends with. His name is Kal Nemer. We lived only a few miles from each other, and we were both builders. I did a lot of his framing in Swartz Creek, the little town that we lived in. We even did model houses together. Kal was a funny guy and made me laugh a lot. He could also be very intense and could get really keyed up. At times, I would help him to calm down. He was college educated and knew the business angle very well. I was a dropout and knew the mechanics of the business very well. Kal and I became best friends and I think we still are. We helped each other a lot.

Ed Dick and I also became best friends. Ed had quit the Buick just before I did, and he got a poured wall business going. I guess you could say that Ed's business was another spin off from Jerry Kubica's business. We all had worked for Jerry at one time or another. I believe that Jerry was the one that gave me enough courage to quit the shop.

I was forming a lot of good relationships during this time in my life. I had a small business, and it did very well for me. One of the people that really helped me make my business go so well was a young guy by the name of Reiner Wedel. This kid was sharp. He worked as hard as I could and always had to prove it. He watched and learned and became a very good framer in his own right. We also had become very good friends and still are.

As I became more and more involved in the Builders' Association, the more time it demanded of me. It kept me away from home in the evenings a lot. I saw that as good, but also as bad. It did keep me away from that little office in the basement of my house, more than I would have liked, and therefore away from my kids. I loved being around them and they I believe, around me.

By this time, Jeff was up and running all over the place. He could do the stairs by himself, sitting on his butt. Julie of course would just run up and down them. So, there was no problem for them to come down stairs and just hang out. Julie loved to draw things in my office. I wish I had a few of those pictures now. That would mean a lot.

THE PPV

One day Reiner and I were driving from a job out on Davison Road in Flint. We came by this little store that was selling these peddle things called a P.P.V. as in people powered vehicle. They were a fiberglass buggy with two seats in it, two wheels on the back, and a single one in front. Both people riding in it could peddle and it could go really fast. I loved gadgets so we stopped. Reiner and I took one for a ride right down Davison Road. It had three speeds, and I was sold. It was a ball, and I knew Jeff and Julie would love it. I bought one and brought it home.

I was right, the kids loved it. Julie could touch the peddles and help power the thing a little, but Jeff was just too small yet. I would put them both in that thing and away we would go, running all over the neighborhood. The kids would be just a squealing! I can still hear Julie asking me as soon as I would get home, "Daddy, Daddy, Daddy can we go in the P.P.V.?" The thing was fiberglass, and it made a lot of noise when it was going.

One day when I was out with just Jeff, I pulled into the drive. I had to run into the house for something quick. I had set the hand brake as the driveway was sloped a bit. Jeff stayed in the seat as I jumped out. As soon as I came back out, I was shocked. No PPV and no Jeff! He wanted to drive and somehow got the brake loose. Away he went, down the drive and out into the street. The street also was sloped a little and so the thing had turned just enough. Down the street he went, backwards. We lived on a cul-de-sac so he couldn't go that far. Jeff was scared but excited about his all-alone ride. It really was funny and we all got a laugh out of him.

There was a little neighbor girl that lived just to the north of us. Her name was also Julie. The two Julies spent a lot of time together. We had a plastic pool for them in the front yard and a really nice sand box for them in the back. Her parents were Bob and Jenny Myers. I had built their house. The two girls would buddy up with little Janie Campbell and the three of them had a grand time together. Poor little Jeff though was left out a lot.

One thing I remember about Jeff was him and the swing set. He could make it all go. There was this little glider just right for four little guys, but he could make it go all on his own. Jeff liked the slide the best though. He would run, climb and slide over and over again. What fun he had.

HBA TROUBLES FOR JANET

The year '74 turned into '75 and I stayed really busy in my little building company. I was gaining more and more knowledge as time went on. I had gotten into the Parade of Homes each year and would build a model house to show off my skills as a custom builder. The parade was sponsored by the Home Builders' Association and there was usually 25 or so entries each year. I won awards every time I had a show house. I also sold six or seven houses off the model each year and that kept me real busy.

Thanks to some of the people I met in the association I was learning more and more how to bid, build and finish my Wallen Builders homes. I was enjoying my work so much. I was outside a lot and I loved framing. I had hired several good guys to work for me. Reiner was good enough by this time that I could leave him alone and he would get the job done right.

The Home Builders Association was getting more important to me, as I conducted a lot of business during the meetings and I was getting into some of the socializing after the meetings. A lot of the guys would go out after the meetings for drinks. This was okay but as time went on, we would stay out later and later.

My relationship with my wife had gotten progressively worse with no closeness to each other both physically and mentally. It was bad. I was finding it harder to communicate with her. Janet did not like my business and she had a real rough time with guys coming to our house to pick up their checks or meet on plans and get work orders. There was no way that we could afford an outside office. We were sort of stuck in that position. I found myself making up reasons not to come home or be with her.

BUILDING THE THIRD HOUSE

8474 Wesley Dr. Flushing, MI– My third house.

I got the idea that if I could get Janet to let me build a new house for us, we could get back to being a lot closer just working together. I could have an office in the new house's basement with an outside entrance so it would not have to bother her in the house. It all made sense to us. Janet was also wanting to live in Flushing.

Our current house would give us most of the money we would need to build the house if I did all the work, and if we could find a good lot for a good price. We found the lot, made the purchase and went to work on the plans. By this time, I had gotten good at drawing plans and doing the layouts. We would build it, about 4000 square feet including the basement finished area. As I had always wanted to have a nice play area for the kids, that was well planned into the lower level. This one would be really big for them. I also built-in a nice large rec room downstairs. It would have a nice bar with its own fridge built in. Just nice if we ever had a party there.

We got the house started late in 1975 and I spent all the extra time that I could working on the house. Ed Dick and I poured the basement. I got it back filled and got into framing the house. I had the whole lower level to frame as well as the upper. It took me over a month, but I got it done. By the next spring I had the brick on and the drywall going in. It was working as Janet and I were spending time together picking out things for the house and discussing things. Janet's mom had no say in this house. It would be just us. Our own design, colors and materials.

Jeff went with me a lot when I was working on the house. He would love to play with blocks of wood. Sometimes nailing things together. Pretty good for a 3-year-old. Jeff had been attacked and bitten by a neighbor's dog on Mac Scott Ct. He was very fearful of dogs after that. One Day when he and I were at the house working, and before the brick was on, a dog came by the front of the house. The front door was wide open. Jeff was standing at the door and the dog scared him. Just behind the front door was a large opening through the floor where the fireplace would go. It was about ten feet down to the basement floor. Jeff turned and ran when he saw the dog. He ran right into that opening and fell all the way to the cement floor below. I remember jumping down there about as shook up as I could be. I picked him up and took him straight to the hospital. He was a strong little guy. Nothing broken and only a few little bruises. I could not believe it. He hardly even cried. We did always have a good time at that house when he came with me. Except of course for that one day.

The day finally came to make ready for carpeting. This to me was always very exciting. Janet and I spent most of the day and a little into the night cleaning everything to make ready for the carpeting. I had felt we were doing well. The next day though, I received a shock. I was on a ladder cleaning the big front window over the front door when Janet announced to me that if I ever again wanted to build us a house, it would end in divorce for us. I had thought that she really liked the house. It was done and we only had borrowed $25,000 to build it. At that day and time, the place would have been worth about $150,000. We had done well in that light. I was stunned and felt that her and I had been set back again. We had a nice house, but so what!

We got ourselves moved into the house. I got the yard sodded and planted flowers and shrubs. To me it was beautiful. The kids each had nice bedrooms and I believe we had gotten each one of them a new bedroom suite. Julie was now in the school system and making friends. Jeff had become friends with the little guy across the street and had a playmate. Janet became good friends with the lady across the street.

I got myself settled into my office downstairs. I had a nice desk in there. There was a wall with a window and a door to the outside in it. I had built a nice big stair well with the steps up to the side of the house and then a walkway to the drive. Janet did not need to be disturbed any longer. I felt good about the set up, but it did not help Janet's feelings about having the business in the house. Julie on the other hand loved it. Almost every evening when I would be working down there, she would come down and keep me company doing her homework or just doodle.

She also loved to just sit there and Jabber. Talk about anything or nothing, just talk. She was 7 years old and Dad's little sweetheart. At this point, she and Jeff were the only thing really keeping me there. Jeff was a very soft and awesome little guy, he and I had a lot of good times together. He was also turning into a little jabber box, just like his sister. My kids had gotten a good start in life and were progressing nicely. They were both making me so proud. Even with Julie kissing the boys on the school bus!

Jeff and Julie loved this house.

CHRISTMAS TIME 1976

It was a good holiday season that year. Christmas was such a joy as both kids were really into Santa Claus. It seems to me that the Barbie doll stuff was in at that time and Jeffery wanted an inch worm. And so on and on. I can still remember being up late that Christmas Eve, working at what I use to call, the Japanese assembly line, putting together all the toys needing assembly. Lots of good stuff. The kids had a ball. Their new playroom would be overflowing with fun stuff. Julie was now seven and Jeff was four. Just right for Santa.

BUILDING MY LITTLE COMPANY

By the end of 1976, things had settled down for us as far as the move into the new house went. My work was picking up just fine but trying to run the field, frame and trim the houses I was building, and doing the counter tops was too much to keep up with. Times were good, but I really needed help. The office book work was another problem for me. I needed help there as well.

Going into 1977, I had quite a load of things going on in my life. There were about 10 houses that I had sold and had to get started as soon as the frost came out of the ground. I felt that I had to hire someone for the office duties, things like bidding, book work, paying bills and answering the phone. I also needed someone in the field to help oversee the building jobs.

The kids were doing just fine but Janet and I had never been farther apart in our relationship. I was losing the care I needed to stick it out with her. Out of my group of friends, almost all the wives helped their guys out with their business. I was experiencing just the opposite. She was hating it more and more. I was very much afraid of suggesting that I hire a girl to help in my office. I was right, she wanted nothing to do with it. There was a lady though, that Janet got along with fairly well and when I told her that Susie Lock would come to work for me, she finally agreed to let her into our domain. I would now have an office gal. I did not need her full time and that was just fine with Susie. I had known Susie for a long time because she had always done our income tax. That is also how Janet knew her. It was really no bother to Janet as Susie never came into the house. Just around the back and down the stairs to the office. I think it worked out just fine.

Janet still did not like the fact that people were coming around the side of the house and into the office. Ideally, I would have had an outside office, and no one would come around her. I also hired a guy to be my superintendent. His name was Johnny Pringnetz and as it worked out, he was very good for me. The money was very good, and the business was running nice and smooth for me. I now could concentrate on selling houses. It also gave me a little more time to spend with my two little ones.

HELPING AT THE HBA

I became more and more involved with the Home Builders Association. There was trouble brewing from the federal government for our industry, in that they were getting to a point where they wanted to impose a 10-year warranty on new homes. The House bill was called the Magnuson-Moss Act. That would have been a real rough one. At this time, I was a local as well as a State and National Director in the Home Builders Association.

In the spring of that year, 1977, a large group of directors flew to Cleveland, Ohio for several long weekends to hammer out our own 10-year warranty. It was called HOW or Home Owners Warranty. This would be a self-imposed warranty, and it worked. The feds backed off. So, I had done my little part for our industry. I continued serving on the boards and it took me away from home in the evening several times a week.

I also had to go to Lansing once a month for the State Director's Meetings. All of these meetings were very helpful for me as I had much to learn. The meetings all would cover things that involved my work. I was also meeting more sub-contractors and suppliers. It all was helping build my company. I was now taking awards with every spec home I built for the Parade of Homes Show. I had also hired a lady to handle my home sales. Her name was Marg Deutch. She did very well for my little company.

There was a bit of a downside to all the HBA activity though. All of us guys that were directors, and even the executive officers, were going out on the town after our meetings. There were the favorite spots and at times we would just stay at the place where we would hold the meetings. That place was called the Country Squire. We had about 400 members total in the association and a lot of them would be out on the town after the general membership meetings. I was starting to drink a lot more than I did before this time and I was staying out later and later on more nights a week.

There was just a bunch of what I felt at that time to be a really good gang of people. A few I had become really close to. We would hang out a lot together. Kal Nemer was probably my best friend out of the group. We worked together. He was on the board with me, and we played together. I had even taken up golf with these guys. I needed the companionship.

I knew this was making things worse at home, but I don't know if I cared. I started stocking more whiskey at my little bar downstairs at home. And on some of the nights that I did not have a meeting, I would sit down there by myself and drink. I knew I was in pretty deep trouble. It was now starting to affect my two kids and that was horrible for me.

I really loved having my little guys around and we still did spend a lot of time together. I would take them at times on an outing out to Mary and Ed Dick's house. We did that alone quite often as Janet would not want to go with us. I did not want to let my relationship with my sister go away, because even after all these years, I still held her as my best friend. Ed Dick and I had become best friends as well.

PREGNANT FISH

Ed had a river running right behind his house. One day when I was out there with Jeff, we decided to see if we could catch a fish. So out to the riverbank we went with poles in hand and we started to fish. I think Jeff was about five then. Sure enough he got a really big bite. He had wanted to know if he got a fish if we could eat it. Naturally I told him yes. So, he has this big ole fish on and his pole was going nuts. It took a little time and with some help, he got it reeled in. Jeff had caught himself a big ole carp. The garbage fish of the world. You just can't eat a carp. How do you tell that to a 5-year-old? I ended up telling him that big fish was a lady fish and it was going to have babies. We needed to return it to the water. That did not go over real well as I recall but he did it. Trying to eat a carp would have been rather rough.

Janet had the idea that Jeff was color blind, and I could just not accept that. I used to put Jeff in my truck with me and as I made my rounds of the job sites, or whatever, we would go over the colors of things along the road ways. Janet was right, as hard as Jeff or I tried, he just could not get the colors right. The poor little guy. He just did not understand. I felt bad for him, but we finally had to give in. He really had tried hard to get it right.

CHRISTMAS IN '77

We had a prosperous year in '77 and by year's end we still had houses to build. That was a good sign for the next year. We both tried hard that year to give the kids a happy holiday and I think it worked for them. I spent time once again on the Japanese assembly line putting all those toys together. I also had given Julie a cat. They really needed to have animals in their young lives and Janet would not allow us to have a dog.

We even spent time with the Korfs. Janet's Mom had a ceramic business where she taught ceramics and also did ceramics to sell. Every year she put on a nice Christmas party for all her students. All the kids had to be there to sit at the head table with her. I guess I did not mind too much because I could then spend time with Janet's Dad. Marv knew that Janet and I were in trouble. He also knew that Jane and Phil were having big problems in their marriage. I felt bad for him.

FORCED TIME TOGETHER WAS GOOD

So the holidays went smooth that winter and Janet and I had

talked it over and decided to try taking a vacation together. We would take the kids to Tucson and spend a few days with my mom and dad. We knew that our relationship was not good and would try and see if this would help. The plan was to leave the kids with my folks and drive to LA for a day or so and then back to Las Vegas for the National HBA Convention. That would be another four or five days alone together before returning back to Tucson. The flight was set and we flew out on about the 20th of January. We landed in Chicago in a blinding snowstorm of which turned into a blizzard. The storm lasted for three days. The Air Lines put us up in a hotel right at the airport. There was no way to get anywhere else. We were stuck. It sure wasn't like a marriage encounter but it really helped us. We had nothing to do but talk. It was like God stuck us there and said, "now, work it out. You're not leaving until you do." It took three days.

We had sort of agreed to try to be open and talk through things. I knew I had to be careful, as the least little hint of criticism, she would go off on me. So, we talked about that some and then tried to analyze where we were. Janet did not like my business. She did not like me in the HBA. She did not like any of my friends. She did not like most of my family. She did not like having people come into our house for business even if it was just downstairs. My drinking was a problem, as well as staying out late. Some of these things were very legitimate for her. I knew that but I also knew what led to some of these things.

My biggest problem started with our closeness to each other. It got much worse as the years progressed. I was still the guy that craved a close physical and loving relationship. She had basically told me to get over that, but I couldn't. I was raised so differently. I also needed her to support me in my business and be there for me in any way she could. In her upbringing, her mother was the dominating person. Marv worked at a granary and then when that closed down, he worked at a tire shop. I used to like to go visit him at his work when I was in Owosso.

I finally reached a point in 1978 where I could build a model house, not sell it, and move the office into it and out of our home. She was very happy about that. The way she treated my clients as well as the subs and suppliers would have to change. I had quit the shop six years earlier and there was no turning that back. I had made a good run at it and made a success of my business. I had spent a lot of long hours working to make a go of it. I had made a lot of mistakes since getting off that plane back in 1966. I could see them. A lot of our troubles were because of who I was. A lot were because of who she was. If she could have helped me in the business and we worked together, it would have been just great. We both knew that we were very mismatched to be married to each other.

So it was, we spent a lot of time talking in that hotel room and trying to see into each other and to see if we could make it. We both had a lot of changes to make, and we would work on it. We also had decided to make this the best trip ever. Our two kids had spent three days totally board with themselves in that hotel. They went up and down the elevator a lot and hit the candy machine a bunch. TV had gotten old for them as well.

OFF TO MOM AND DAD'S AND THE CONVENTION

On that third day, we made our way back to the terminal for our flight. I think that ours was one out of maybe six flights that made it out that day. God let us go. He said, "There, go forth and try to get along." The Airport was shut down again a short time after our departure. I don't think that we would have been on that plane either if we hadn't had the two little ones with us. That Airport was a mess, with people all over trying to get a flight out.

We made it safe into Tucson that afternoon, both trying to put on a new face and have a good time together. It was another new start in our lives. It showed, we did have a good time. Mom and Dad could tell the difference. They seemed relaxed around us and really enjoyed Jeff and Julie. I do have to say that, at that time, I was very unsure if it would work again for us. I had felt finished with it. This though, could be a new start and I was willing to try it again. More for the little ones than for us.

After a few days of visiting with Mom and Dad, we borrowed Charlene's car and drove to LA. We spent a night in a real expensive hotel named the Bonaventure. It was an awesome place. We checked in, got a bite to eat and went to our room, dead tired and we went sound asleep. So much for a really nice place. That ten-hour drive was a little too much for us.

The next morning, we had to head right out to the convention in Vegas. That blizzard wiped out a lot of our play time. We had to register at the HBA and get checked in. We were staying at the Star Dust Casino. I could sense for the first time in a long time, being away from everything, Janet wanted to have fun. We were rested and got right into things.

There was a Michigan Room set up at the hotel and we got into that. A lot of hometown folks were there. Janet knew several of the people there, such as the Wallings. She then had other people to talk to besides me. We spent time walking the strip. I remember checking out the little wedding chapel on the main drag. We even done some gambling in the different casinos. We did some of the shows on the strip and enjoyed them. I think one of the shows we seen was Redd Fox. He was nasty but funny.

The convention that year was great. I took in some of the seminars and came away with a lot of things that would help in my business. Janet and I spent several days going through all the exhibits and brought back a lot of flyers on new products. We had a great time together. We even had a great time doing things that can't be mentioned here. It was all good. I think we both felt that just maybe we could have a fresh start out of this. If only she could join in and help me in the business. Both of the Walling wives helped their husbands in their companies.

After four days in Vegas, we returned to Tucson and the kids. Mom and Dad were happy to see us being happy together. Julie and Jeff had a real good time with them.

There was a really rough winter happening back in Michigan. It was not fun returning to that super cold February of 1978. It seems like I can remember nine straight days in a row that never got above zero degrees during the day. Nothing was moving in the building industry at that time. I decided to get a new model house going for the parade of homes for 1978. It would be about 1700 square feet and I would finish off the garage for the new offices.

Then disaster struck me. I ran into our neighbor, Dennis Miller, a week or so after we got back. Janet was good friends with his wife, Marilyn. I was totally shocked when he told me that he had heard our trip was a bad one. A total bummer as he put it. That is what his wife had told him that Janet said of our trip. This was a devastating blow to me. Why she needed to tell that to our neighbor, I don't know. To me it was a setback. I don't remember if I confronted Janet about it or not. It just really hurt. I would just dig in and move forward. After a few weeks I could tell that things were still not okay. Once again, I was scared.

HOMEOWNER WARRANTY PROGRAM

Things were popping at the Home Builders Association that spring. The National Home Owner Warranty Program was coming together and we needed to elect officers and hire an administrator. Norbert Walling was selected to be president and I was to be the vice president. We put out a search for a person to be the administrator. It would be about March when we hired Mary Ann Schorr for the position.

Also, in the spring of that year I was elected to the position of Secretary for the regular Board of Directors. The Association had given me a lot in helping me out in my business. I figured it was time to give a little back. That fall I would be on the executive board. This also would mean more meetings for me to attend. I hated to tell Janet of my new positions and she was not happy when I did tell her. Maybe I did take on a little more than I should have. I was learning though and I really needed that.

Spring finally broke and building was under way. We got started on the new model house in late spring and by the fall we would have the new office going. The year was going smooth as far as the business was concerned but sales were dropping off a little. It was a bit of a worry in the industry. Interest rates had started to climb and that was never a good sign.

NOT LOOKING GOOD

Things again continued to go bad in my relationship with Janet. I know that I was around the house a lot more in the evenings but mainly with the kids. Julie and I had such a wonderful bond and Jeff and I did too. Weekends were really good as we usually had time to spend together. Janet seemed to keep herself just at the edge of things though and I felt a dark distance forming between us again. This time there was just nothing left there. My time at home was uneasy and except for the kids, I did not want to be there. Julie would really cling to me when I would be home and in the living room. She was eight years old that year and such a pretty kid.

Janet completely redid our living room at one point. It was either '78 or '79. She spent a good bit of money on new sofas and bookcases, end tables, lamps and she replaced my easy chair that I really loved. It was a chair that was from the first house. I believe we had had it recovered. In its place was this really big, overstuffed leather recliner. If I wanted to sit in my old one, I would have to go downstairs. The other stuff looked okay, and I could live with it. The new chair was big enough for Julie and me to sit in together. And sometimes Jeff could fit in as well.

When Janet was a kid, she had to clean house every day at home. I liked "clean" but it was a little rough some times. I remember one Saturday when I was going to sleep in a little, I got up about 7:30 and went to the bathroom. When I came back to bed a few minutes later, the darn bed was already made. She used to also fold up the newspaper behind me as I would finish reading a section. I also hated having the table cleared before the kids and I were done eating. These are petty things to talk about, but it might give a little insight into our lives together.

Julie, this may be a little embarrassing to you, but I should bring up the time your Mom told me I had to do something to make you change your undies every day. Remember, you had to hang them on the stair rail every day for a little while.

Janet loved to clean or at least it appeared that way. That took over for her for times when she could have been in the living room with us in the evenings. It could have been sort of an escape from me, for her. Sometimes She made me feel like she was our maid, or like I was her father.

That spring I was instructed to get rid of the cat. It was Julie's Christmas present, but Janet did not want us to have it around. I was basically told to "handle it." I had brought it into the house, I could get rid of it as well. Poor kitty, it got dropped off over in Brent Creek. It was such a nice kitty, I am sure it got a good home in that little village of about 40 people or so, only five miles from home. It never did find its way back. We sort of let Julie know that it probably ran away. Jeff and I were never allowed to have a dog either.

INDUSTRY SLOW DOWN

Going into January of 1979, I had a few houses that needed to be finished. There were also a few that needed to be started. We had some locked in mortgages at lower rates but nobody else seemed to be able to get qualified for a loan. I needed some cash flow as things were getting a little tight on us. I had thoughts of laying off my two employees. We had payments on our personal house as well as the model with the office in it. After those good years we had, I could see where we could get into trouble.

I still decided to go to the home show in Vegas. Janet at first decided not to go, but then changed her mind. She would go. I took in a lot of seminars that year as well as H.O.W. programs. Norbert Walling and Mary Ann were doing the same. A lot of the programs that year were on ways to survive if the slow down got worse. We learned about ways to protect ourselves. I only had personal property and a model to protect, no subdivision or lots anywhere. Inflation was going crazy and it was getting to a point where you could not bid a house and rely on the outcome. Lumber pricing was going all over the charts. If you bid a house too low and lumber went way up, you lost. If you bid the same house too high, you would not get the job. They showed us in those seminars how to include an escalator clause for protection.

I was rather busy on that trip, and Janet and I did not do much together. Maybe a show or two and some dinners. We did not have a really good time. Certainly nothing like the year before when we had a great time. I was sorry. It had really fallen apart. I knew it would be a bad trip this time.

THE H.O.W. PROGRAM

The Association had gotten a good start on the Home Owner Warranty Program. It was set into place and Mary Ann was doing a great job as administrator. We had taken in maybe 300 houses by that fall, under the program. By the start of '79 we needed to have a H.O.W. conciliator on hand and then paid arbitrators if the conciliation did not work. I became the conciliator for our Association. I was good with people and could settle almost all grievances, as I had learned a lot about housing. A lot of the times I would meet Mary Ann at the HBA office, and we would ride out to a claim together. We settled almost all claims at the job site with no arbitrator needed. We worked good together. There was almost 100% participation from the builders. If things picked up at all, the H.O.W. program would do well.

Mary Ann and I got to know each other well and we became good friends. We did our jobs very well. I believe that the board was happy with what we did. For a fledgling company the H.O.W. program was doing nicely across the whole country. Being tied to the Home Builders' Association, it had to work. Mary Ann had to travel around the country a bit, learning more about the program and going to national meetings.

Julie turned ten that spring and Jeff would be seven in the fall. There were not a lot of happy family times, but I still had a lot of fun with those two. For example, I had gotten Jeff a B.B. gun. He did not shoot his eye out, but he sure did pop out a window in my little storage garage, out behind the house. He had a boat load of little match box cars, and he had several plastic cars. I remember he wanted them to look like they had been in a wreck, so he and I heated the fronts of the cars up with a torch and bent the plastic so as to look like a major wreck. He got the biggest kick out of that. Julie, even at 10 years old, came down to my office just three houses away from home and would spend hours just sitting and talking. Sometime she would bring her homework to work on there.

BUILDER OF THE YEAR AWARD

The 1979 annual Officer Installation and Christmas Party for the H.B.A. was set to be at the Grand Blanc Country Club that year. I was to be installed as the 1980 Treasurer of the Home Builders Association. I had to be there. It was black-tie. Janet and I both got dressed to the max for the gala. We had to sit at the head table for the event.

I actually thought that we could enjoy the party. Everything went really smooth through the dinner and then the award plaques were presented. There was one award that was very much coveted. That was the Builder of the Year Award. I had done a lot for the Association in 1979 but I had no idea that my peers had chosen me for that award. I could not believe that I would be given that coveted plaque. I think I went nuts with joy. It was the best award. When I looked over at Janet though, I could tell she was not happy with me getting it. Maybe she felt that I had done too much or would now have to do more for the Association. All I know is that the rest of the night went really bad for us. We went home in silence that night. I had pretty well made up my mind. I could not go on like this. She hated my company and did not like the building industry. She still wanted me back working at the factory. I just couldn't do that.

The Holidays were so-so that year. We didn't know how the kids were feeling about us, but they could feel the tension I am sure. The office had been moved down the street into the finished garage of the model home. I had a company Christmas party there that year and it was nice. Most of the subs and suppliers came. We were going into 1980, with runaway inflation and interest rates that had climbed to 14%.

Mary Ann had come out to the party, and we spent a good bit of the night talking. We were good friends and got to talking a lot about our personal lives. She had noticed what had happened at the H.B.A. Gala. She was in a marriage that was five years old, and she had been forced into an abortion by her husband. She was wanting out of her relationship. I was wanting out too, but I had two great children which made it an extremely difficult choice to make. They were the only thing keeping me there as it were. We talked a lot, not knowing where this would lead us. We had developed some strong feelings for each other, but we were still both very married.

A NEW MODEL FOR 1980

Marge, my sales lady, and I met and decided to build a new model house. If things took off again, we wanted to be ready. There were some nice lots just a few blocks away from the office model there in Flushing. There was a chance that the interest rates could drop again soon. So off to the banker I went. They knew my financial position fairly well. I had real good equity in my personal house and a decent amount in the office model. I knew in the back of my mind it could be risky. I was doing my banking with Detroit and Northern Bank. I had been using them for quite some time. They told me that if I wanted to start a new model for the Parade of Homes, to go ahead and do it. They would back me. They were not lending as much as they had been, for specs, but I figured I would be alright.

I made a very big mistake as there would be no recovery for years to come. I now would have three big house payments a month. I was heading into big trouble but did not know it. 1980 would turn out to be a year like no other in my life. In a normal year, just getting that Builder of the Year award would have boosted my sales. But not with the interest rates we were experiencing. Little did I know that they would be reaching 22% by the start of 1980.

1981 VEGAS CONVENTION

The builders show in Vegas was once again at hand. I was excited to find new products to put into the new model. That model was going to be really something. I figured it would sell during the parade of homes. Janet had decided that she would not go with me to the show as we were miles apart in our relationship. I only booked one seat for myself and the charter plane that we were taking completely filled up. At the last minute, Janet announced that she would be going. She got really mad at me because I could not get her on the flight as it was completely full. A lot of people from Michigan were going that year. We were all booked in at the Maxim Hotel and Casino and I believe we were all on the same floor.

FALLING IN LOVE

Everyone got signed in at the center and the show was under way. They always had a great opening ceremony. Mary Ann and I hung out during most of the convention. She went with me to all the exhibits, and helped me collect material. I did some of the seminars that I thought were important to the business and some important to the local Association. Mary Ann and I also took in things that were needed for the H.O.W. program. There was only a little optimism for the coming year for the building business. There was a lot of talk about remodeling.

Mary Ann and I stuck close to each other for the whole four days of the convention. I think we were both smitten a bit this time. We just had such a nice time together. Everything we did was fun. We enjoyed the exhibits a lot, with all the new products coming out. We even enjoyed going to the seminars, maybe because we were just together. We did some of the evening parties put on by the suppliers, such as cabinet companies and such. We did some dinners with some of the hometown gang. We took in a couple of Vegas shows and did some gambling. That part was funny, because whenever we gambled together, we would win. When we gambled on our own, we would lose. I had never in my life enjoyed spending time with anyone as much as I did with Mary Ann for those four days.

The time finally came when we had to talk. We were coming out of the convention center on about the third day and Mary started to cry. She had a guilt trip coming on and we had to talk about it. I was feeling sort of the same thing. We both knew we had a big problem on our hands. We were falling in love with each other. Where would we go with this, we were both married. We went back to the hotel together and went to her room where we spent a good bit of time just talking. We talked about our present marriages being what they were. We already knew about that from other conversations with each other. Maybe that was why we felt so free to be who we were to one another on this trip.

We talked about my kids and what Janet and I were doing to them with our dislike for each other. Mary would not go on with her husband George, and I would not go on with Janet no matter what happened between Mary and I. We also both realized how good it really could be for us if we ever became as one. We both had not counted on this happening. We were both just looking for love, caring, affection and understanding, and a forever closeness. We talked about all those things we could feel from each other. This is the way it would be between us. We finished this talk and these feelings with some of the mushy stuff that two people in love do. I know that both of us were ready to recognize that we were really in love with each other. We had gotten to be such good friends. We talked about what a really rough road we would face if, in fact, we tried to make it together.

For me, just the thought of being out of a relationship that I hated to be in was so up lifting. A big part of the blame could have been placed on me, but just as big a part or maybe even more could be placed on Janet. Maybe even some of our family members.

With the guilt thing hanging over Mary and I, we finished out that trip on the highest note that either of us had ever experienced in our lives. It was just awesome. Some of our friends told us that we looked like our feet never touched the ground on that trip.

Our return flight home to Detroit was delayed for four or five hours that evening and Mary and I just sat in the terminal and talked. I think we were both scared to death, but as high as a kite. Everything seemed so exciting and fresh to me. We sat together on the plane on the return trip home sort of cuddled up and dead tired.

It was at least zero degrees out when we landed in Detroit that night. My little truck was encased in ice when we retrieved it. After a warmup, we piled in and headed for Swartz Creek. Kal Nemer was with us, and we had to drop him off at his place. Kal was a close friend and knew a lot about Janet and me. He now knew about Mary and me as well.

After dropping Kal off, Mary and I drove to a side street in Swartz Creek and just sat there for a while, cuddled up, and talked a little. Our wonderful time together was at an end for now. We knew that if we did not try to get together, we would just always be in love, on some other plain in our lives. It was going to be rough but at that time we did not know just how bad it was really going to be.

I dropped Mary off at her apartment and went on home. We only lived about a mile apart. It was about time for the sun to be coming up and I just went in and straight to bed. I don't even remember seeing Janet. I was dead to the world in just a matter of minutes. I don't recall what was going on with Janet for the next few days. I took Mary to lunch the next day and she was very distraught but determined to do the right thing.

WE CRASHED, SORT OF

When I dropped her off that early morning, she went in to her apartment and was confronted by George, her husband. She told him everything about our trip. They talked it out and she decided that she was going to give it a real try with him. She felt she owed that to herself and her marriage. After lunch that day, we would not be seeing each other again, unless it was just for work related things. I was still her conciliator and the Vice President of H.O.W. We would have to be around each other on a professional basis but that would be it.

She left the restaurant crying that day and I sat there in total shock. I went from the highest high a few days ago to the lowest low. That afternoon, I just drove and drove, going nowhere. I guess I was shook beyond belief. So, where do I go from there in my life? I was even more sure that I would be leaving Janet very soon. I thought that maybe it could be good to see a marriage counselor. I knew though that it would just not be possible to stick it out with her. The last seven or eight years had completely taken its toll on both of us.

I had my two kids still very strong in my life. I had to hang onto them at all costs. I know at that time Julie could really tell that there was something wrong with me and that nothing was right between her mother and I. Janet and I did not talk much after I returned from Vegas. She was upset that she could not go. It wasn't my fault though. She had made the choice.

The next few times that Mary Ann and I saw each other it was really strange. Everyone knew what had happened and knew that we were trying to stay apart from each other. It was not very comfortable for either of us. We both had to sit at the head table at the general membership meetings.

Then one day we had to go out together on a H.O.W. problem.

At the head table.

We tested things as I picked her up and we drove there together. We joked lightly about her having to sit way over by the window. We had put the retractable center counsel down in my El Camino. We actually made it through that trip okay, but wow were the feelings ever flowing. I think we knew then that fighting our feelings was not going to work. I was doing my best to honor Mary Ann's wishes and stay away from her.

I found out a little later though that in spite of her efforts to make a go of it, she had left George and moved out of Flushing. She moved into an apartment over in Grand Blanc, alone and some 20 miles away. That came as quite a surprise. I think our relationship as it had emerged over the last months had shown her what a real loving union could really be like. She had told me none of this.

PARADE OF HOMES MODEL

The new model was started that spring, as soon as the frost laws came off the roads. This was something that happened every year. The frost would go deep into the roads and cause them to heave. Then when the temperature would warm, things would be soft, and the roads would break up with the real heavy weight of the cement trucks. We had to wait till everything settled down. We would get an all clear from the state and could go to work. I think there was only one other house to start that spring, so money was very tight. I had to lay Susie, my office gal, off. Johnny had a few houses to finish up and then he had to go as well. I picked up some remodeling work that I would do myself. And that would hold us over a little.

MOVING OUT FROM HOME

I was honoring Mary Ann's wishes and staying away. We did see each other at meetings and at a few conciliations. By the time April came around though, I could no longer stay with Janet or be home. I knew it was going to be hard on the kids, but I had to leave, at least for a while.

We would go to a marriage counselor. I moved out, and in with a friend of mine. To me that was like a breath of fresh air. The only time I got to see the kids though was when I came to the office model to do work, or sometimes on the weekends. That gave me the idea to move into the model house close to the kids. The model was just 4 houses down from the office. I talked it over with Janet and she let me take the furniture from the basement to put into the model. It did not go well there as the colors were bad, but so what. I had a place to stay. Julie, and some of the time Jeff, would come down right after school, if I was there, and we would spend time together. I was in such a confused mess at that time. I loved those kids and did not want to be apart from them. I knew though that I would never win in a custody battle over them. Besides I don't think I could have done that to Janet.

Janet and I, at that time, started in with a marriage counselor. First she went to him and then I did. After that we would both go. When he seen us both together and how we were, he was blunt to us both and said that there was not much hope. We had destroyed our relationship. I had told him our whole story from the times back to my military days. He knew that I had worked too hard and too many hours.

TO SUM IT UP

Janet had put up with me when I worked so many hours those early years. From the start with working in the shop and trying to get a house built for us and then I started a side business. After that I got involved in the H.B.A. It all took a lot of time away from us. Even though we had spent those four years apart when I was in the Service. She had come to dislike any interruptions in our life from outsiders. Mainly the ones that would come to our house. After I had quit the shop, I did not work much at nights. I would just work some in my little office at times. She also had to put up with the fact that I was not thrilled with her family and did not want to see a lot of them. As time went on, and we became further and further apart, she had to put up with some late nights out and my drinking as it got worse. The further we grew apart, the more I seemed to drink. Though I never was drunk around her or the kids.

As for me, I saw our relationship as actually just starting when I got out of the service. We knew nothing about each other. We built a relationship from that point forward. She was happy with me when I did an eight hour a day shop job. When I started my own business though, she became very unhappy even though the money was much better. She did not like the people that I had to have involved in the business. She treated most of them in a very rude manner. Some even refused to come around. I had to meet them elsewhere. She did not like the Home Builders Association at all. I had a lot of good friends there. That was the place where I learned the most about my building business.

If only she would have jumped in and learned and helped me. It could have been wonderful for us. If I were to stay with her, the building business would have had to go. I would have had to get a "real" 8 to 5 job. Not much chance of that.

Janet was a super clean person and I sort of remember myself as a slob at times. That was a problem. She also could not take any criticism at all. At the slightest hint of it, I would be in big trouble. I think the biggest problem that I had with her though, was very personal. That marriage counselor called it "frigid" I believe. That was the one thing that pushed me the farthest away from her. It really built up over the years. That was the one thing that brought us to a really cold union. I still remembered that night of the barbed wire in my feet, years before. We had a dislike for each other. I hated all that it made me feel. She had come from a family that showed little emotion toward each other. I came from a family that was always close to each other. That was the one thing that I could not live without, and she could not live with. Even when she tried. Her mother always had those twins on display as kids. She was very proud of them. I even remember most of Janet's letters to me in the service were just sort of matter of fact. If you were to take a close look at the family, I think you would realize why all three of the Korf kids got themselves divorced. It is a wonder to me that ole Marv did not walk out on Janet's Mom. At times, he was not treated very well.

We fell out of any good feelings we ever had for each other. Janet is a good person. She loved her two kids and wanted the best for them. We were just way too different in our personalities. We had those differences, and it was affecting the kids. Jeff was having some really bad nightmares. Also, I could never handle a regular job. I could not be what she wanted me to be, and she could never be what I needed her to be for me. That is all I care to say about that.

FAILING BUSINESS

It was time to start worrying about money. Our bills were starting to fall behind a little. I kept all the subcontractors paid but some of the suppliers had to wait. I had the new model going and one other house and we had several to get closed but there were no new sales. Yes, I was worried. I worked on some projections. I had to sell that model and even the office model if I could. The parade of homes would be coming up.

Mary Ann and I had managed to stay apart for some time. She had needed this time to be able to think and concentrate on her own future. Without pressures from either George or me. A cooling off time if you will. We had been on several H.O.W. problems in the field and did well staying apart. The only talk about "us" was light or in joking. After one of the builder's meetings though and probably after a few drinks, we sat together in the bar and talked. We wound up in my truck for a little while. After that time, we relaxed and started seeing each other more. Mary knew that the marriage counseling had fallen through for Janet and me. She was talking some with George, but it was not going at all well for them. We were both just sort of in limbo.

I think that it was some time around June that I met with Janet. We had a very long talk. I told her about Mary and what had happened at the builders show in January. She seemed to accept it.

Interest rates had climbed to about 20% and there were almost no homes being sold anywhere. The Parade of Homes was about to start, and I had my house ready. All but the touch up.

Mary Ann came out on an afternoon to help. Poor babe, she was up on a ladder doing a little paint touch up and the paint bucket slipped out of her hand. Down it went and hit just right so as to splash paint all over the brick on the front of the house. That was a no-no. She was scared to death. I grabbed a water hose and went to spraying and Mary started scrubbing. It was latex paint and we managed to get it all off without a trace of paint. We actually got a big laugh out of it afterwards.

That year of the 1980 Parade of Homes, we had a good show with a lot of traffic in and out of the house. There was a demand for housing but with that high interest rate, no one could buy. My interest rate on that house was heading up to 21%. I was afraid it would cause me to go broke. A $2,000 a month payment on just that house alone was not bearable, let alone the two other houses. I was then forced to take out a loan on the house Janet was living in, just to make our payments.

Nothing sold during that home show but in July, Marge had a buyer that was very interested in my model house. They were either going to buy mine or another house by Jim Gray, another local builder. After about a week, the buyer decided on the other house because their furniture fit better in that house. I dropped the price on mine to just what I owed on it and still no deal. I was sunk.

We made it through the summer with odd jobs that I could come up with, and a cash deal that we got. The H.B.A. was having its own problems as membership was falling off. H.O.W. was going very slow. Enrollment of new homes had dropped off to near zero. Income had fallen off to nothing. Mary Ann would be laid off soon.

PROTEST TO WASHINGTON

There was a big campaign going on during that spring of 1980. All the builders nationwide sent a message to Washington D.C. in one massive effort. Our messages were written on 2 by 4 blocks that were 12" long, pertaining to our plight. The boards were sent by mail to every Senator and Congressmen in D.C. They all received thousands of blocks. Then in July or August, we all descended on Washington en masse. Thousands upon thousands of builders doing a follow-up on our blocks of wood. We met with every single legislator and a group even met with Carter. Some called him President but most of us had no use for the man. It was his policies that put us all in this mess. Interest rates would top out at 22% in that year, and it would spill into 1981. We had a huge, massive meeting at one point and there were several congressmen that delivered a statement to us.

They told us that as long as we were having double digit inflation, interest rates would stay high. The economy would go from hot to cool and then to cold. At that point things would start back up again. Wowzer, we were all in trouble!

As 1980 rolled along, we, as an association, spent a lot of time looking for ways to try to survive this mess. Personally, I felt that I was sunk. I was thinking about what it would be like to go bankrupt. I still had bills that were late on the new model on Apple Blossom Drive. It was very embarrassing for me to let Mary know that I was going broke. As we got into September, the hammer dropped on Mary. The H.B.A. had to lay her off. There were no jobs to be had for her.

We then did the one thing that we both regretted doing later. Mary and I would live together. Just down the street from Janet. In the office model that I was living in. Our choices were extremely limited. Mary could no longer live in Grand Blanc. The money was just not there. I told Janet of our decision and the reasons why we had to do it. She was very angry with me. It was like a slap in the face to her. I understood. But with money running so low, what else could we do. I had to keep all the house payments up. And I managed to do that.

Some of my friends had simple things going at times and I got some hands-on work from them. Things like trim work and cabinets, as well as counter tops. It kept the heat on and food on the table. We were getting along. Mary also had an unemployment check coming in. We had to keep money going for the kids.

TRYING TO MOVE FORWARD

With Mary and I both living there in that model, the kids came down almost every afternoon. Some of the time I would not be there, and they still loved to come down. They had gotten to know Mary real well and enjoyed being with her. She, as well, loved having them come down to our place. One day though, they did not come down and when they finally did, they were not allowed to hug or be close to Mary any longer. They were told to stay away from her. We of course honored that but it put a bump in their relationship. They did not know why.

MARY'S DIVORCE FINAL

Going into December, Mary became free, as her divorce was finalized. She received a settlement of $10,000 and she had her car. She felt a little better knowing that she was moving ahead in her life. I was the one stalling out on her. Janet had filed the papers, but we were not close to a final agreement. It was a sad time for me. I had a hard time accepting not having my kids with me. I did, however, feel that it would be better for them not seeing their mom and I fighting all the time.

OUR FINAL PARTIES

We had one very fun time that December. Mary and I went to the H.B.A. Christmas party in downtown Flint. We had hotel rooms on about the 10th floor for that night. Ed and Sister Mary also had a room. There were a lot of members with rooms that night, all on the same floor. I was installed as the Association's vice president for 1981. We all had a really great time. It was a lot different from the year before.

Mary was just a lot of fun to be with. We did a lot of dancing and carrying on. When we decided to go back up to our hotel rooms, Ed and Mary were with us and for some reason we decided to take the decorated Christmas tree from the lobby up to the 10th floor to our rooms. We had some whiskey for drinks up there. So, the two Mary's convinced Ed and I to take the tree. Into the elevator it went, and we continued our party upstairs. I think word got out and we had a lot of people up there that evening. It was a really fun night with not much sleep.

We had two other really fun parties that fall. One was for Mary's 29th Birthday. It was on the 4th of October. We had it at the model house in the basement. There was lots of booze as everyone brought their own stuff to drink. That party went on all night. Well, almost all night. When we got up the next morning, there were a few people sleeping on the floors and couch. We didn't go downstairs for several days after that because we knew it would be a mess. Yup, it was.

So, if that was not enough, we somehow got talked into having a Halloween party. It would be in costume, and we really put on a party. We had a dance floor downstairs, and it was sorta dark. We hung black thread all over the place where people would be dancing. So, as you danced, it felt like cobwebs hanging down all over, just for fun. It was great watching people swatting the cobwebs away. We also had an old wooden casket down there with the devil laying in it (one of our friends). He would come up out of there to tell people about one of their sins. It was hilarious. We had told the guy playing the devil little stories that we knew about some of our guests. We also had a fake swami to tell your fortune. That party also went on into the next morning. It was quite a hoot. Maybe we were having a coming out party of sorts. There were probably 70 or 80 people at each of the parties. Clean ups were some job after each party, stale, spilled booze. Really bad.

Mary and I set up a Christmas tree that year but with little money, the decorations were a little slim. I had a few things and Mary did too. So, maybe it looked like a Charlie Brown tree. We did not care. Presents were also a little lean that year, but we were together and that is what really counted.

ROUGH TIMES

The winter was a cold, brutal time for us. I remember coming home from a framing job several times, froze to the bone, as I would have been working outside all day. We had a small bath in the kitchen area with a shower. I would turn the water on hot in the shower until it steamed up so much that you couldn't see. Then I would jump in there and steam for 20 minutes until I was too hot. We had one of those tankless hot water heaters. That winter was really cold. I hated snow and cold.

1981 turned out to be a very slow year for having any work at all. I don't think a single mortgage was taken out that year in Flint. It could not have been worse. We put that model house in the parade again, but it was for not. There were not a lot of people out looking. There were a few odd jobs around. Some small remodel work. By mid-year, we had gotten far behind with some of our bills in the building business. Janet and I had agreed that I would build her a house as soon as I could. There would be no mortgage and we had a lot picked out. I had put 3 or 4 thousand dollars down and was making payments on the lot. The big house on Wesley Drive, where Janet was living, did get sold on a cash deal and we then had a little cash plus we got a few bills paid off. We tried to save as much as we could for living expenses. Janet moved into the model house on Apple Blossom Drive. We now had only two house payments.

Mary had gotten her divorce all finalized out the past December. Janet and I were still in limbo. I knew I was needing to get it over with. Maybe I was afraid to do so and just did not want that last big confrontation. I don't know.

THE RIGHT DECISION

That July I went on a fish trip up into Canada with Ed Dick, Jerry Tucker and Bob Paradise. One evening I took one of the fish boats out for a ride and after a while I just shut the motor off and sat looking to the heavens. I got myself deep into some serious thought. The guys had set a lamp out on the dock so I could find my way back in. It looked very bright from afar. I sat there for maybe two hours. I was praying and thinking. As I look back, everything came into sharp focus for me that night.

I thought over my past with Janet and how hard it was for us, our families and of course our kids. It was so fresh in my mind how wonderful it was to be around Mary. She just gave me so much love and so much caring in my life. That is exactly what I had so desperately needed. She knew what my life was all about, and she knew what I needed. When I finally started that motor and went on back to camp I felt completely refreshed. I decided on what I had to do, and I was ready to take on the world again.

The guys in camp did not say much as they knew why I was out on the lake so late that night. In searching through my life with Janet, it was very clear how really mismatched we were. We would be getting divorced no matter what Mary and I did with our lives. I had turned into a complete drunk living with Janet. The last eight years or so were horrible for both of us. This was the end, no matter what.

I thought about all the friendships I had developed over the years with all the people in my industry. Most of those people were really good and hard-working folks. Some I had become very close friends with. Jerry Tucker, Bobbie Paradise, Berry Simon and Kal Nemer. Ed Dick was relation, but he became my closest friend. I knew that Janet could not stand to be around any of them. That was something her and I could have never gotten over. My job and all the homeowners. She could never accept any of that.

I had built that nice house for her, and we had a nice rec room down stairs with a cute little built in bar. All but one time, I sat there at that bar by myself. Berry Simon was the only guy to ever come and visit me there. I can still remember him calling and asking. "I am coming over but only if she is not there." Janet had a reputation of treating my business associates really badly. So, they would not come out to the house, only to the office model.

One of the last times she and I went out together was at some sort of a dance, maybe a wedding party. I don't remember. It was at a dance hall, way west of Chesaning. I used to love to fast dance with my sister Mary. We always had a ball dancing. I had danced with Janet that night, but one of the times when I gotten off the floor with my sister, Janet had picked up and drove herself home. She left me there, maybe 45 miles from home. I think it was Ed Dick that drove me all the way home that night. I didn't go in; I just got in my truck and drove around till the sun came up that morning. I did not want to go into that house.

All those thoughts went through my mind that night on the lake. These were all the negative things along with the much deeper personal problems. On the other side of the coin though were my two little guys that I loved very much. How could I leave them? We always had so much fun together. I thought of how living with the parents they had would affect them. I remembered Janet slamming Jeff down in his chair because someone had come to the door at breakfast time. It was rough on them, and I knew it would be affecting their lives. To leave would be better than having them grow up bitter with life. Maybe Jeff's bad dreams would stop.

I also knew how bad things were in Michigan. I knew that if I was ever going to make it in life, good enough to support the kids and Mary and I, Michigan would not be the place I could do it.

I was excited to get back from that fish trip that year. Mary and I had a good talk and yes, she said "yes" she would marry me. She was already divorced from George. I just needed to get myself right and we could go ahead with our plans. I don't think that her and I had ever talked much about marriage until that time. Her and I had had a lot of fun together over the span of time we knew each other. We now had to get serious about our future together.

PREGNANT

The big bomb would drop the next month. Toward the end of August of 1981 we learned that we were pregnant. This really sealed our plans. My divorce from Janet became final on August the 31st, I believe. We started making wedding plans as soon as we knew we were having a baby. We had about 6 weeks to put it all together.

WEDDING PLANS

We found a church in Flushing. It was the United Methodist Church on Main Street. Then we had to have a place for a reception, and we found that in Clio, not too far from Flushing. We hired a disc jockey for our reception and found someone to cater the meal. I think we put the whole thing together for around $2,000. We chose the guys and gals that would be in the wedding with us. Ed Dick would be my best man and Mary chose her best friend Debbie Stark as her Maid of Honor. Invitations, tuxedos, dresses, flowers, center pieces, the booze and all the whatnots were put into place. We had done it.

All the plans for the wedding were coming together nicely. Mary was a little worried about it all happening as planned but we had worked it out very well. My ole buddy Gary McEldowney was coming up from West Virginia for the wedding. He was going to be in the wedding party. We invited some special friends from Canada, and they were coming. Some other good friends from across the state also would be there. They were old deer hunting buddies. Mary's Mom and Dad were coming up from Ohio and the whole thing would wind up at about 250 guests.

We would be married on the 10th of October. I could not believe that I was going to be married to such a wonderful gal. She had been treating me the way I always wanted it to be treated. She liked my business. She liked my friends. She loved my family, and I did hers as well. She worked in the office all she could, to help me out. We both wanted God to be in charge of our lives. We both wanted kids as well. We told no one about the pregnancy, not even my sister Mary or Ed.

Mary and I spent a lot of time talking during those next few weeks as a lot of decisions had to be made. We could not afford the house we were living in on Wesley Drive and hoped it would be sold soon. Marge was trying hard to sell it for us. We had gotten way behind on both house payments. Mary had put her $10,000 into the company as a loan. Somehow, we had to get that paid back to her.

We talked about all of our friends and what they would mean to us if we lived around Flushing. They were wonderful folks, and we always had a lot of fun with them. We both felt, however, that they would be very distracting to us if we were trying to build a life together. We were looking for a complete new start in life. My kids were the only real worry we had. We both wanted to stay in the building business, but we knew that it would be a long time coming back in the Flint area, and maybe never would come back.

I knew that there was no way possible for me to make enough money in Flint to keep two families going. Our thoughts turned to moving. We both loved the mountains and we both loved the west. We decided to go west on our honeymoon and look it over out there. Mom and Dad had moved to Tucson, but we felt it would be too hot there for us. I found a book on the 10 best places to move to in the country. Albuquerque was voted the second-best place to move to according to that book. We decided to go down to Tennessee, visit my Niece Cindy Kubica, look Nashville over and then head south and west on our trip. We made plans to spend some time with Mom and Dad Wallen in Arizona, then head up north and come through Colorado. That would be a good place to move to, but it could get awfully cold there in the winters. So that was our plan for the near future. We wanted my folks to be the first to know about the baby we had on the way. We would not tell anyone until then.

JULIE AND JEFF

One weekend we had Julie and Jeff at the house for dinner. Mary and I cooked a nice meal for them and for some reason I remember having apple dumplings for dessert. We told the kids that we would probably be moving somewhere, and it would probably be out of state, where I could make a living for all of us. I told them that I would do everything I could do to help support them. We would be back to see them, and they of course would be coming to see us. We had no idea where we might live but hoped to know fairly soon. I know they did not understand a whole lot about the economics of why we had to move but I tried to explain as best as I could. I also told them that I would help them with their education, again as best as I could. I told them that we would have to be moving out of that model house soon. It was very hard to talk about those things with them and they tried to understand as best as they could. It was a sad day for all of us. They had to know.

We told them that they would be coming to the wedding only if they really wanted to. Julie chose to be there, and Jeff did not feel like he wanted to attend. I knew there would be trying times for all of us as time moved on.

I would once again work as hard as I could to make all the ends meet for both families. I knew how hard it was going to be not having the kids around any longer. We had been so close. If I tried to stay there, there would be no work, especially trying to feed two families. As it turned out, I was right. Michigan never did recover to any decent point in the housing market. It would have been really rough trying to make a living there.

OUR WEDDING

Time passed quickly those last few weeks. My divorce became final, and all of our preparations were paying off. We had bought very cheap wedding rings and bought lots of party stuff. It was one or the other. Kal Nemer got us all the booze real cheap from his store. A lot of the out-of-town folks came to town the day before the wedding and we had lots of help decorating the hall. Gary McEldowney was a big help. He and Jeanie stayed with us at our house.

The wedding that next day was wonderful. Cindy Kubica was there to sing at the wedding, and it all went off so nice and so fun. I believe we were all waiting in anticipation for the party. What a party that one was! The people who did not know a lot of folks that were there, soon did and it was like one big happy gang. We all danced until early AM, and I think Clayton Rutherford was the only one that had to be helped out of the hall. Well, maybe Jerry Tucker and Berry Simon were that way too. It was a mid-October night, sort of cool but with all the dancing going on everybody was a little sweaty and jackets and ties were removed. All the decorations were tore down by 1:00 am and Mary and I made our escape. We hit the hotel room that night totally exhausted. It had been a wonderful Wedding for Mary and me.

Happy Days

Mary's Mom and Dad, Harold and Virginia Grater

HONEY MOONING

We had my little 1977 El Camino all loaded and ready for a 3-week honeymoon. I had put a cover over the back of it so we could safely store things there for the trip. After a late morning rise, we were up and ready for some time away from Michigan and all that downer stuff that covered the land. I had never been away from my kids this long before and that would take a little getting used to. I was, however, very excited to see what lay ahead for us.

I had married the love of my life, my very best friend, someone that wanted all the same things in life that I did and was very excited about sharing a new adventure with me. It was hard for me to believe that this was really happening. I felt that I had gone through so many unhappy years. This was very exciting for both of us. We drove south across the state line and wow, we were on our way.

We spent a few days with Cindy at her place. She showed us all around Nashville and spent a lot of time with us. It was a great time. The city was really nice, and I could see how she loved it there.

We headed south and west from there and got into the blue grass country. I can still remember how hard we laughed when we came to a little town called Buck Snort. I think it was in Arkansas.

Mary made me stop the car the first time we saw cotton growing in a field. It was along the expressway, and she had to run out into the field and pick some cotton. Being October, it was ripe. She was so funny. She just had to experience everything we came across. We were tootling down the road listening to some down-home country blue grass music. There sure was an excitement about us.

We traveled across Texas and got to experience what totally boring land looked like. It was flat, dry and nothing there for miles. We got excited though when we made it to New Mexico. The landscape started looking a lot different. I got a kick out of Mary. Every hill over 50 feet high, she had to take a picture. I knew she would be excited when we seen mountains.

We had bought this coupon book of some kind. It had special hotel rates in different cities. We were heading into Albuquerque and had a cheaper hotel picked out. It was awesome pulling into town and going through the pass, as we entered the city right between two really high mountains. They were beautiful, the pass was beautiful, and the city was beautiful. We found the city to be laid out all west of the mountain range, in a slope to the Rio Grande river.

Our hotel turned out to be at the base of the foothills and it was an old jewel. It was a two-story, rambling, very old structure. There were pictures hanging in the foyer of a lot of movie stars and one of John F. Kennedy, all taken at that hotel. In its glory days it would have been really something. They said that Marilyn Monroe had swam nude in their now empty pool.

The room they assigned us was on the upper floor and when we went into it, we didn't stay long. The wallpaper was rolling off the wall. It needed paint really bad and was dirty. They gave us the owners suite after that one. It was large but also a mess. We found bullet holes and knife cuts in the walls. Mary re-arranged the furniture a bit and we lasted 2 nights there, fascinated by it but it was a little frightening for us.

The next day we drove around Albuquerque and developed some car trouble. We had lost about 50% of the engine power. That little truck would hardly go over 30 miles an hour. I thought I had blown something in the engine. We finally found a fix-it shop over on Central Avenue and they got us right in. After a short check out, the guy figured out that the motor was not blown. The muffler had become plugged with some sort of muffler packings. What a relief that was!

We left the truck there and took a bus over to the mall. This was something important to Mary. She loved to shop. She was happy to see such a nice mall in town. We shopped around the place for a little while, got something to eat and found our way back to the fix-it place, on the bus again.

It was really nice to meet such a nice honest repair shop owner. They had replaced the muffler, and the truck was running just fine. We were very thankful for such a cheap bill and such a nice guy. That truck had over 90,000 miles on it . It could have been anything.

We were finding that all the people in town were very friendly. People on the streets would wave to us as we drove on by. Everything in the downtown area was clean and neat and busy. We were liking what we saw.

We found the Home Builder Association office and stopped in there to check on work in the area. We were told that things were very slow for Albuquerque. They sent us to the west side to a place called Paradise Hills and to Rio Rancho. We decided that the next day we would go out there and check it out.

After the second night of staying in that big old hotel, we decided to make a change. That place was just not right and besides we were about the only ones there and it smelled old and bad. We relocated to a much nicer, cleaner and non-smoking place. I did not know a non-smoking place existed at that time. I remember the manager telling me that if I were to smoke in that room, he would hunt me down. I was a smoker, but I did not smoke in that room. It was a comfortable room.

We got to do a lot of sightseeing during the next day. We found the Tram that you could ride to the top of the mountain. There was a restaurant at the summit, and we decided that we would like to go up there for our evening supper. That was exciting for us. We noticed that there was a lot of open space, just right for development and building.

We then drove to the west side of the river and drove through Paradise Hills. Much to our surprise and delight, we saw a lot of home building going on. We were told that it was very slow but for Flint Michigan standards things were on a boom. We then drove north to Rio Rancho and were really surprised by the amount of construction going on there. We stopped in at the Amrep main sales office and talked to the folks there. Once again, we were totally surprised by what they told us. It was slow for their usual pace. We saw it as a great opportunity for us if we were to move here.

We checked into rental units and again were surprised at the rates. We got back to the hotel that afternoon feeling very positive about this place. It was a neat, clean and very friendly place with what I considered lots of work. We were quite excited.

We got dressed and headed for the tram that evening with another excitement. We were going to the top of the mountain, 10,000 feet up, to have our dinner. Mary was feeling a little overwhelmed by the mountain. The western slopes were a lot of huge rocks and not much trees. The eastern slopes were heavy with trees. We would land at the top of the tram in a heavily wooded area. The trip up the tram was awesome. The sun was setting and beautiful. All the city lights were coming on and we knew how gorgeous it was going to be.

There was quite a chill in the air as we walked to the restaurant at the top of the mountain. We had sorta forgot that we might need reservations to have dinner up there. They were filled up when we asked for a table. After a little conversation with the folks there we told them we were on our honeymoon. They went right to work on a table for us and we were very thankful that they let us in. People really were very nice here.

The sun had set and from where we were sitting, we could see a sea of lights thousands of feet below. It turned out to be absolutely beautiful, much to our delight. The meal was great and as we headed back down in the tram, we saw many different views of the city lights.

This city was clean, beautiful and friendly, and the cost of living seemed reasonable. The work opportunity looked great to me. The weather was awesome with something like 88% sunshiny days. The average cold winter days ranged around the 55 degree mark. Outdoor work would be great. I felt I could do very well here. I would just need the opportunity to prove myself if we were to move here. The thought of it was very scary for me but I was excited. This was the place I was ready to call home. I could work hard and get a company going again out here. Mary liked it as well. Little did we know what this place held in stock for us. The good Lord was keeping an eye on us and his guiding hand was there with us.

After four days in Albuquerque, we left with the early morning sun at our backs, and we headed west going to Tucson. Mom and Dad would be awaiting our arrival. Western New Mexico turned out to be one heck of a beautiful drive. Taylor Mountain loomed over the desert floor and then on into the red rock area toward Gallop. It was just one really neat thing after another until we broke out into the high desert of Arizona. It had its own beauty but did not compare with the red rock mountains. We passed through the petrified forest and the painted desert on the way to Holbrook. That would be our turning point for heading south to Tucson.

Mary and I stopped in Holbrook for a true Mexican dining experience. It was a little restaurant in the downtown part of the town. I was wanting to get the full experience. I ordered a combination plate with green chili. It was HOT. Really bad for me, a tourist. I sat there vowing to eat it all. I wanted the experience, I guess. At any rate, I remember breaking out in a hot sweat and a very hot tongue. It tasted so good. I just had trouble with the heat. I would definitely be trying it again. Mary was smart and went easy on herself.

We then headed south toward Sholow, a little town that was named after the Sholow card game from the old west days. South of that town we started to run into a very pristine forest of Pondarosa pine trees. Just a beautiful forest as it were. Dad had told me that this drive south from Holbrook would be great, but we had no idea what lay ahead. We came down through the Salt River Canyon. When we made our first turnout stop, it was just beautiful. Mary sat on the stone wall along the road and exclaimed. "Bring me food and water. I am staying right here." It was probably the most beautiful place that we had ever seen.

As we drove on, we got further down into the canyon and the prettier it looked. We crossed the salt river (not salty) and drove out the other side. It was all so cool to us. We were falling in love with the Southwest. The forest finally played out and we found ourselves back in the desert.

When we got into the Sonoran Desert just outside of Tucson, we really found out how gorgeous that area was. All the different kinds of cactus and other plants and bushes and trees. We loved it, especially the old men of the desert the cactus they called the saguaro. The big, tall dude with several arms sticking out. Mary just loved all the different plants.

The best of our trip was now at hand. I was driving into Tucson and about to introduce my new bride to my Mom. I had no doubts that Mom would also fall in love with her.

We got to their house late in the afternoon and they were all waiting for us. I had heard that Mom had a few preconceived ideas about Mary, but I was not concerned. I was right. When we got out of the truck at their house everyone was excited, and Mom and Mary hit it off from the very minute they saw each other. Of course, it is a well-known fact that my Mom loved everyone when she met them. Well, almost everyone.

Those two hit it off, and by the time we left a week or so later, they were best friends. Mom even made a point to let us know how well she liked Mary. Years later, she would say how comfortable she was when we would come out as she did not have to spend two weeks cleaning before we got there. She felt like Mary was just one of her kids. Dad really liked Mary as well. He was really surprised to find out that she could keep up with him all the way when it came to the Bible. Mary had a very good Christian upbringing.

When we told them that we had something special to tell them, Dad interrupted by saying, oh, you mean because she is pregnant. We were a little surprised that he should know but then like a lot of pregnant women, Mary had that special glow. The glow that would say, "Hey, I am P.G.". They were both really happy for us. We were about three months P.G. by that time.

Mom and Dad took us all over sightseeing while we were there. We did the desert museum, the old movie sets at Old Tucson, and we went to Aravaca to visit with brother Ed. He took us on a back road trip from his place down to Nogales. We also went out with Charlene a time or two, on the town. All in all, we had a wonderful time and Mom and Dad were delighted to know that we were maybe going to move out west and that we liked Albuquerque.

When we left, after a week or so with them, I had such a glowing warm feeling. My Mary had fit right in. She had made such a wonderful bond with everyone there. That bond would last and grow till the day my folks passed away. They loved her very much.

What a honeymoon we were having! We drove northwest from

Tucson and headed to Page Arizona. We visited the big hydro dam there and headed north into Utah. Everything we saw was so pretty. We saw one thing there in southern Utah, though, that we still laugh about. We were coming into this little town and there was a little gas station restaurant combo store with a big sign that read "STOP, EAT and GET GAS". That sign just really hit us funny. Naturally we had to stop, eat and get gas.

We drove up through a beautiful Utah and headed over into Colorado. We wanted to do the Rocky Mountain National Park. We drove on and on through the mountains and when we got there, we were disappointed. That big ole park was closed for the season.

We then headed north again and on into the Black Hills of the Dakotas. We did all the tourist stuff; drove out to Devils Tower; took in Mt Rushmore; and found Calamity Jane and Wild Bill Hickok's grave sites. We also did the Badlands National Park on our way heading back east. Mary took a zillion and one pictures on our tour. Heading back, we went through Chicago and on up into Michigan.

We had seen tons of really cool sights. We passed through 23 different states and had been on the road for a total of three weeks. Our plans were to now sell the model house, find a place to live, and as soon as we could get ourselves freed up, we would move to Albuquerque. That would be our new home. Away from all the business grief of Flint. Away from all the distraction of the friends that we loved, all the connections I had in business and all the wonderful people that helped me out so much. We would really miss the Home Builders Association where I had learned so much about building. I was supposed to be the H.B.A. president in Flint for 1982. I had to resign that position. I felt that I would not be in Michigan for much of '82.

I knew that we would really be missing Ed Dick and my sister Mary, that would be really hard. Most of all, my little guys would not be around any longer. I knew how really hard it would be on them. Julie, now twelve years old, had stuck by my side as close as she could be. It seemed to me that the harder things got between Janet and I, the more Julie tried to be close to me. I didn't know how hard it was going to be. Jeff and I were also very close. Maybe in a little different way. He always loved it when we did things together.

One time we got a hold of this old copy machine. We tore it completely apart. Then we started with all sorts of different parts and made an operational "whatchamacallit" out of the parts. It had lights that flashed and blinked and one that would blind you. There were lots of gears and chains and fans and whatever moved all over the place, a metal bar that would rise and fall. We even had an electrical arc that would occur every few seconds on the thing. Jeff was so delighted with it. We had had a lot of fun making it. The time was soon coming when I would be missing a lot of that with the kids.

HONEYMOON'S OVER

We had driven long and hard that last day of our trip and we got back about 4:30 in the morning. We drove straight to Ed and Mary's house in Chesaning. They were sound asleep that early morning. We pulled into the yard and went to their big bedroom window. On que, Mary and I started to sing "Ya picked a fine time to leave me Lucile". When they finally woke up, we changed our song to "A baby, a baby, we're gonna have a baby." They were shocked but let us in. We all sat there 'till the sun came up.

Had a few drinks and told them all about our trip and about our plans. They were both sad. They did not want to lose us to the West as they had with Mom and Dad. Mary and I were really close to Ed and Mary.

We made it back to Flushing and our little home on Wesley Drive. I am sure we slept for several days after our return. It sure was great to see my kids again. They came and stayed with us that next weekend. That gave us time to talk to them about moving to Albuquerque and what it was like "out west." Julie was very interested in it.

BACK IN FLUSHING

One of the first things we did was to have a little best friends get together. We had about 15 or so folks over to our house and we made our announcement about having a baby on the way. Then we told them about our plans to move west. We also had found out some other good news that we shared with our friends as well. The house on Wesley Drive had sold while we were on our honeymoon, and we had to move soon. There was a lot of emotion at that little party. To top it all off, Mary's best friend Debbie Stark made an announcement that night. She also was expecting a baby and she and Denis, her fella, would be getting married soon.

I made plans with my hunting buddies to go north for a last shot at the deer hunt that year. It was mid-November. It would be hard the next few years, not being able to go, as I knew it was for my Pop when he could not make it any longer. Ed had made a camp mounted on the bed of a trailer that would sort of pop up and then a tarp would be placed over it for a roof. This was also the last year I would be able to go hunting with Gary McEldowney. Jerry Tucker was there as well as Harry McEldowney, Gary's cousin.

I had driven up north that year by myself and I am glad I did because my heart was just not into having a party with all the guys. My mind was full of my kids and my new bride and all that had to happen before we could move west. I think I said my goodbyes about 3 days early that year and went on home. I knew it would be a long time before I would see Gary Mac again.

A LITTLE HOUSE TO MOVE INTO

My good ole buddy and best friend Kal Nemer came to my rescue early that December. Our house on Wesley Drive was closing and we had no place to move into. We also had very little money to go on. Kal had a little house in Durand, Michigan that he had taken in on a trade and he told us that if we wanted to, we could move into it until we were ready to move west, and we could use it for free. What a friend he was. Mary and I drove out and looked it over. It was a three-bedroom, 1000 square foot little house and it needed quite a little work to make it decent for us to live in. Mainly, it was dirty and needed some paint. We were very happy to have it to live in.

The house on Wesley closed and we had some money in our

hands. Yea! So, we paid off what bills we could and I paid Mary back for her loan to the company. She had given me $10,000 and I was able to give her back only $8,000 of that money. She stuck that money away so we had something to move west on. Thank God for that. We had no more house payments as the fancy house on Apple Blossom Drive was going back to the bank. What a mess.

We spent four or five days really cleaning in that little house and patched some walls and done a little paint touch up. It really did come out looking cozy in there and we were happy. We moved in and got it all set up with enough time to spare so we could set up a Christmas Tree. The season was upon us, and we were happy. Our lives together were finally settling down and we could think a little about the direction we had chosen.

We knew that things in our life together would be very different now. We had a bit of a feeling of isolation living way out where we were. I still owed over $50,000 from the building business and I planned on paying that off when I got back on my feet, some day in the future. I felt like I was running from things of obligation, but I also knew it was the only way, the only real chance I had, to make it work. I had absolutely no chance to make it in Michigan, at this time.

We had a nice quiet Christmas that year. I knew it would be the last one that I would ever spend with my kids. That part was really sad for me, and I never brought it up to anyone. I goofed up as I recall with what we got Julie for her Christmas present. She had thoughts of forming a band, so we got her a drum set. The only problem was, we had gotten her a juvenile set. I don't think she liked it very well and was disappointed. Sorry Julie, we did not have a lot of money.

Our thoughts were that we would wait till the baby was born and then make our way west. We did not have the money to buy the baby furniture, so in January of 1982, I decided to make it myself. There was very little work going on anywhere, so I had a lot of time on my hands. We could afford to buy the materials I needed to do the job, so I got started on it. The house had a full basement, so there was plenty of room to do my work.

DEB CAME EARLY

Deborah Marie

Then things started happening. On the morning of February the 9th, Mary went into labor. We still had 10 weeks left till the baby was to be born but it was too late. Mary's water had broken, and we made a mad dash to the hospital. Our little girl was born very prematurely. She only weighed in at a little over three pounds and then, as all newborns do, she lost a few ounces. When she stabilized, she was 2 pounds and 10 ounces.

Mary and I were scared to death. We really wanted to have that baby. We said lots of prayers from that moment on. The hospital gave her a chance for surviving but we wanted her to have more than just a chance. I called Mom and Dad in Tucson and asked them to pray for us and Mary did the same with her folks. My folks were in the Catholic Charismatic Movement at that time and had lots of friends that would pray for us. One guy stayed up and prayed for us overnight. He did not even know us. It was wonderful all the support we were getting to help our little lady pull through.

This all brought into focus something that Mary and I had talked about but had not implemented into our lives as of yet; God. You might say that God just put it all together in a plan for us to grasp and to move forward with. We did just that. Days turned into weeks and our little Debbie was gaining in weight as well as in life. We went to the hospital every single day. Even when the roads were near impassable because of bad weather. We spent many

Such a beauty.

many hours with her and just loved her into living.

OUT OF MONEY

We had run right out of money and were afraid we may have to use some of our moving money to live on. Things along that line were not looking very well. So as the hand of the Lord moved once again to help us, our neighbor just behind our little house, had a fire. The damage was to the complete garage and a little of the house and attic. I had met the guy several times out in the yard, and he knew I was a carpenter. He gave me the job of restoring his place. What a break! I did almost all of the work by myself and made enough money to get a little ahead. We were smiling again. I worked on that job and worked on our little Debbie's furniture and made that trip into the hospital every day. It was really fun making that furniture. I think she still has it today, 40 some years later.

We had gotten a puppy that last summer. It was something that Jeff really wanted. It was a female black lab pup. We picked her up from a guy that I had built a house for. Jeff insisted on calling the little girl dog Jessie. So that is what she was named. She turned out to be a little terrorist and destroyed a lot of things around the house. Sadly though, when we were having a large garage sale at the Wesley Drive house, a month or so before our wedding, Jessie was taken from our yard. We were all really sad to lose her even though she destroyed everything in her path. Jeff and I drove all the roads around us for miles looking for her with no luck. We finally gave her up as lost for good.

Then one day in about March of '82, when we were living in Durand, we got a call from our old neighbor on Wesley Drive. There was a black lab dog hanging around our old house. Mary went over there right away and sure enough, there was our Jessie dog. She had grown to full adult by that time and was very happy to see us. It took her 6 months or so, but she made it back to our old house and we got her back. Maybe the guy that stole her just couldn't take it with her anymore and brought her back. We loved having her back home but wow, what a handful she was. That dog was into everything.

One day we got a call from a busy body neighbor of ours and the lady was mad. Our Jessie was being mated in our backyards by another neighbor's dog, she said. Such a display in the openness of our adjoining yards was very immoral. We paid little attention to the neighbor but now we had a pregnant dog on our hands. We also had a cat that we had brought from Mary's folks farm in Ohio. He was a Tom cat and also a little wild. His name was Fred. So that set the stage for our pets.

Jessie had six very cute little black and white pups. That gave us 8 animals living with us. Jeff was ecstatic with that as he loved critters very much and was not allowed to have any at his house. He would miss his Jessie dog when we moved west. Those six pups would be only about 3 weeks old when we moved.

LONG HOSPITAL STAY

For the next 45 days, after our little Debbie was born, we ventured up to Hurley Hospital, day after day. It was so heartwarming to watch that little one struggle and grow. It was also disheartening to watch some of the other little babies wither and finally die in that ward. Some of the parents just would not come up and be with their little one. Some did not even have a name.

We watched Debbie's charts every day, when we got there. We needed her to get to 5 pounds and then she would be ours to take home. By the end of March she was almost there and we were allowed to take her home a little under the 5 pound mark. That was a very exciting time for us. Even Jeff and Julie were happy to see her come home. I had finished most of the furniture for her room and we had a nice little nursery set up. It sure was good to not have to make that drive every day into Flint to see her.

MOVING WEST

For the next few weeks, we managed to get everything finished up that we had to do before our departure. We hired a moving company to move everything to our new home. It was very scary looking back on the move. It was sort of like back in 1966 when I got off that plane from the military, no job; no place to live; no education; and we did not know a soul in Albuquerque. This time I had two wonderful kids that I had to leave behind in Michigan. I had a brand-new baby that was going with us. I had a new wife, a new dog, and 6 new puppies and a cat. This time though, I would have all my skills and carpenter tools with me. I would have to put all my faith in God and in myself and my tools. You will see later how God helped me out.

We set the move up for the guys to pick up our things on about the 22nd of May. It was almost 20 years to the day from the last time I moved out of Michigan, for my four years in the Air Force. That date was May 28th, 1962.

Our furniture and things were all picked up. I still had my little El Camino pickup truck with a camper shell on it and Mary had her little VW Rabbit. I had built a little wood center console for my truck and that would be Debbie's bed for the trip. She would ride right next to me, all the way. I had a built-in place for her bottle and a little shade to keep the sun off her. She would be not quite 6 pounds by the time we left. Mary would bring Fred the cat with her and I would have the 7 dogs with me in the back of the truck. They were way too young to ween as of yet.

We said our goodbyes to Jeff and Julie the day we got all loaded up with the movers and then we drove out to Ed and Mary's to spend our last night in Michigan. It was so exciting to head out to a new life. It would be lonely without my kids and it was also really creepy knowing what I was about to go through. We only had Mary's money to go on, and that money would not go far. The trip with two cars would be expensive. The movers would be expensive, and we had to have money to live on until I could get some sort of an income. There would be rent to pay, and we had to send Janet money as well. Scary huh?

Mary and I each had a C.B. radio in our cars as we headed south down 23 and on into Ohio. It is still very clear to me, passing over the Michigan Ohio state line. We were well on our way to a new life and a new chance to make a living. Mary and I both cheered as we continued on south. After a brief stay at Mary's folks, we were heading for our new home state.

We were able to talk to each other with the C.B. radios as we drove. I was excited to have my little angel with me and we talked a lot. Well, she jabbered a lot. She was such a happy little lady. We had to stop at various intervals as there would come a familiar smell every so often. I could feed her her bottle as we drove but no way to change a diaper.

The dogs were a little warm but did just fine in the back. That turned into a bit of a mess but we cleaned out the big plastic tub every day as we went. Jessie was a good mama dog and stayed right with those pups. Mary had the cat in her car and even though it did not like to travel, it did okay. Once, when we stopped, I think for lunch, the cat got out and ran away. It took a little while, but we got him back.

The miles clicked on and soon we were at the New Mexico state line. Our new home. It was really great driving that last 200 miles to town. Having the dogs and all, we stopped at an old motel, and they let us spend the night with the dogs in the truck. We did let them all out for a little walk about. We were finally in our new hometown.

We found a dog kennel the next morning and dropped the dogs off. That was a relief not having them with us for a while. After checking on rental properties we decided to take a place out on the west side of town. It was in a newly formed town called Rio Rancho. We wound up in a little 1000 square foot, three-bedroom duplex for the price of $325 a month. The place was brand new and never lived in. We were delightfully surprised and happy to have it. We had our furniture coming in just 2 more days from the time we got the house. It had a fenced-in back yard, about 4 foot tall, and we thought it would be just right for the dogs.

Mary found a used mattress in the paper, and we bought it so we had something to sleep on till the movers arrived. We knew we would need an extra bed anyway, so it worked good. We did a little grocery shopping, picked the dogs up and we were in business. Our new home, in our new city. Just the three of us with 8 animals.

The pups were now about a month old, and we could give them all away in just a few weeks. The cat was very independent and we could let it outside and it would return on its own. Jessie was real good and stayed in the yard very well. We were hoping that it was not just because of the pups. No one lived in the other half of the duplex so we had it nice and quiet. There were no houses behind us, and the street was not traveled that much.

I think it was on the 27th of May that the movers arrived. What a thrill that was. We got Debbie's room all set up and then could take a little time doing the rest of the house. Those two couches that we brought from Michigan looked really bad. They had been in the basement at the big house in Flushing and we still had them. There was no way that we could have afforded to buy anything different. One, I think, had big flowers on it and the other one was burnt orange. It was our new home to us, and we were happy. Besides, Debbie did not mind.

She, by the way, was doing just fine after being only a 2 pound, 10 ouncer at birth. Her little frail body was filling out and she was getting cuter by the day. We still had these little, tiny baby bottles to feed her with.

We took 4 or 5 days to get all settled in and the place was feeling like home. Small but cozy. There was just a one car, attached garage on the place and there was a washer and dryer hookup in there; we had our own washer and dryer. We had also went to a used appliance store and bought a $75 fridge. That old thing actually lasted us several years.

SHORT VISIT TO TUCSON

After a few days of settling in, we loaded Debbie and the 7 dogs into the El Camino and went to Tucson for a long weekend. It was Mom's Birthday. Mom and Dad were happy to see us and get to meet their new grandkid. They also got to meet all those dogs. It was getting close to the time we could get rid of them.

It was great to just jump in the car and be at Mom and Dads in just 7 hours. It was great to just sit and relax with my folks. We would find that going to their place would always be a soft, easy place of escape from the world out there. The last three years or so were really rough on both Mary and I, so it was great to be there. The big load was on my shoulders now, so you might say that this was the calm before the storm.

We talked some, on the way back to Albuquerque from Dads place, about what had to happen next. The biggest item on the list was to get a job. Things across the country were really rough in the building business, but Albuquerque was moving along some and I just needed to get out there and knock on doors until I landed something. I knew I could get a regular job, but I needed something where I could get a crew going and do some framing. There was just me. I had no crew, so it would be a little hard to get hired to frame houses. I had had no work for a long time and Mary's money was running low.

OUR FIRST TRIP INTO THE DESERT

Our first trip out into the desert after arriving here in New Mexico was rather remarkable. We got our first good learning experience that day. We drove west out of town on Southern Blvd. As far as one could drive, about 8 miles, I guess. We parked the El Camino at the foot of the sand dunes and decided to go for a little walk up a hill of pure sand. We soon found a set of squiggly slanted lines about 4 foot long each going up the hill in the sand. We had no idea what it was, so we followed the lines up the hill and almost at the top, they suddenly stopped. Big mystery. No further sign of whatever it was. We stood there looking around when suddenly we heard little Debbie crying from the car. Mary had left the door open so Deb could get a little air and she decided to roll off the seat and into the sand. So, we rushed back down the hill to find Deb lying beside the car. Poor Babe, she had a mouth full of sand but was otherwise fine.

About a week later, we were watching a show on TV telling about snakes of the south west. We found out that those marks we had seen in the sand were actually a sidewinder rattlesnake and we had been standing right on top of it. Those snakes will back themselves down under the sand and wait for prey to come along, Yikes!

GETTING MY FIRST WORK

It was a bit of a rough position to be in. I knew it was showtime for me. Brother Ed's son, Dave Wallen had told me when I was in Tucson, that if I got any work, he would be happy to come over to Rio Rancho and go to work with me. At least I had that going for me.

I spent the next three weeks or so traveling all over Albuquerque looking for work. I had visited and revisited every builder I could find. I knew things were a little tight and I also knew that if I just kept looking, I would get a break and find work.

One day I decided to try something different. I drove up to Santa Fe. I found some building areas and checked in with the builders and their superintendents. I did not have any luck. I took a break and found the Sisters of Loretta Chapel. This was the place that had the miraculous staircase built into it. Those stairs were something that I had wanted to visit, ever since I was a kid in school. I think I had learned about it in history class.

There is a circular staircase built in the chapel that makes two and a half turns from floor to the choir loft, about 20 feet up. It was built in the late 1800's. The wood used in it is of an unknown species and there are no nails in it anywhere. The nuns had needed a new staircase to the choir loft. No one could figure out how to build it, until one day this guy shows up and convinces the nuns that he could do the job. The staircase was completed in a few months and upon finishing the job, the guy vanished, never asking for a dime for his pay. He had

Loretta Chapel Staircase

furnished the material, did the labor and left the city. In the eyes of the church, it was considered a miracle and after seeing it I thought it was as well. The credit was given to Saint Joseph. The stairs were magnificent. I sat there in the church for a while and then I prayed to Saint Joseph to help me find work. I was a good carpenter but could never have done a job like those stairs. I was overwhelmed by the work and beauty of it.

I returned home that afternoon in awe from what I had seen. When I got home, I started to tell Mary about the stairs and that I had prayed for work. God does answer prayer, because that afternoon, I received three phone calls, all within a few minutes of each other. I had three job offers, just that quick.

The next day, I met with a superintendent from Presley homes and was hired to install a fireplace in an already completed home. That job took a little over a day to complete and I had earned my first $200 in New Mexico. It felt really good to have finally made a little money. I had been living off my wife's money for long enough.

I did not have a builder's license to work in New Mexico and they told me I had to get set up so I could get paid. The next little job they gave me involved working on a model house. This was a stroke of good luck for me because that is where I met a wonderful little Mexican guy by the name of Gil Trujillo. We became best friends almost as soon as we met. I was working in the garage on that model house, and he was working on the house next door. I can still see him as he came walking up. The first thing he said to me was, "I love to bullshit, you got time?" Yes, I did, and after talking to him for a while, he offered for me to use his builder's license until I could get mine. He was a trim carpenter and did trim work for Presley Homes. Gil was a hoot. Just a really funny guy. My first close friend in my new homeland.

I now had a license to work under and a company that would hire me as a carpenter. I did a few other small jobs for Presley and then hit them up for a full framing job. I convinced them that I could get a crew together and I would do them an excellent job. They gave me a set of plans and a job address, and I was off and running. What a big break for me. It was now up to me to really prove myself and make a go of it.

Mary was really excited for me. We both knew that we were going to make it in our new home state. God was watching over us and helping to make things happen. I was becoming very optimistic and rearing to get going. The building business was still in a big slump in the nation, but New Mexico was doing okay. Michigan was still in the pit of depression. I was so happy for making a really hard decision to move here. Building was really the only thing that I knew how to do, and I could work really hard.

MY FIRST FRAMING JOB IN NM

I called David Wallen In Tucson and invited him to come over and help me frame. He was a carpenter and was needing work. He came over right away so we could get started on that frame. The two of us built the whole house in about 8 working days. It was about 1,500 square feet with a garage and was fairly easy to build. My years of framing back in Michigan were now really paying off for me.

Presley gave us more houses to frame. All I had to do was to get our overall time down a few days and they would be real happy with us. I started to look for guys to hire and that was a big problem. The work force in New Mexico was not up to the standards of us ol' Michigan boys. I had to get used to that, and I learned ways to get them to produce and give me the quality I would need to keep our builder happy.

Before long, we had Edward Wallen the 3rd working with us as well, and our crew swelled to about 6 people. I was starting to make some money, at last. Mary was happy and I was feeling secure in our life together. There were weeks, though, that all of our income had to go to just payroll and there would be very little left over. We tried to keep up with our payments to the kids.

It was hard to keep that money flowing, plus keep our payroll up, pay our workers comp insurance and still have money to live on. I just had to produce a little more. I started working the weekends, by myself, to cut down on payroll and still get the job done. That did help some. It was really hard on Mary when I did that. I came home dead tired and just wanted to crash almost every night.

I was working on the east side of Albuquerque and we lived in Rio Rancho, so I had a long commute every day. I started thinking about moving to the east side so I would not have such a drive. It would save on gas and give me an extra hour and a half with my wife and little miss Debbie. We only had a six-month lease in Rio Rancho, so when that was up, we could move. We really liked that little house though.

Dave and Eddy worked really well for me, and they soon got their own place on the east side of Albuquerque. Soon, my brother Edward Jr. would be joining us as well. The work was coming in very fast for a rather crashed building industry. Albuquerque was doing nicely, and I sure was thankful for that. I knew that God must be watching over Mary and me.

The months started to roll along, and we were keeping our work up, making our builder happy. I had not seen Julie and Jeff since I left Michigan in May, so we planned a trip back to Michigan around that Christmas time of 1982.

VISIT TO MICHIGAN

We flew back to a cold place that December and stayed with my sister Mary and Ed Dick. It was a joyous reunion to see my kids and also to be with Ed and Mary. I had really missed all these people right from the time we left to start our new life together.

We did not know it then, but we had another baby on the way. Mary was sick and grumpy that whole trip and we soon found out why. It was not long after our return to New Mexico that we found out. We had a one-year-old and another one on the way. I felt good about it. I was already 40 years old, and it was good for me to have our kids while I was still fairly young. We were due in September, it was 1983. Debbie, by this time, was doing very well. She was gaining weight and had no problems from her two-and-a-half-month early birth.

It was really great to be with Jeff and Julie again and we spent as much time as we could with them. It seems like we had gone to the mall and got a Atari set for them for Christmas. I remember thinking how good it would have been if they could have came back with me to New Mexico, but that, of course, was just not possible. We did make plans for them to come out that next summer. We would have some really good quality time then. Julie was getting right into the teenage scene. She was having a good time with it.

BUILDING THE COMPANY

So, after a cold vacation back in Michigan, we made our way back to New Mexico. The really hard part was leaving the kids again. I had six months or so to continue working the framing company into a success and save enough money so we could have Jeff and Julie out for three or four weeks in the summer.

It went really well that spring and we were soon doing over a house a week. I loved working with my little crew. My only problem, as I recall, was I just wasn't making enough money to keep my workers comp and taxes paid and send money for the kids. I was paying my guys cash at that time. They loved that.

With traffic and all, it was taking me 45 minutes or so to get across the Rio Grande River and make it to work, so we decided to make a move to the east side of Albuquerque from Rio Rancho. We made that move in February of 1983. We moved into a nice little three bedroom house in Cherry Hills in north east Albuquerque, just off of Wyoming Blvd. That was great, as I could make it to work in just a few minutes.

Presley did move us around a lot, but I was keeping my guys busy and keeping food on the table. The bad part was that I had to work six or seven days a week to keep my builder happy, and to make decent money for myself.

So it continued and by summer I had enough money saved so I could bring Jeff and Julie out to be with us for a three or four week visit. They came right after school was out. The time went so quickly during those four weeks. Soon the kids were off again heading back to Michigan. We had so much fun on their visits. We traveled the state a lot, visiting different places. Lots of pretty sights and a few ghost towns along the way. We got to see some really neat New Mexico ghost towns and did some good ol' mountain camping. I think we all had a great time. It was so good to have them with me. I just missed them so much when they were in Michigan.

Mary was very pregnant that first summer and suffering a lot, but we still got out and had a good time. Little miss Debbie had her fun with the rest of us. I think she really enjoyed their visits. Mary has to have her mountain fix every so often, even to this very day.

JESSIE HAD TO GO

Our black Lab dog, Jessie, was such a friendly dog and she wanted to be with anybody that walked by. We had gotten rid of all the puppies in '82 and she became a problem for us. We had to go get her from the dog pound three or four times. She was always jumping the wall and wanting to go walking with whoever walked by. We decided that she was too much for Mary being home with the baby, and we felt we needed to find her a new home. Then, to make matters worse, she turned up pregnant and Mary and I both were too busy to handle that one. There was a young feller working for us at that time that lived east of the mountains and on a ranch, so he offered to take Jessie to his place and keep her with them. This all happened while we lived in Rio Rancho before the move to Albuquerque.

SAMMY DOG

One day, the next year, when I was going to the grocery store for Mary, there was this guy parked in front of the store and in his car was a beautiful little pure white Samoyed puppy. She was for sale for just $50. I got the guy's number and went on home. Mary got as excited as I was. So, we wound up with a pretty puppy of which Debbie was very happy. She made us a wonderful dog for the next ten years. Mom and Dad had two Samoyeds and when we visited them, those dogs had a great time. We named her Sammy.

ANNA'S ARRIVAL

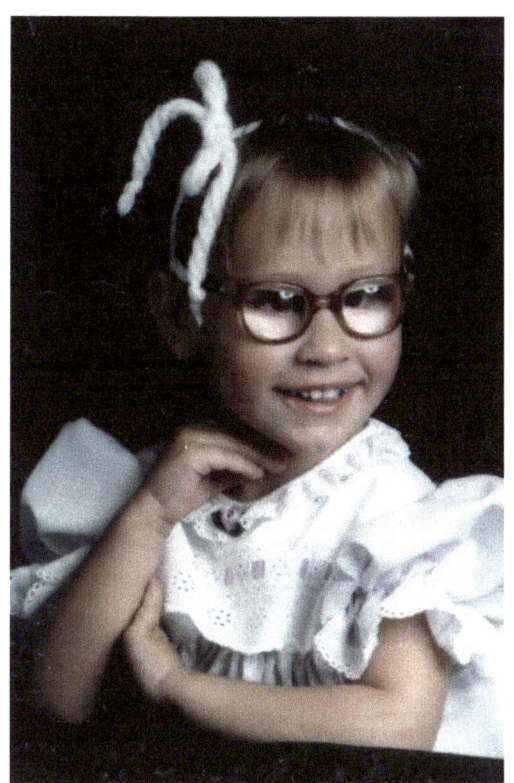

Totally sweet Anna.

Looking back at 1983, Mary and I were excited to have our next little one born. She was due in mid-September. We knew we were going to have a little girl and selected Anna Marie for her name. That name was chosen in respect to my grandmother, Anna Marie Wallen, my Dad's mom. Things were readied and Mary was suffering from the heat, but she was excited. It was so hot that summer. As with Debbie, Anna was born early, a little over a month.

Our excitement was dimmed a little as we soon found out that Anna had cataracts on both of her eyes and her eyes were small. Basically, she was blind. We knew that this would be a lifelong problem for her. They soon performed and eye operation on her and removed her lenses. She was blind at birth but soon could see with the aid of glasses. They gave us a lot of bad predictions for Anna, as to what to expect, like never being able to get a driver's license. Our little lady has far out preformed what they told us. She also had some hip problems but with the help of some braces, she came out of that part really well.

At that time, Dad and Mom Wallen belonged to the Catholic Charismatic Group over in Tucson. It was a great group of people and we decided to look up a like group in Albuquerque. We found them at the Risen Savior Catholic Church just a few blocks from where we lived. After meeting with that group there were lots of prayers and hope for Anna. We got really involved with them and it sure was a blessing for us. Anna was improving very well, and we thanked God for that. She was prayed over, often. We became really good friends with those folks. Mary and I felt really blessed to have found them and we were thankful to Mom and Dad.

We had other exciting things happening in our lives that were related to our faith in God. Mary was brought up Christian and I was raised Catholic so we both knew God. This group helped us to bring those beliefs and feelings right to the top. Wonderful things were happening in our life together.

My rough and tumble kiddo.

GETTING A TRUCK

My 1977 El Camino truck turned over a hundred thousand miles on our trip moving to New Mexico and it was fairly well over the hill. We were way too broke to buy anything else, so I just kept praying that it would keep going. I really needed something better to drive. So, with that in mind, during the summer of 1984, I took some of my crew on a camping trip up into the Jemez Mountains. It was a three-day outing and on that Saturday we went exploring, looking for this old ghost town called Albermaid. I knew about where it was, according to this old map. So off we went in Tommy Thompson's Jeep. Everybody had to really hang on as the trails back to the old town were extreme. Some very steep areas and lots of huge boulders and large rocks. We had barely made it back to this one really steep drop in the road, several hundred yards long, so we decided to walk the rest of the way to where the old town should be.

When we got to the bottom of that long and steep hill, we found a three year old Chevy ½ ton pickup truck. It was only a two-wheel drive and there could be no way to get it out of there. It looked very suspicious to me, so after we found the little old town, we walked back to the truck and I dug out the registration and took it with me. The next week I checked it out and found out it had been stolen.

Someone had managed to get it way back in there and couldn't get it back out. I bought the salvage rights to it for about $2,500 and then I had to get it out of there.

One Saturday, shortly after that, we took Tommy's Jeep and a few tools and went back in there. This time we drove the Jeep down that steep hill with concern of getting back out. I guess I had the faith. We got the ignition switch and lock out. The battery was still up. The tank was almost full of gas and we started er up. It showed about 28,000 miles on it. We got both vehicles pointed up the hill with a tow rope hooked up between them. The jeep started spinning even before the rope got tight. That's when I started really praising God. All of a sudden, both vehicles were going up that hill, almost too steep to walk up. Sure made a believer out of me. I finally had a good truck for my work. I Thanked God.

NO MORE SMOKING

Another wonderful thing that happened to me with that prayer group had to do with my smoking. I smoked for 26 years and had tried to quit for 25 of those years. One night, after a prayer meeting, some of the folks came up to me and said they were supposed to pray over me to heal my smoking habit. So they did and that was cool.

I went on home and the first thing I did, as usual, was to light up a cigarette. I always smoked by the fireplace so the smoke would go up the chimney and not into the house. So, I lit up and I would like to have thrown up. I can still taste that awful taste in my mouth from the cigarette smoke. After studying it a bit, I threw it and my pack in the fireplace, remembering how I had been prayed over. I have never smoked again from that day forward. The desire, the dependency, the habit, it was all gone. Two packs a day for a lot of years was wiped clean from my life. I thanked God over and over. Nobody quits 2 packs a day cold turkey like that.

GROWING

Riener Wedel, who worked for me in Michigan, came out to

New Mexico and wanted to get his own framing crew going. He worked for me for a while and then in '83 went out on his own. He loved framing large houses and was soon doing it all on his own. He didn't have a builder's license either so that was a problem for him. Riener was one of the best in framing and I had wished he would have stayed with me. He first went to work for me back in Michigan when he was fresh out of high school and 17 years old. I have never seen a guy that could learn as good and as quick as he could.

By this time, we had been in New Mexico over a year. With my work being outside, I quickly learned to read the weather. Our first summer was really hot but very dry until the monsoons moved in. Then it turned slightly cooler, but we had rain almost every afternoon. The rain would hit and soon be gone, so we learned to pick up all the tools and wait a short time in the trucks 'till it stopped and then it was back to work. The Fall season was wonderful up until about December. Working outside in the winter months was mostly great as well, as the temperature usually stayed moderate and we had very little rain or snow. Springtime turned out to be our worst season. The temperature was usually nice but oh the wind. Sometimes you couldn't even see for 20 feet. The blowing sand was awful.

Our framing crew was doing very well and from our first work in July of 1982, with just Dave Wallen and I, we never went without work. I felt really blessed and we kept our quality top notch as our reputation for being excellent grew. Dave and Ed, as well as Brother Ed, went back to Tucson as work there began to pick up.

1983-84 was a good learning time for me as the framing crew grew to about 8 guys. We had plenty of work to keep us all busy. I was even getting calls from other builders wanting us to go to work for them. By this time Presley homes seemed to be running out of building lots.

AMREP FRAMING

The AMREP Corp. in Rio Rancho seemed to have a lot going on as they were building almost a thousand homes a year. Their houses were smaller and looked really easy to frame. I met with them and soon had a contract for their framing. The sky seemed to be the limit as to how much work we could do for them.

The guys on the crew kept coming and going though, a lot of turn over, even with all the work we had. Shortly after I started work for AMREP, over the course of the next month or so, I hired four guys that really made a big difference for me. Clifton Thompson "Tommy" was the first and stayed with me until I sold the company in 2007. Tommy was very quick to learn, and he was one of the best. Then came Joe Lucero and he was really a good learner. Manuel Jojola was the third and was just a ball of fire. Very hard-working kid. We then brought on Rick Vigil. Rick had some problems but turned out to be a good employee. So, with these 4 guys and a few others, we were really good and really fast. AMREP had one house with about 1500 square feet plus garage that we could frame complete in less than 8 hours and it would be a good frame. I was really happy with my guys by then and AMREP was really happy with me. They were giving us whole streets of houses to frame, and I had to start thinking about expanding.

Pricing competition was really tight with AMREP, at this point, and I had to keep my pricing low. We were a little behind on taxes and insurance payments but keeping everyone on the crew well paid. AMREP had three framing companies working for them at that time and I needed to keep a sharp eye on the competition. AMREP seemed to play one against the other. Both of those other framing companies had a large group of [Native American] Indian folks working for them. I paid my guys a little more and we could out produce them. We just had to work a little harder and we did it.

I hired on more guys. Lots of work and lots of fun. By this time in '84 and '85 we were only working five or six days a week with Sundays off. My company was moving along nicely and I was home a little more.

In 1984 a few of the companies, back in Michigan, that I still owed money to came after me in New Mexico and this was a real low point for me. I had hoped, by this time, I would have been able to start paying off bills that I had to leave behind. The housing crash in 1980-81 was so bad for everyone and I didn't do well at all with it. I had no choice but to file for bankruptcy. I knew that would ruin my credit, but I had no other way out. At this point in our lives together, Mary and I had no assets, only a car and a truck with tools. So we had nothing anyone could take. It was a really sad situation for me. I had never wanted to mess over anyone. So that move cleared up my past and ruined my credit. I now could only look forward to growing a prosperous framing company and it was working.

By the beginning of 1985 our lease was up on our little house in Albuquerque, and I was driving all the way across town to Rio Rancho for our work with AMREP. So once again Mary and I decided to move back to Rio Rancho.

SPOOKS AT HOME

I think I should mention a happening in that house in Albuquerque that we were renting. I don't have a lot of belief in spooks and such but there were times in that house on Yeager Drive in Albuquerque that either Mary or I would wake up in the middle of the night and see and feel a dark presence at the side of the bed. That was an awful feeling. And Debbie would also wake up a lot of nights, screaming, even more reason to move.

MOVING BACK TO RIO RANCHO

We moved out in February of '85 and moved into a nice rental house in Rio Rancho, on Sienna Ct. A little over a year later there was a nice young couple that moved into the house right next door to us, and we got to know them. It shook Mary and I both up a little when we found out that they had moved next to us from the same exact house that we had rented in Albuquerque. Amazing. They also had the same experience we did in that bedroom and their daughter also woke up screaming at night. Yeah, I know it sounds a little farfetched but it's a true story. Another YIKES!

We had fun in that house on Sienna Ct. Julie and Jeff were with us for several summers while we lived there, and we had fun times. We got into the mountains a lot, camping and doing old ghost towns.

Debbie and Anna were both doing fine and loved camping. We also had several really great Christmases while living there. We went into the mountains to get our Tree and the girls always remember Mom's great chili that we would enjoy after the tree was cut and loaded. Those were fun times with our little ones. We always had snow in the mountains on those outings. Deb and Anna had great times in the snow.

There are lots of cool memories of family time and of work time as well. We were there for 2 years and Jeff and Julie came out both summers while we were there. I believe Julie's friend Jenny came out to visit one year while we were there. I think Jenny went camping with us at some point.

Jeff and Julie were into their teen years and the girls were growing so fast. It was just such a joyful time in our lives with all that was happening. Having two teens and two young ladies to keep us entertained, life was good.

JULIE'S FIRST CAR

Julie was visiting during the summer of 1985 when we lived on Sienna and she was needing a car. She had just turned 16. Wow! So Mary took her shopping and they found this pretty little red car. Julie fell in love with it and so we got it for her. The problem was, the front-end suspension was shot. So, Julie went back to Michigan and I had the job of putting new struts and linkage on the car. What an awful job that was. So the little jewel was made ready for a trip to Michigan. Mary and one of her friends and our two girls made the trip. The car ran great, and they made a stop at Mary's folks on the way up. Mary finally made a rendezvous with Julie in Flushing and Julie was excited to have her first car.

Something went really wrong from that point on, and I felt so bad. The car ran very well for Mary on that whole trip to Michigan but when Julie started for home that day, it quit on her and she couldn't get it running. Sorry Julie! I believe she sold it about six months after she got it and she had to replace the alternator three times. I didn't blame her for selling it.

THE TUCSON EXPRESS

I had my truck and Mary had a little VW Rabbit to drive. It made it really hard to go anywhere with the kids, especially if we were going camping. When Jeff and Julie came out, it just didn't work out. I had gone bankrupt and had no credit to buy a bigger auto. We visited the banks and were turned down everywhere we went. It just so happened that one of the leaders of our prayer group was a vice president of one of our local banks and we knew him well. So, one night after a prayer meeting, I asked him for some advice. Maybe he could tell us what we needed to do to get a loan. We were so surprised when Dave Wintermute said, "Well just come on down to the bank on Monday and ask for me". Wow! He got us a loan for a big ole Chevy Van. Mary found it in the papers and we got it. It was five years old and ran great. The interior had been converted with a bed in back and four really cool seats. We loved it and it was really good for us, room-wise. It was great for going to the mountains and our drive to Tucson to visit my Mom and Dad.

We loved traveling the state with that thing. It was roomy and fun. It was soon called the Tucson Express. We even made three or four trips back to Michigan and Ohio in it. Trips out camping and into the mountains for the Christmas tree each year were awesome. We all loved the ole black van. Well, that is until it needed an overhaul and some body work done to it. We were going to drive it up to Michigan and help Julie move out to attend Arizona State University after her graduation from High School. So, I redid the engine, put new shocks on it and other little repairs.

The problem came when Mary and I took it to a paint shop to get a repaint on it. It was black and we selected a blue trimmed in silver. Lovely colors until we went to pick it up. It was a bright blue color and not what Mary expected. She cried and wanted it repainted. I thought it was okay, just a little loud. Mary got to drive it that way for a number of years. I think we sold it in about 1993.

We all really did love that ole Van. She did a lot of miles for us. The kids still talk about that ole van. Mary took it for a run to Ohio one year to visit her family and to help Marcella move to New Mexico. She came back pulling this great big trailer behind the ole Van. I believe the girls got to experience the farm life on that trip. I know grandpa took them for tractor rides and they got to try playing with barn cats.

EXPANDING THE COMPANY

Work was strong during this time, and we were finally making good money. We branched out to several other builders and kept AMREP happy. It was at this time, in 1986, that I had finally gotten my Builder's License. There were a couple of guys that came to me and were needing to do work under someone's license. I let them use mine and made a couple hundred bucks each week with their work. They were good and I got to know their builder. That's when I met Jim Brown from Preferred Building Systems, Inc. Jim was a great guy and we became good friends. They were doing trim work for him. Within a year or so we would be doing all of his framing.

By this time in 1986 I put Tommy out there with a crew of his own and wow, he was doing great. Then I got Manny out there with his own crew. We were rollin' along great. Joe Lucero was next out the door with his own crew, and we were getting lots of houses framed every week. I still had my own framing crew, that I led, going. Keeping up with all of this turned out to be overwhelming after a while. Things seemed to be a bit out of control with all this happening. Every job had to have lumber, windows, siding, etc. ordered every day, plus running a crew. I was getting tired. I then hired a fellow by the name of Bob Hopper to handle running the crews. He was good at inspecting completed frames and keeping up with all the ordering of the materials. It was working great.

The time was passing quickly and work continued steady for us. I was feeling wonderful. We were still paying the guys cash and it was time to think about getting everything completely legal. That was a rough thing to consider as most of our competition was doing the same thing as we were, paying everybody in cash. It would take a lot of doing when we decided to make the switch to a regular paycheck for the guys.

We had caught up with our workers comp payments for our

company, but we were still far behind in keeping our taxes paid. Keeping everything else paid but the taxes was a real no-no as we were starting to get those IRS notices and some were threatening letters. We knew we were going to have to do something fairly soon. Penalties plus interest, it was looking nasty. Mary and I had been talking about maybe getting our own house. I knew that with the IRS looking at us, and the bankruptcy just a few years ago, it would not work getting a mortgage. So we sorta just kept it on the back burner for the time being.

We continued to expand the company. There was no end in sight for work being available and I took advantage of it. I think by '87, I had six crews going and I needed another man in the field to help out. My thoughts turned to my ole Air Force buddy Gary McEldowney. I spent some time trying to locate him. I was really surprised to find him living in an apartment in Cleveland, Ohio and absolutely hating it there. His wife Jeanie had gotten a real good job offer there, with her nursing. Mac was a West Virginia country boy and loved the outdoors. He caught the first flight he could get and flew out here. He spent a few days and decided this would be great for him. A year or so later, Jeanie would be moving out here as well. With her background she could get a job anywhere. Mac jumped right in helping me keep things running smooth. It was so great for him and me to be working together again. He had a pretty good understanding of building and framing, so that was great. He had built a few houses in West Virginia. Just what I needed. Mac stayed with me until I sold the company in 2007. I guess we sort of got old together.

We were really enjoying our home on Sienna Court but in '86 we were notified that the owner was going to sell the house and we had to move. Mary got busy and found us another house in the same neighborhood, just a block away. It was on Black Hills Road and also was a nice house. It would be our sixth move since we were married. We settled in and the girls soon found new friends, it was great. They got to play with the kids of a young black couple who were our neighbors. Our little guys sure gave us a lot of joy, watching them get their start in life. We lived there for the next two years.

I think it was in '86 that Julie's boyfriend Jamie came out and went camping with us. I can still remember all the excitement those two had running all over the hills and the red rocks in the Jemez mountains. I was excited for them but also a little scared especially on those red rocks, 60 feet in the air.

Jeff always enjoyed just sitting around a nice glowing campfire. Jeff even enjoyed getting up the firewood. I think he just liked to chop wood. He did love camping.

Our favorite camp site was at a place in the Jemez Mountains where a turn of the 19th century sawmill was run. And just down from it was a generating plant for electricity. There was a nice flat spot there for the tents and a stream ran through it. Everything was gone from the mill except for some old foundations and there was an ever flowing well with a pipe running from it that provided good drinking water. We loved the site and Debbie couldn't get enough of that fresh drinking water. She was funny. That also was the camp site where Anna attempted to swim in that creek. She actually fell in headfirst and it scared the beegeebees out of Mary. Poor Anna, she was still in diapers at that time and wound up with a big goose egg on her head.

LOSING MARY'S DAD

The two years that we lived on Black Hills Rd. were fairly uneventful for us except for loosing Mary's Dad. It was in 1987. He was 78 years old. He had angina with blood clots to his lungs and we lost him. Harold Grater was a wonderful man and we all loved him very much. He worked hard all his life, farming. When I first met him, he had about 30 cows and worked a hundred acre farm. It had all the outbuildings and about a 10-acre woods on it. He was really proud of his farm. He was a good Christian man with high moral standards. Mary had a really rough time with his passing.

Mary lost her birth mother, Francis, when she was only 8 years old. Losing her Mom at that young age had to be really rough for her. About four years after Francis passed, Harold married a wonderful lady by the name of Virginia. She took over as best she could with Harold's five kids. I thought she was a great lady from the time I first met her until her passing in 2005. Mary was lucky to have her for her stepmom.

I should mention here that Mary was fourth in a family of five children. Marcella was the first born. Then her oldest brother was Donald, we lost him in 2003 from the Vietnam war agent orange mess. Next in the lineup was Norma, followed by Mary, and last is younger brother Chuck. Chuck has run the farm since Harold passed away. Chuck also has leased other farmland in the area to raise corn and beans. He has done well most years but has had a few bad years as well. Farming can be a gamble at times depending on pricing and of course the weather.

CAMPING

Mary and I and the kids spent a lot of weekends camping during the years we were renting. We had favorite camp sites in the Jemez mountains, in several locations, as well as up on the San Mateo Flats of Mount Taylor. Another place we loved to camp out was down in the Gila Wilderness area. We even took large church groups to several favorite camp sites for weekend camp outs. Those were really fun times. I think the largest camp out we had was with about 60 or so church members. Great times in those days. I even built plywood outhouses for those gangs. The mountains are so awesome for camping. We sure did make a lot of memories there.

THE BIRDS

One time that I have to mention was a trip we were on, down in the Gila area, where we were camped along a stream. Anna and Debbie both had a ball building a damn in the stream. It was on a beautiful evening with a wonderful campfire and there was a bird, of unknown origin, that had started to sing to us. It was a rather strange sound though. So as evening came on, the bird picked up its singing and we thought it was so cool. Soon there were several birds making that same sort of annoying sound. It kept up over the next several hours and became really annoying to all of us.

Bedtime came and the birds were still at it. I think that there may have been several more birds to chime in. Berrip bruu, berrip bruu. It was driving us nuts and we couldn't sleep. I got My 44 mag pistol out and fired all six rounds into the tree from which the noise was coming from. Wow! Quiet, for about two minutes and they started right back up again! We finally gave up in the tent and all four of us climbed into the van to sleep. We could still hear the darn things but finally made it to sleep. We never did find out what kind of "songbirds" those things were. This was late May and Memorial Day weekend. We woke up that next morning with snow on the ground. We were at about 8,000 feet in elevation. It was cold out and we packed up and went on home.

We can laugh at that trip now, but it was no fun at the time. I remember one other funny time when we had Jeff and Julie with us, and we were way back in the Jemez Mountains. We woke up with a whole herd of cows surrounding the tents. They were all over our campsite and did not want to move. I believe breakfast was stalled for a while that day until we finally got the cows to move on. They left us plenty of cow poo, but they did finally leave.

One other time when Deb was just a baby, we were way down in the Mogollon Mountains, about 2 miles off a main dirt road and down this big hill. When I pulled off the little trail, driving that El Camino, I ran over a good size rock. It hit the transmission and pushed the pan up against the shift linkage. We were stuck in high gear. That left us with very little power to climb back up that big hill. After a nice weekend at that site, we got all loaded up and Mary and I pushed the truck back onto the trail and after several attempts to get up the hill, I got turned around and drove back aways and give er all she had. We finally just barely made it to the top and back to the main road. With a little relief, we made it out of there and drove home all the way with just high gear. That was a task just in itself.

Camping will always hold a lot of good and fun memories for all of us. Some of the old campsites, that we loved so much, are no longer accessible to the public. It sure would be nice to go back and visit them again. With all the worries of forest fires these days, many areas of our mountains are closed off.

FINALLY OUR OWN HOUSE

Our House-Before the Remodel

In the latter part of 1987, Mary came across an ad in the paper for a house for sale just a few blocks from where we were living on Black hills. It was on Twisted Juniper St., three blocks over. It was advertised by owner with an assumable mortgage. She got excited but I had to tell her that there was no way we could come up with the down payment. She wanted to go see it anyway, so off we went. It turned out good for us as the owner was a builder himself. His name was Emil Hargette. He had a small company. Emil had his plans drawn up for a new house he was going to build for himself. He just had to sell his house on Twisted Juniper, and he would be ready to build. It turned out great because I could give him a price for framing and roofing and trim for his new house as the down payment on his old place. We then could take over his mortgage and we would both be happy. It turned into a done deal. We were allowed to assume Emil's mortgage and I had lots to do to satisfy the down payment. Emil was really happy and it gave me a wonderful opportunity to get a permanent place for us.

That house was in decent shape, but it was only about 1,000 square feet in size with a two car garage but it had a large half acre lot. I knew when we made this deal that a lot of our exploring and camping would be coming to an end. I had tons of personal work to do, as well as keep the company going and all that work on Emil's house.

Emil and I became good friends over the next 6 months or so. Emil and his family moved out in early December and that gave me plenty of time to get that house painted and we got new carpet installed before we moved in. It was January of 1988. It was Mary's and my first house that we actually owned. Yippie! But now I had to earn the down payment. It was called sweat equity. We were happy.

THE ANEILLOS

The house just to the west of our new place was empty when we moved in. About a month later some folks moved in. Gary and Janet Aneillo were our new neighbors, and it turned out that they would be our lifelong friends from that point forward. They had bought their house years earlier and were New Yorkers. They talked funny. They drank "wooder" instead of water!

I made lots of plans for additions and remodeling on our new home. The kitchen was real small and I planned a bigger new one at the other end of the kitchen dining room. I cut a deal with a guy that had a big stack of red oak and he wanted to get rid of half of it. It was all rough cut but would be great for the new Kitchen cabinets. I came home one day with a trailer loaded with red oak. I had backed the trailer in beside the house to unload all that wood and my new neighbor came over to offer a helping hand. We introduced ourselves to each other and unloaded the trailer. That was my first encounter with Gary Aniello.

We sat down and talked about ourselves to get to know each other. It turned out he was a CPA and did taxes. He knew a lot of the ins and outs of the IRS. How lucky could that be for me. I explained my situation with the taxes I owed and he said, "Hey, no problem! I can help you out of that mess." There was a thing called, "offer in compromise" with the IRS that could possibly help us out of our debt. Gary offered to help us get it through. By that time, we were up over $120,000 due to the IRS. Wow. It looked like we may have a way out at that point. Getting my little company up and running with the builders, all the new employees, office work with Mary, material orders, punch lists on completed work, and on and on was a lot. The IRS worries just seemed to always slip by the wayside but now it was getting serious and they were looking really hard at us. Gary came into our lives just at the right time. We had lots of paperwork to get together. Those interest and penalty charges were huge. Mary and I finally felt that we may get past this really big problem.

Over the next few months, we got to know Gary and Janet really well and spent a good bit of time with them. They both liked tequila and so did I, so we kept a supply on hand along with my crown royal whiskey. They had two boys that were close to Debbie and Anna's age and those guys got along really well and had much fun together.

After Gary Aniello got settled in with his move from New York, he went to work on my tax problem. Naturally I was quite uneasy for a while. It was all going to come to a head soon. I knew though that I might even get my life back from the IRS. Those three letters, IRS, gave me the shivers. Gary got it all together for us and then he went in and presented it to the government folks. They accepted it and then we just had to wait for their determination. I think I may have drank a good bit of whiskey during those days of waiting for the reply.

The day finally came and Mary and I had to go in and meet with them. I think Gary A. was with us during that meeting. With penalties and interest, we owed over $120,000 and they made us a settlement offer of just $20,000. They gave us 30 days to accept the offer and come up with the money. Naturally we wanted to settle with them and we had to get the money up. We managed to get it all put together including the money and came out of the IRS Building all smiles. We had gotten our lives back and a future for Wallen Builders. I was ready to push on to bigger things.

We stayed squeaky clean from that day forward and it sure felt good. The IRS came in and audited us for 3 consecutive years shortly after we got everything completely legal. They found nothing wrong every time and we haven't been bothered by them ever since and that was in the early 90s.

A NEW PLAN FOR WALLEN BUILDERS

During the late '80s and early '90s we were doing our payroll by hand. For each guy we had working for us we had to collect hours from each crew chief for the guys on his crew and do all the tax with holdings by hand. That was a big job for Mary and me but we stayed on top of it. We had over 50 guys working for us by then.

It was very hard managing that many guys and getting their

pay right every week. We had to check every job under each crew leader and make sure we were making money. I finally came up with a plan that really worked good for Wallen Builders and also the crew leaders. I had a good meeting with the crew leaders to explain it and they were all on board with me. All of the guys on each crew would stay as Wallen employees and the crew leaders would become self-employed. They would be responsible for getting the house complete, including the punch list. They then would be paid the full contract amount for their completed house after all the deductions. This included $200.00 taken out for Wallen Builders, all labor costs for the men under them on that job, and all taxes and workman's comp cost. They would have to furnish all their own nails and furnish all their own tools. Whatever amount that was left on that particular job would be the crew leaders pay. It worked so well that some of the crew leaders were now making over $100,000.00 a year. They all loved it. Houses got done quicker and cleaner. My builder, AMREP loved us. We were doing 12 or 13 houses a week and I was bringing in about $2,500.00 a week. It was making Mary and I really happy.

REMODELING AND BEING HAPPY

Going into 1989 and '90, I took enough time to build a nice laundry room onto our little house so Mary would have a nice indoor room. The kitchen dining area in that house was strange. The room was really long. So, I built a new set of cabinets out of that oak that I had brought home, where the long dining area was. It worked out great and I built a nice little fireplace and installed patio doors off the area that was now our new dining room. This made a good addition to our little house, and we were enjoying it.

Looking back over the '80s, I feel that I was really blessed. It was rough getting started in a new life from Michigan. Tons of good ole hard work. A new business to start. A bankruptcy. Being blessed with two beautiful little girls. Having some really good quality time with Jeff and Julie and watching them grow into young adults. It felt so good watching my little business expand. Mary was just wonderful for me. We shared such a strong love for each other and worked so well together. She made me so happy. I really felt a good, renewed love for God during this time and felt his hand in much of what I did. It was great exploring our new State. So many new things to find. All the camping we did. Watching Deb and Ann as they grew. And winding up with our own house after so many moves. It was quite a decade. Mary and I worked very well together.

AMREP AND BIG CHANGES

It was in about 1992 that AMREP called me into the office to notify me of a new change they were making to our framing. Oh great, not what I really wanted to hear. They had done material take-offs on all of the houses and with those lists, they wanted us to be responsible for all framing materials. They would cut us a check for the amount they thought it should take on each job. Done deal, take it or leave it. So, at this point I did my own take-offs for what I knew it would take on each job. I was very surprised when I got done. I found that AMREP was willing to pay us anywhere from $300.00 to $800.00 dollars more on various different models than what those houses would take. I think they goofed up on their take-offs. The contracts were written and away we went. At this point I was making $2,500.00 a week from the crews and adding sometimes another $3,000.00 or so on lumber. This of course had overhead deductions. Wallen Builders was turning into a great success.

EXPANDING THE COMPANY

We had other builders calling and wanting us to do their framing for them and I also had other framing companies wanting to go to work for us. Everybody liked my system, and we were good folks to work for. So, if you came to work for Wallen Builders and had your own crew, I would hire the crew and you would be self-employed running your crew. You would have no worries about paying your comp or withholding taxes. That included Federal, State, Social Security, Fed and State unemployment Tax. We took it all out of the frame amount and the crew leader got what was left over. Good incentive to really work those crews efficiently. It took a lot of worries off the crew leaders. They all loved it, and I did too.

By 1995, we were working 20 or so crews and working for four builders. Our framing company, starting out with just me and David Wallen, would at some point reach over two hundred guys on our payroll. Gary McEldowney and Bob Hopper played a big part helping me keep it all rolling along and running smooth.

I put Joe Lucero working for Jim Brown at Preferred Building Systems LLC and he handled the whole account for me. Jim was a great guy to work for. One or two houses a week. Jim had a great system of building his houses on his big lot, on blocks with a wood floor system. Then when the house was complete, he would have a house moving company move the house out to a remote lot in the boonies, where stick building would not be possible. He had a great market for his product and done very well.

Wallen Builders was the largest lumber consumer in this area for a number of years. We used a company called Lumber Inc. Really great people to work with.

MORE HOUSE ADDITIONS

After the Remodel

We were using one of the three bedrooms in our little house for our office and it was really tight working that way. Poor Mary. With all the company expansion during those years, we had to add on an office room to the house. I decided to make the master bedroom larger and have a door going from our room into the new office room. We added four feet to the bed room in front, plus the office space of 12 by 20 foot. It came out great. I had a door in front to access that room from the driveway. We then started looking for a full-time office girl and lucked out with a new neighbor that had just moved in. We became good friends with Kathy and Bob Lindig. Kathy would be with us for a number of years and did a really good job for us.

While we were at it, the next year I actually cut the house in two at the living room and added four feet to the front and put a cathedral ceiling in there. The house was way different now than when we bought it.

It was around this time in the early '90s that I stumbled across a 1957 Chevy 2 door hard top. Just like the one I had as a kid. Mary gave me the thumbs up to buy it. Yippy, I loved that car. So, once again I needed to add on to the house with a third car garage. That house really grew from the 1,000 Sq. footer it was. It actually looked quite nice from the front. I had completely redone the yard as well.

YARD WORK AND HORSESHOES

The back yard on that house was mostly dirt and goat heads. You sure couldn't walk out there bare footed. I first added on a nice patio of a good size and then went to work on the yard. It took a lot of weekends but after a lot of good ol' toil with the soil work, I had it really nice. I built a retainer wall between the Aniello's lot and ours and put up a new wood fence with a gate to his back yard. This allowed for a nice big flower garden along the west side. The back of the yard had two really nice sized peach trees and most of the yard was grass. On the east side I built a nice garden. It took a few years to prep the soil just right, but after a time, I got it right and we sure had nice gardens for a lot of years. The kids just loved the yard. I also installed a set of horseshoe pits, of which we had tons of fun with. I even put lights out there so we could play at night. Right in the middle I planted a globe willow. It was just a twig when I planted it but by the time we sold that place, that tree was huge.

Those two peach trees required a lot of babying, but wow. We had the best and largest peaches I have ever seen. Deb and Ann still talk about them. In about 1998, those trees set fruit in the spring but then they both started looking sick. So, I talked to the folks at the nursery and they told me to check for trunk borers and if they had them, then look for a ring of sappy stuff at the base of the tree. If that was the case, there would be no hope for the tree. So, I checked and sure enough, the trees were full of borers. We were all sick because we loved those trees so much. Then I got an idea. I drove 16 penny nails into the trunk where the borers were, from top to bottom. I then wired and hooked 120 volts of electric power to the nails. I left the trees like that for a full day and then unplugged the cords. Wow, it worked, crazy as it was, the trees perked up and once again we had great peaches. Even the neighbors were happy. The trees lasted another 3 years before they gave up on me. Sigh.

That yard was a great joy for all of us. The kids had lots of fun out there. I had built them a swing set and Anna had her rabbits there. Old Sammy dog enjoyed that yard and stayed outside most nights except in the cold. The kids would have sleepovers and set up tents and we had campfires there.

Just too much to mention, except for the horseshoe pits. We had lots of nights out in the back yard with the pits. Gary Aniello and I would invite friends over and sometimes play until mid-night. One night when I came home around 9 pm, there was a lot of noise coming from the back. When I went back there, I found Aniello there with a bunch of friends that we knew from our local pub, The Anchor Inn. They were all drunk and playing horseshoes. The Aniello's and us had a really great relationship going and he knew I wouldn't mind. Great neighborhood, great friends and lots of fun. The kids as well as us enjoyed it.

One year, Mom and Dad came over for a few days at Easter time, and I had gotten the garden all ready to plant. Mom and Dad helped in the planting. They would have been well into their 80s by then. It sure took me back to the days as a teen, helping Mom plant that huge garden that we had every year. I can still remember Mom and Dad trying to decide how far apart we used to plant the potatoes. What great memories.

That back yard was awesome with the grass, the horseshoe pits, a little shed, the swing set, the patio, that nice garden, all the flowers (I planted lots of morning glories), Anna's rabbits, that Globe Willow, the apple tree I planted, the sprinkler system, the fire pit, and on and on. Well, it turned out to be a wonderful place for us. Lots of work and it took away most of our camping time, but well worth it. It reminded me of Michigan. We also had several company parties back there.

THE UPSET DOCTOR AND MY FOOT

There is one thing I should mention here that was so cool. When I was working on the roof of the addition for the little office space, I was cutting the valley out with my skill saw and the blade got into a bind and the saw kicked back on me. I wasn't holding onto it very well and it cut into my shoe, almost cutting my large toe off. It was nasty. So, Mary took me to the hospital, and I went right into surgery. It was bad as the toe was held on only by a little bit. Almost off.

So, they called this doctor in. He was a grumpy little India guy. He did the operation. I think they took about four hours or so to do the reattachment. He put a cast on it all the way up past my knee. He scolded me with, "Don't touch that cast". It was summertime and it was hot out. How could I not at least scratch down in there. So, I had made an appointment to come back in for a checkup in two weeks.

I hobbled around for a few days on crutches and the darn cast got to itching on me, so I did the coat hanger thing and itched it. That next Sunday we went to church. I was sitting in the aisle seat, when this doctor friend we knew came down the aisle. He stopped and turned around and walked up to me. He said, "I am supposed to pray for you". So, I told him what had happened. He bent down and put his hands on my knee and prayed for a healing. Little did he know that I was healed right there. The pain was gone and it felt normal. Well, that didn't help the itching, and I started cutting the cast down, a little at a time, during that next week. By the time I went back in for my two-week checkup, the cast was about the size of a tennis shoe. It didn't itch anymore; besides it was healed.

I went to the doctor's appointment and that little Indian doctor saw it like that and got really mad at me. He also had put a stiff wire under the toenail and up about 3 inches into my foot. Well, it had come loose and started to come out, so I just took it out. He was so mad he almost refused to see me, but he did and he took the rest of the cast off. I told him about my healing, and he sort of glared at me. It looked great with the cast off. He sent me in for some foot x-rays. When the x-rays came back, he put them up on his lighted glass and studied them for several minutes. He mellowed out a little and told me that the x-rays didn't look right and he needed to take another set. So off I go again and when those x-rays came back he really studied them. Finally, he turned around and said, "Well, It looks like you could be right. This showed that you have healed already". I don't know if he was a believer or not, but I sure was. I have never had another problem with that toe. It is about a half inch shorter though. God is good.

MOVING TO A RENTED OFFICE

During those early years of the '90's, I had the company running quite smoothly and I could relax a little more with most weekends off. I had hung up my tools pretty much for good in '87 and concentrated more on running things. I was bringing plans home to do bids and material take-offs for frames and payroll with all the paperwork that entailed.

Our little home office just was not big enough, so we started looking for an office spot to move in to. We really didn't want to spend a lot of money but Mary and I both needed our own desk as well as Kathy Lindig. We found a little office for rent just a half mile from home and it was reasonable. We bought some desks and a few chairs, and we were in business. It was great having the office out of the house and some set hours for people stopping in. Kathy was there full time and Mary and I came and went as business needed. I had lots of meetings with the builders, keeping plenty of work out front.

GROWING EVEN MORE

We continued to add framers and the workload kept increasing on McEldowney, Bobby Hopper, and a new guy we put on to help out in quality control. His name was Steve Lane. Doing all the framing lumber for the AMREP houses had turned into a really wonderful thing for us. It allowed us to pay well and really make good money. My crew leaders were all doing really well making money. I hired a guy by the name of Brady Hayden and his crew that really helped increase production. He had a bunch of Hispanic carpenters and knew several other crews that wanted to go to work for us. So, the push was on to get more work lined up. By 1995, we were producing 15 to 18 good quality frames a week. That was a lot of houses, and we managed to keep it running well.

Things rolled along well during those years and our company was making really good money. When I look back at all that took place to get to this point, I felt blessed and successful. A lot of my ways of doing business were not by the book but I understood them, and we stayed legal. Mary saw to that part. She kept the office running straight. Gary Aniello even contacted the Feds and the State to confirm that I was doing things legal. They gave us the go ahead. The biggest question was having crew leaders operating as self-employed and working for only one company. The good part of it, as the Government saw it, was that all those framers were having taxes taken out and their comp was being paid on them.

Most of the other framing companies were not doing taxes and they were cheating on their workers comp. Under my system, everything was legal, and those crew leaders worked the framers right to a peak for performance. We worked our way up to becoming the largest framing company in New Mexico and we had it running smooth. A lot of the builders were wanting us to frame their houses for them.

HUNTING

Starting back in the late '80s, I was getting the itch to get back into some hunting. All I had was a 30.30 rifle, a pistol and a 12-gage, black powder shot gun with an interchangeable 58 caliber barrel. Those were the guns I had brought from Michigan. So, I got myself all the stuff it took to load a 12 gage, black powder, double barrel shot gun including some number six bird shot.

On September 1st the season for dove opened. The whole area just outside of Rio Rancho was just plain desert with plenty of water holes to dove hunt by. What a blast! The dove usually flew in flights of three or four at a time. So, with that big ole blunderbuss of mine, I had two shots to get off.

If I got one or two birds I would first have to go get whatever I had knocked down. Sometimes they would be hard to find. Then I would run back to my little stand and have to reload real quick before the next flight would come in to the water. That part included dumping powder down both barrels then pushing a wad down and pouring in the BBs. Then top it off with another wad to hold the BBs in. Those things had to be metered to just the right amounts. Then after putting two percussion caps on the nipples, I would be already for the next flight. It sure kept me busy but what a lot of fun I had.

I had a special way of baking the dove and it came out really well. Anna used to ask me every year to make sure I was going to go dove hunting. She really liked it. I used that ole black powder gun for a few years and finally bought myself a nice Browning 12 gauge shot gun. It sure made hunting a lot easier. After Gary Mac moved to New Mexico, we went every year during the '90s. What a great time.

I had heard a lot about elk hunting in New Mexico. One of the guys that worked for me was Jim Tyson and a really nice guy. We decided in '92 to put in for an elk permit. We lucked out that year and drew our permits. Wow was that ever exciting. We had lots of preparations to do. We decided to put together a little 8 by 12 plywood camp that we could frame up once we got into the mountains. We prefabbed it at home and it was ready to set up. We even made a wood stove out of an old hot water heater. It was great. Our hunting area was up on Mount Taylor out on the San Mateo flats. Mary and I had been up there some and loved the area for camping. We saw lots of elk.

I remember that exciting day Jim and I left for the mountains. It was Oct. 3rd. I remember the date because the next day was Mary's birthday and opening day for the hunt. Mary didn't mind as she was excited for us too. We got our little camp all set up that day including bunk beds with mattresses and a supply of fire wood. It was awesome but a little scary knowing the next morning we would be out after the mighty elk. We had elk cow tags and there were plenty of them around. As I recall, we sat around that campfire making plans for the next morning and I had a good idea exactly where I wanted to go. There were very few hunters up there and lots of elk. I headed out of camp that morning maybe 30 minutes before first light. It was so awesome, as I could hear elk running around. It wasn't quite shootin time and I literally walked right into a heard of cow elk. It was ruttin' time for them and they paid no attention to me. They soon ran off and morning was lighting up for my first day of elk hunting. Wow I was excited.

I hunted through the day but never got close enough for a good clean shot. The next morning was different though and I got a good sized elk. What an exciting time it was. Jim got his on the last day of the hunt. With the two elk packed in the back of the pickup there was no room for the camp so we left it and came on home. Got the meat into the butcher shop and I had a happy wife. We had heard how good elk meat was.

The following weekend Mary and I went back up the mountain to pick up the plywood camp. That little trip will always be easy to remember for us. We got the camp tore down and went for a walk. I had the big ole camcorder with us and we saw tons of elk. Wow, they were everywhere. Mary was so excited and we got a lot of footage of the herd. There were quite a few bull elk just milling around. We even got fairly close to some of them. They were in full rut. Their song is so beautiful. And we heard lots of calls that morning. I still have that beautiful tape here somewhere. I will never forget that hunt and the day Mary and I spent with the elk.

I should mention, at this time, that a good bit of the hunting for elk had to be done with black powder guns. I had bought myself a nice 54 caliber Renegade, side winder, black powder rifle. Those guns were a little bit touchy as you had to keep everything real clean because it was easy to get a misfire. That ole gun was really good for me though, as I went on to bring home a lot of elk in years to come. I loved that gun. It was one shot and a quick reload but I learned it well. There were lots of fun and successful days ahead for me with it, with deer and elk.

Over the course of my hunting time in New Mexico, I brought home 19 elk and I don't know how many deer I took. We didn't care that much for the deer meat, but oh, we sure loved the elk meat. I tried to get one every year because the girls really loved it and a freezer full was always great for us.

After that first year hunting with Jim Tyson, a bunch of us guys started putting in for the draw. Back in the '90s it was fairly easy to get drawn. It gradually got harder as more and more folks found out that hunting around Albuquerque was great.

Gary McEldowney got himself a Renegade 54 Cal, just like mine and we hunted together ever after. We always put in for the draw together. We had lots of experiences and stories to tell over the years. We hunted a good bit down in the Monzano Mountains right at the top. There were two trails going up there. The one we usually used was Red Canyon Trail. It rose about 5,000 feet to the 10,000 foot level but was a nice clean trail. It was three and a half miles long. A long walk but oh so beautiful. When you got to the top, you could see everywhere. We would pack in our tents and sleeping bags and food. One time I even toted a 12 pack of beer up there. I stuck a few cans in different old, rotted stumps across the top trail and they stayed really cold in the old rotted saw dust. Mac and I would enjoy one every so often, but only one.

One day I went hunting up there with Brady Hayden. Brady was a good hunter and a great guy. So, there was this one spot on top of the mountain that had a spring running out all year round. The water came out of the ground and ran about 200 yards down the slope and then disappeared back into the ground. I had ran across a black bear of respectable size at that water the year before but didn't have a bear license so this year I had gotten one. That fateful day, Brady went on down farther than me and I stayed at the spring water laying in deep grass. I waited. Sure enough, about an hour or so later, that big ole black bear came back to the water hole. He was a big ole boar. He sensed something was wrong and got his front feet up on an old dead log and he was sniffing around. He was facing me with his head in the air and it was just perfect for a shot of about only 30 feet. He ran about a hundred yards and down he went. I sure was glad it only took one shot because I would never have had time to reload. I had gotten him in the heart and he died in just a few seconds. Thank God for that! I consider the bear a majestic animal. I would never do it again and sometimes when I see him hanging on the wall, I sort of wish he was still alive roaming in the mountains. He was about a 300 pounder, and I waited until the next day to go up there with horses and bring him down. Brady helped me get him down. He had died so fast that there was no adrenaline in the meat, and we ate the whole bear. It was better than deer meat. Even the girls liked it.

Another good hunting memory was up in the Jemez mountains. I had a young Jemez Indian working on one of the framing crews for me and I knew him fairly well. So one year, in about 1996, I was not successful in the draw for elk. This young guy worked as a guard on the weekends for the Valle Grande during hunting season and they would give him a free hunting tag for that year's hunt. The tags were worth about $500.00 dollars. This kid offered to sell me his tag for three hundred and, oh ya, I took it. It consisted of a one-day hunt, and you had to go out with a guide. It was always a sure kill at the morning hunt, and always for a cow elk. They would gut it for you and skin and quarter it for you.

That's when I met Dave Collis. He managed the elk herd for the owners of the Valle Grande. The Valle Grande was a cattle ranch at the time, with a lot of elk on it. It was 144 square miles in size, 12 miles by 12 miles. To hunt a bull elk there they charged $8,000.00, but they always got huge trophy bull elk. So, Dave guided me on that first hunt and we soon became good friends. Every time I put in for an elk tag and didn't draw, I would call up Dave and he would set me up with a cow tag on the Valle. It worked out great and I loved going up there.

Dave even had me guide other hunters a few times. The Valle Grande was finally sold to the Federal Government and it was converted into a National Park. It was a beautiful spot and the Feds have kept it up pretty well. Dave did a great job keeping the elk herd up on that land. They usually sold around 200 cow elk tags a year for $500.00 per tag. It was always a neat experience to go there with Dave and all his guides, usually eight or so good guides and those guys were a lot of fun.

Mary went up there with me a few times and really loved it. She watched me take a nice cow Elk at about 500 yards one time. That was a fun time. I was using my 300 mag. on that shot. I had done a lot of practice shooting at 500 yards. Mary even helped gut a few elk by holding the legs apart during cleaning.

That was great, but really our best times hunting were when we drew our own tags and went deep into the mountains for the hunt.

Leon Kulhanek, Mike Koviack and Leon's son Scott drew one year, for elk, and we had a fun time up on Mt. Taylor. I took Scott on a long walk deep down into Salado Canyon which is about a 2,000 foot drop off the mesa. We spent the night down there and it was a great time huddled around a small campfire. I guided Scott for several days and on about the fourth day he got himself a nice 4 by 4 bull. He was satisfied.

I think that the most fun elk kill I ever had was up on Mount Taylor. I was hunting with my 54 cal. black powder rifle. I had a bull tag and had taken a bull and a cow call with me. One morning, before daybreak, I started bull calling and within a short time I was getting a bull calling back. It was rutting time and those bulls go nuts. So that morning I started out toward the return call from the bull. When I got fairly close I realized that he had about 20 cow elk with him. That made it really tough because the cows were always on guard and one little sound, and they would spook. Well, I had spooked them three or four times, but the bull still kept a response back to me every time I would bugle. He was really angry that another bull was following him and his harem. He was getting louder as the morning went on. There were times I would crawl to get closer and sneak and run and break branches from trees and then bugle and sometimes cow call. He didn't like it very well. He finally burned me out, I had to stop, sit on a stump, and rest. He and his harem had gone over a hill and a little far away. Well, that big ol bull must have wondered why the bull (me) stopped following him and he came back to see what was going on. He walked right into my view. He was magnificent and I brought him home. Both of his eye tines were broken off from fighting other bulls and his whole belly was soakin' wet from all of his mating. What an animal. And I sure messed up his party!

Speaking of the bulls fighting, I did happen to see two large bulls go at it a time or two on the hunts. You could almost feel the power those guys had in their fighting. The clacking of the horns and the grunts that came out of them. Awesome! The bull elk bugle is one of the most beautiful sounds there is.

Another really cool memory I have from hunting was on a nice bright sunny morning when I was just out moving really slow and quiet going up and down a lot of valleys and slopes deep in off the road. I got a little hungry and decided to sit on a stump and have a candy bar. I came up a slope and found myself on an old logging road or fire lane. It was pretty well overgrown. So, as I was sitting there, very quiet, eating a candy bar, I caught some movement out of the corner of my eye. Thinking it was a nice elk, I slowly reached down and cocked the ole Renegade leaning up by my side. I stayed froze waiting for it to move out in front of me. It was not an elk. It turned out to be the biggest, most beautiful mountain lion I had ever seen. He walked right by me about 20 feet away. I was in total awe, his tail had to be at least five foot long and at least six inches thick. I know he weighed at least 250 pounds. So big and so beautiful!

When he got about 40 feet in front of me, he stopped. He turned and looked me straight in the eyes and as he stood there he blinked twice. I think I was too much in awe to even be scared. You should never make eye contact with those guys, but I couldn't help it. He then looked straight ahead away from me and moseyed on his way. I watched him for about three or four minutes until he was out of sight. I must have just sat there for a half hour thinking of what had just happened. That was a true God given experience. It is really very rare to ever see a lion in the wild. In all of my hunting experiences, I have only ever seen three.

One other really remarkable happening was down in the Monzano Mountains. I was walking up the Ox Canyon trail for a rendezvous with McEldowney. I was in a switch back part of the trail. That trail was three miles long to the 10,000 foot level. Puff! Puff! So, I had a full camping pack plus the ole Renegade 54. As I was walking the switch back area of the trail, I could hear sort of a scurry type noise up ahead. To my shock, as I rounded a little curve in the trail, there just ahead and about 20 feet away was a beautiful large black bear. He was sitting on a rather large fallen tree trunk. He was sunning himself. I stopped in my tracks and watched as he stretched his front legs way into the air and turned his belly to me. That was a very different thing for him to do as they never expose their underside to what could be a foe. He was like that for maybe a minute and then he got down and sorta rambled up the side of a hill. It sure gave me a thrill to be that close to a completely wild bear. I could tell a lot more neat experiences being out hunting but I would be rambling on.

It has been a few years now since I last went hunting. We don't eat a lot of red meat anymore. I don't think I could actually go out and kill another animal again. Hunting is a really good thing as it keeps the animal population down and that helps in disease spread and starvation, as well as deprivation. I took my last elk in 2018. I was on a hunt with my only buddy that was still alive or around, Bob Lindig. We were down at Slater Mesa south of Quemado. New Mexico has given me so many truly remarkable and wonderful experiences in hunting with my buds or camping and exploring with my family. It's been a God given gift to us. I love it here!

Leon and Mike and their wives would meet Mary and I for a number of years up in Salida, Colorado where we would go deep into the mountains fishing. We had a truly beautiful location that required walking about 2 miles up a trail to a series of beaver dams. There we would spend the day fishing the ponds for brook trout. Usually, we each would have 15 or 20 fish to carry out. Brookies are a small fish and the way Leon would fry them up, Wow! They sure were good! I sure miss those trips. Leon and Mike were really good at cleaning those little buggers. We always ate well and had some to take home.

Leon invited me back to Michigan for a few hunts with him and Mike. So, Mary and I would head up there. They had several hunting blinds set up in a woods and I guess I took several deer back there. We always left the meat there so Leon and Mike could make a lot of deer sausage. It was always really good stuff.

I guess that is about enough about my hunting exploits! It was a great time in my life and lots of good buddy time. I miss it.

JULIE MOVING WEST

Julie's Graduation

So, my little best friend, Julie Wallen, grew herself up into a fine young lady and graduated from High School in 1987. Julie had been out west on our "Daddy time" a number of times and she felt compelled to move out this way. That made me really happy. First of all, for her graduation and then, because she would be a lot closer to me so I could see her more. A lot happened to her that year. She graduated and we were there to help her move out west. We drove the ole van to Michigan to help her move. She decided on living in Tucson and made arrangements to stay with Cousin Dominic Wallen at his apartment.

Julie's best friend Jenny had come to Michigan to ride west with her on the move. Jenny and her mom had moved to Phoenix earlier. So, Miss Julie, ready for any adventure, decided to go exploring and wanted to see a lake. She and Jenny went to a lake called Canyon Lake close to Phoenix. As I understand it, the two of them were on the shoreline when these guys in a boat came zipping on by. When the driver of the boat saw Julie, he made a quick turn around and pulled up to shore. I haven't been told this, but I think the boat driver fell head over heels at first sight. I believe it worked the other way also. The girls got into the boat and the rest is history, so to speak.

The boat's driver was Julie's future husband Don Holthusen. The two hit it off right away and they started seeing each other. It wasn't long 'till she was living in Scottsdale, and she went to work for Astro Blue Printing, a company that belonged to my sister Char's husband's family. The next New Years Eve, Don proposed marriage to my little girl, and she accepted. They sure had my full approval.

The next year they had gotten their own place together, it was 1988. Don was really good at maintaining swimming pools with repairs and cleaning, so they set themselves up a little business, which they really made grow and do good. It was a good money maker for them, but it was also a lot of work for Don. Don had a great work ethic and that's what it takes. They called their little company D & J Pool Service. Phoenix and the area had tons of home pools and that is what they needed.

On June 10th of '89, I gained a son-in-law, as the two love birds got married. I was very happy for them. I felt that they made a great couple together. She had chosen wisely. Their wedding day would be the last time I got to see Julie's Grandfather, Marvin Korf. I loved that guy.

Julie worked for several construction companies over the next few years including Golden Heritage Homes. I think she really enjoyed working there. She continued helping Don run the business and worked for Golden for about six years. At this point they had made a wonderful life together. Parents are always happy when their kids do well. Mary and I drove over to visit them a number of times. They bought their first home in 1992. I remember going over to visit them and help Don put a covered patio on the back of the new house. Don was a "go getter" type of a guy and I really admired him for that. I knew how hard it was for a person to start a new business and make it pay off enough to make a decent living. He done well!

Don and Julie Wallen Holthusen

JEFF MOVING WEST

Jeff's Graduation.

Jeff was having a bit of a rough time in high school keeping those grades up there. But he made it through and graduated in 1992. In 1993 Jeff moved to New Mexico and went to work for Wallen Builders. Several years later Jeff was having more and more of a problem with his social anxiety and he returned to Michigan. He got a job working with Sears in their parts department and he seemed to be really happy there. He had good people skills and had to work with the public. He even learned how to deal with "know it all grumpy folks". Being a builder, I knew what that was like. Jeff was quite interested in art and decided to go to Baker College and get into a program while he was still working at Sears. After several years at Baker, the college told him he shouldn't go on because he was color blind and would never excel in what he liked. He was totally bummed from that happening. He really loved the arts. Jeff stayed with Sears for a total of almost 15 years between Michigan and Oregon, where he would later move.

THE EMPLOYEES

Building my company from the ground up was quite a challenge for Mary and me. We put a lot of work into it. We tried hard to make every employee feel important and needed. That feeling helped them all want to be the best that they could be and want to produce. We gained a great reputation as good clean framers who were quick to complete each job. We were now working in volume.

I had to be at the AMREP office building a lot and I got to know most of their staff. There were a lot of really good folks working there.

Knowing them and becoming friends with a lot of them would really pay off in the future. Their company was based out of New York and a lot of their clients were folks that moved here from that state. Yup, they all talked funny. Of the builders that we worked for, including Centex Homes, I stayed closest to AMREP. I felt that I had a good future with them even if the economy turned bad again.

TAXES AND CRUISIN'

In 1993, the New Mexico State taxation department sent us a bill for over $100,000.00 dollars in back taxes. They were sort of reneging on what they had told us a few years earlier in regards to our crew leaders, as they were self-employed and working for only one builder. That really scared Mary and me but my buddy Gary Aniello jumped into action for me. Gary got all of our papers together and went in and met with the head gal in Albuquerque at the State Tax Revenue place. He explained our history to her and then when he went to open up the folio with the papers, he sort of dumped it all over the floor. He was putting on a show and she told him after he came up with a handful of papers to just pack it up and leave. The State wrote it all off and canceled our liability. Wow! That was close and we skated through it.

I went down and got Gary a large bottle of Tequila. Gary had helped me an awful lot in my business since we became friends. So, I gave him his bottle of tequila and told him that we were going to buy him a cruise in the Caribbean with his wife Janet. He got really excited. After I talked it over with Mary, we decided that we would go along with them. Then to top it off, Gary and Jeanie McEldowney decided that they would like to go cruisin' along with us.

So that made it Gary, Gary, and Garry going off together. None of us had ever been on a cruise before so we got it all set up. We did Cozumel, The Grand Caymans and Jamaica. The first cruise is always magic and wow, ours sure was. We all sure had a wonderful time. I think the three Gary's made an impression at every bar on that ship.

Mary and I fell in love with cruise ships and the islands. To date, I think we have been on over 30 of the Caribbean Islands. We have taken many island tours and never had a bad time. We have cruised with a lot of different couples since that first one and now that I am 81 years old, (I 'am writing this now in the year 2024) I plan on doing more. Just gotta stay in shape.

So, on that first cruise, our first stop was Cozumel. We did a catamaran snorkel dive and were in total awe. They taught us how to do the Macarena dance and we got fairly drunk. They did a beach party for us and then back to the dock. The three Gary's stopped at this little outdoor bar right on the water and we had a ball. The girls went shopping and we did Tequila shots all afternoon. The girls helped us back onboard the ship. We all let go and had a ball. The rest of the cruise was about the same way. I will never forget it, nor will the gals.

Don and Julie went with us one time and we took Deb and Anna on a cruise as well. A lot of our friends were cruisers with us. Those islands are so beautiful. I think if we didn't have a lot of our family here in New Mexico, I could live on one of those islands.

KIDS MAKING IT A GO

By 1996 Deb and Anna were getting it going in school and making lots of friends. Don and Julie were getting their little business going and doing very well and Jeff was happy at Sears but having lots of trouble with his phobia. I felt so bad for him.

FIRST SPEC HOUSE IN N.M.

I kept building the framing company a little at a time. We had everything running really smooth. I was thinking about building a spec house at some point just to see how it would go. We were building a fairly nice nest egg and an investment in a spec house just might pay off. I began working on some plans for a model house and decided to build one almost like the big one I had built for Janet before our split up. I had really loved that house. I think it was about 1996 when I finally did build my first house in New Mexico. It really felt good to be doing that again. It was about 15 years since the last house I built. It was great because I got to know more suppliers and subcontractors. I didn't make a lot of money on that house, but it was fun and it got me involved with a lot of folks I would need to know a few years later.

NO MORE PUB

I had developed a bit of a bad habit with some of the framing crew leaders and other staff, as well as some of the guys from AM-REP around the mid '90s. We all would meet about 5:30, or so, at a little pub called Phil's Pub in Rio Rancho. Mac, Bobby Hopper, and I were there most afternoons after work. It got to be a problem for Mary and the kids because I would be coming home late and sometimes fairly well tuned up. I don't remember what year it was but one night when I got home, the kids said to me, "Dad, we gotta talk." So, I listened. Mainly they wanted me to know that I was coming home late often and sometimes I would use words that maybe I didn't mean to. I guess, with everything that was going on, I was not paying attention to what I was doing to my sweet family. So, that was it. No more Phil's Pub except only once in a while. My little family meant everything to me and no more making their lives miserable. It was a good let down for me after a busy day and I enjoyed it but not at my family's expense.

MOVING THE OFFICE AGAIN

During the next few years on into 1997 everything ran really well for my company. We had ample work for every crew and were doing almost 600 frames a year. I couldn't have been happier. The company net worth had grown to over $700,000.00 and it made everything comfortable for Mary and me. For once in my life, I felt that maybe I would be able to retire at some point. Little did I know what would lie ahead for me.

After a few years or so of having the office in the little plaza off Southern Blvd., we needed to get a bigger office space. We found a place on Unser Blvd. that worked out just right. We rented a nice space upstairs and soon after, we had to expand in that building even more. One big problem though was, on the lower level, there was a beauty shop and some of the smells that came out of there were downright awful. Fridays were especially bad. That was the day all the old ladies would come in for the "blue hair special". Yuck, I can still taste that perm smell. Yuck. As business expanded for us, we soon were renting several rooms downstairs in that building as well.

OUR LITTLE CHURCH

We had joined a little Church called New Beginnings Fellowship and they were meeting on Sundays in a day care place. It was hard for our little group as we had our own chairs and a few tables that had to be set up every Sunday and then taken down after service. We had a tight little group and folks just pitched in. So, on the back section of the place where we moved our offices into, there was a large room just right for a group of 50 or so church members to hold church. We, as a little Church, rented it and I spent several weeks remodeling it so it would be great for Church meetings. It turned out very well and our little group grew in size. We felt blessed to have a really cool group of Church goers.

Deb and Anna got right into the youth part of it. They had a great time and it was so good for them. We had a good group of kids. We did group camping trips to the mountains that always turned out awesome. Prayer sessions around a campfire can be a wonderful experience. One year we had rain, rain, rain and still had a lot of fun in the mud.

We had a lot of fun, but maybe a little too much, as one day we all learned that our pastor was having an affair with one of the parishioners. He was single and she was married with a son. The marriage was ruined and the pastor and her ran off together. So much for our little Church group. Mary and I tried several different Churches after that and finally went back to the Catholic Church. Deb and Anna still carry a great faith in God and for that, we are grateful.

JEFF TO OREGON

Jeff had fallen in love with a movie from the '80s called "The

Goonies" and really wanted to go and visit the place in Oregon where the movie was filmed. The little town on the coast was called Astoria. With his agoraphobia being really bad, he had no way to go anywhere, especially all the way across the country. That went on for him for several years and he kept on talking about Astoria.

So, one day when I was talking to him on the phone, I told him that if he ever got to a point where he thought he could make that trip, he should let me know and I would go and meet him there. He didn't think he could do it. Well, several weeks later I got a call from him and he said he really wanted to try the trip. He knew he would have a really rough time especially on an airplane, but he said, "Let's do it". That made me really happy, and I knew if he made it and we had a good time and saw lots of places, all the old movie sets and things, it just might help him out of his social fears. I was excited and so was he.

I went ahead and set up the flights. I planned it so my flight would get in before his, so I could be there for him. I also had found a really nice motel in Cannon Beach, right on the ocean. We would be there for four or five days. I had rented a car as well.

So, when Jeff got off the plane in Portland, he was white as a sheet. He was a sick boy. He had thrown up a good bit on the plane. We made our way out to the ocean and found our hotel. It was a really neat place with a great beach, plenty of food, and shops. After Jeff got settled in, I went out and got some dinner for us for in the room. The next two days he was still fairly sick but was coming out of it. That was a really good sign. I had gone out and bought two kites that we had a great time flying on the beach. The next few days we drove all over the coast seeing all the locations the movie had been filmed at. He knew all the spots. It was a great time, and he really came out of his social problem. Our little trip was very successful. I think at that point he broke his bond with the phobia. He had a little trouble on the way home but soon became a lot better. Thank God for that.

ALL HISPANIC CREWS

1997 rolled around and everything business was doing very well. Housing was going strong, and my company was still doing very well. Lots of framing going on all over the city and we were keeping up. McEldowney and Bob Hopper along with Steve Lane were keeping things running very well in the field and I mostly kept the work out front.

By this time, we were using almost all Hispanic crews. A lot of our guys were illegals from Mexico. Those guys worked really hard and when they got their paycheck on Friday, they would mostly send half of it home to Mexico and live on the rest. Those guys were great. We even sponsored some of them to become U.S. citizens. We also had it set up so some of those guys could learn to speak English. I had hired a teacher for them. They were making good money and so was I.

BIG, BIG CHANGE AHEAD

About September of 1997, AMREP made a big announcement. They were going to close their building company and only sell land after the first of 1998. My biggest builder was going out of the building business. It started out as a really big shock to me, but as the dust settled, I could see a real opportunity for me. So, I went in and met with the President of AMREP. They would have about 800 houses that were still under warranty at the start of the year that would need to be taken care of. They also would have about 30 houses still under construction and another 35 that were under contract to get started into construction. After that meeting, I spent several weeks running the numbers and formulating a sort of a plan. This was big stuff for me. Really scary but what an opportunity it could be.

Putting it all together would be a ton of work. I knew all of the AMREP folks very well and I trusted them very much. I had worked for them for almost 17 years, and it went very well. So, we started out by working out their warranty responsibility. They offered me $200,000.00 to take care of that part. The warranties covered 2 years but some of the houses were already at the end of their 2 years and the number would decrease fairly rapidly from that point. Only a few would go the full 2 years. There was good money to be made in this deal. Most of the warranty work was still the responsibility of the sub-contractors. I just had to get them to do the work.

Next was the houses under construction. I would take them over and complete them out at a set price, depending on how far along each one was. That also would be good money for us. Then there were the contracts that they had, but had not started. They would give me all the contracts and I could consider them all as new builds from start. I would be starting out a building company with 35 houses already sold and ready to build. I did a lot of praying about this deal.

AMREP also had five models in their model village and they would sell them to me for a mere $25,000 a house. They always built their model houses with wood floors on stanchions so when the model was outdated, they could move it out to a permanent foundation on one of their lots. Then they could build a new model in its place. It worked rather well. I had bought houses from them in the past and moved them out myself.

This whole thing was rather overwhelming for me to start with, but I felt I could handle it. It would mean me putting all of our saved money into a venture that could possibly not make it. I really did a lot of praying and I came up with a peace of mind about it. I, at that time, had to get into the banking system and get some rather large construction loans set up. AMREP also gave me all the remaining lots that were not under contract, with no overhead. Just pay them off when the house closed. It really was an awesome deal for me. I just had to make it work and wow, work it was.

I started out by hiring their sales manager and several of their sales staff. I knew those guys well and they were good. Then I hired some of their office staff. A gal by the name of Marlene was already taking care of their warranty program and doing walk throughs. She was the next one to hire. She stepped right in to handle warranty problems. She was great at her job. I also got several other staff from them for payables and closing paperwork.

So, we started out 1998 with a ton of work just getting things rolling right. Wow, what a job that was. I gave complete responsibility of the framing company to Bob Hopper and he handled it very well. I hired a few folks to help him in the field. The framing company was doing well and making good money. I used Gary McEldowney for helping out in the new building company.

At this point, to make the new company work, I needed a lot of land to build on. AMREP had set aside the completion of their last subdivision which had about 35 lots left and with my sales force of three or four people we started selling those lots out. With all the rest of the things going on, I had to find and buy land. After a good bit of research, I started buying land. I wound up with several ready to build areas and one ready to build subdivision. I sure spent all my money rather fast. Getting all that going, along with making contracts with all the suppliers and sub-contractors, I was running around like crazy.

I hired Gary Aniello to meet with and handle the banking end of things. He had a good knowledge of contracts with banks, including construction loans. Gary really helped me get the business off the ground. I hired a guy by the name of Russ Marks as a general manager. This guy seemed to be doing great and doing what I told him, but it turned out that he was a big mistake for me. After less than a year I had to fire him. He was giving things away to home buyers with no trace of paperwork and no charge. He cost us a lot of money in a short time. I then hired Hank Axen as general manager, and he worked out very well over the years to come.

Our payroll really went up fast but with my little office staff we started closing houses and it looked well for making money. The next three or four years kept me so busy that I had very little time for myself and family. I didn't like that part of it very well. Our construction loan ceiling was about to reach way up into the millions, but we were selling and closing houses.

That first year I think we closed around 38 houses. Considering the fact that we had to get the company up and running plus complete and close houses, it was remarkable to me. I had selected a good staff, and they all worked really well together. I did all I could to make our work environment as nice as possible. Everybody had health insurance, and I set up a good vacation plan with sick time off. My goal was to make everyone comfortable and want to do their best for the company. I tried to make everyone feel like they were in a big family all working for the goal of being the best and producing the best homes possible. Our reputation for having a great product spread fast and it helped sales really well for being a startup company. We were getting folks from other builders wanting to come to work for us. We paid well but expected, and got, top quality work.

The second year, we closed about 70 houses and in 2000 we hit about 90. We had made it through what I considered the roughest part of getting the company up and running, but there was still a lot to do. Finding land and getting it developed into building lots was a big part of my responsibility.

In 1999, the framing company was running a little slower and, I didn't have the time to keep the work out front for all the guys. We had about 250 guys working for us at that time. So, we lost a few crews, mainly because of work. Bobby Hopper was talking about being burned out and maybe going back into trim work or framing. That could lead to a big problem. He was really good for me. He was also drinking a lot of the evenings.

THE LAKE HOUSE AND BOATING

The Lake House

In about '96, we were with Don and Julie on an Arizona Lake and we went boating. It was such a great time! I even got up on the skis one time. I liked it so much and thought the kids would enjoy it so much that I started looking for a boat. The next year we were back in Arizona, and we found an older boat for sale that seemed to be just right for what I wanted. So, we bought it and drug it on home.

It was an old boat that hadn't been run for a while and I spent some time fixing it all up. Anybody that wants to get into boating should start out with an old boat. You're gonna give it lots of dents and scratches.

Julie was over one weekend and we took the old blue boat up north to Abiquiu Lake. It was a 21-foot Sea Ray with a cuddy cabin on it. We got it in the water and out a little ways and she stopped running. The fuel filter was full of rust. After a good cleaning we were off again and had a great time a boatin'. My first time.

My neighbor, Gary Aniello, wanted to get a boat too. So, we found him one in Arizona as well. One weekend we set out to go boating down on Elephant Butt Lake. One of my frame builders, Jim Brown, had just built a new house on the lake. After having some fun on the water we stopped by Jim's place for a visit. Jim and I had become good friends and while we were at his place he told me about a cabin for sale just across the road and thought I should buy it.

Later on that week, Mary and I thought about it and talked about it. We decided to check it out further and maybe it could be a nice lot that we could build on later. We knew it had a trailer house on it. Well, we wound up buying the place sight unseen. That might have been a little silly but we were really surprised when we closed the deal and went out to spend our first night at our new cabin. It turned out great as it had a total of four bedrooms and a nice big 24 x 24 party room that was only screened in, great for summer use. It even had two garages there. One place for old blue and one for when we would get some jet skis. We made plans to build a nice deck over the party room and then install doors and windows all the way around the party room so it would be good for winter use. With everything else that was going on, it would be a great place to escape with Mary and the kids. It was great.

I had gotten all the materials down to the cabin that I would need to glass the party room all in. Don called and said he would like to come over and help me get the job done. He and I had a great time working together and we did a good job of it. We had it all glassed in and sealed up. That big ole room was now ready for winter.

DON AND THE FRAMING COMPANY

It was during this time that I got to thinking about Don maybe moving over and running the framing company at some time in the future. I knew I had a few really hard years ahead of me yet and I could then train him in that company. He had already proven himself as a good businessman and he was really mechanical minded. Just what he needed to take the framing company off my hands. I figured I could get Bobby Hopper to stay with me for at least a few more years, then Don could take it over. So, I talked to Don about it and he really loved the idea. He was already making a great living for him and Julie. After they talked it over, they both wanted to do it. I told them that it could be several years though, until I would have time to work with Don and train him.

Then came my big mistake. They got really excited and so did Mary and I. They first called and wanted to know if we could make it only one year until I would be ready. I knew it would be tight, but I said ok. I really wanted them to be here in New Mexico with me. Then it was down to six months. Soon Don called and told me that he had sold his pool company and had the house on the market. It sold right away and there in, was our big mistake. It just didn't go well for us.

I had a spec house that I could sell them for my cost which helped them some and they liked it pretty well. I wanted to do something really nice for Don and Julie so we could really get to know each other and enjoy our time together. I set up a 7-day cruise and we ran off to the Caribbean for a really fun week.

I knew when I got back, I was really going to have to perform. I was really hoping that I could spend three or so days a week showing Don the ins and outs of framing a house and how to deal with the builders we had for our work. I wanted to do a few frames with him. I knew he was a fast learner. I thought the best place to do that would be at Jim Brown's building Company. It could be more controlled, and Jim would understand what I was doing. Jim knew Don from the lake house.

When we got back from that week-long vacation everything was a buzz. As I recall, I was needed in every corner of the company, and I really had to get to work. We were a pretty new building company, and I had really good people but they still needed a lot of guidance in what was going on. That included the framing company as well. I kept Don with me those first few days so he could get an idea of what I was all about and so folks could meet him. Then I made another even bigger mistake with Don. I had shown him all the framing locations and I let him know what the crews all had to do to meet the OSHA requirements. I wanted to keep a check on all the crews for things like safety glasses and hard hats. Everybody took him to be the enforcer, and they didn't like it. Right away everybody on the framing end of it considered him the kid with the golden spoon in his mouth. Bob Hopper let me know that they didn't care for him or what I was doing. Bob refused to train his replacement. I think by then he had changed his plans and did not want to quit Wallen Builders.

I wanted to spend a good bit of time showing Don how to frame a house and I gave it a shot. There was just too much stuff going on in the building company to be able to spend time showing him the ropes. I was in trouble. Sales were going good but I needed more land if we were to survive. I had to hire superintendents for the building field, and I needed several punch list guys for the closing clean-up. To top all of that off, our office space was way too small for our growing company. At that point I really needed two of me. My son in law was getting really frustrated with me. I pulled one of the crew leaders that was on payroll and had him help Don with learning the framing end of things. That didn't go well either. I didn't have time to keep enough work out front for all the crews and so we started losing some of them. I had just bit off way more than I should have. It was straining my relationship with my son in law, and I couldn't blame him for feeling bad.

OFFICE MOVE AGAIN

We had every room being used in the building we were renting and needed much more. I checked out an older building over by the AMREP offices. It was an old armory at one time, and it had lots of smaller rooms that could be used for offices. Yea, it would work. The office move was on. So I went to work renovating it. Added a few walls and did a repaint as well as some new flooring. It also had a large storage area behind, that worked out really well. We spent a full weekend making the move. Everybody jumped in to help and it went smooth. I had hired a young guy by the name of Quentin to do all of our IT "computer" work and he got all the computers set up just over that weekend. Well, it worked out great, we were up and running really fast. I didn't think it could be done. I had to be there a good bit while the work was being done and happy to say our new offices came out really nice.

Hank Axen was working out real well as our general manager and we decided we needed a person to run the construction bidding department. Someone that would be good at getting our new plans bid out for pricing. Hank knew just the gal for the job. Her name was Janice and wow! Did she ever do well for us. We stole her from KB Homes.

RUINED RELATIONSHIP

During all of this hectic time in my life, I knew that I had really messed up having Don and Julie move to New Mexico when I was covered up with so much to do. The whole framing gang was down on him and Don had never been treated like that before. Even Julie was getting upset with me because I just didn't get over to see her very much. I was in a bad place with them. Don was making his rounds everyday trying to keep the lumber and window orders up and he did okay, but Bobby Hopper just wouldn't help or give advice. Looking back, I would have been better off if I had fired Hopper and then let McEldowney train Don to run that company with all the lumber, windows, scheduling, and keeping the builders happy. Keeping the work ahead, I think he would have done very well with that. The biggest problem I had with that is the crew leaders didn't care for him. I think that was Hopper's fault as well. It might not have worked out any better, even if we would have waited those two years. Running the big company took a lot of doing all the way till the time I sold the company.

I ruined a relationship during that time in my life and because of the way things turned out, I would not get to see them for a number of years after they moved back to Arizona, feeling really defeated and very upset at me. I learned a big lesson there, but it didn't help the situation. I could not blame Don or Julie for what they felt. It would be almost 10 years before we got back together again. Sigh.

Julie's Baby Shower

It was during this time in the year 2000 that Julie delivered Abby, my very first granddaughter. She was a sweet little lady and it made me really happy. With all that had gone on with Don and Julie and me though, I would not get to see her after those first few times, for the next nine years or so. That hurt a lot, but I really couldn't blame them. They did come way too early for me, and I couldn't get the time to do Don justice. It was just a sad situation. Julie had a second daughter born to her and Don in 2003 her name is Gracie, such a pretty kid.

DEB HIGH SCHOOL TO COLLEGE

Deb graduated from high school in 2000 and headed straight into college. She had done fantastic in high school and would go on to do the same in her higher education.

She got overwhelmed and sick the next year with all the pressures and took some time off. Deb just needed to get away from it all. She had a friend that she had met at the lake and also I believe she was still very much in love with her high school sweetheart Scott Brenna. The guy she had met at the lake turned out to be quite a pest. So, with all that being said, she went to Michigan for a little over a

Deb's Graduation

month and stayed with my best buddy Leon Kulhanek and wife Diane. That did her a lot of good and she came home feeling much better about things. I believe it was during that time she decided Scott would be in her life forever.

She also had a bad accident the next year when a cement tanker rammed into the back of her car when traffic was stopped on the expressway. We had gotten her a shinny new red Mustang and it was totaled out. I believe she is still having some problems from the accident to this very day.

Leon and Diane Kulhanek

ANNA HIGH SCHOOL TO COLLEGE

Anna's Graduation

The next year, 2001, Anna graduated from High School. She had gotten really interested in artwork and even with her bad eyesight, she had done some beautiful work. She went right into college pursuing the study of art. She had gotten so good at it that she had some of her work on display for sale in Old Town, Albuquerque.

Anna also had a high school sweetheart. Andy Sloan was her true love, and he was also going to college at the University of New Mexico in Albuquerque. Ann became an excellent artist but after 2 years of college, she decided to drop out and her and Andy made plans to be married in May of 2004. Anna would be getting a job and support Andy in his schooling.

I had bought 2 AMREP houses in the mid-1990s and rented them out so the mortgage amount we had on each one would be lowered. They were nice little 1,400 sq. ft. starter homes. We bought them with the intent of giving each of the girls a home for their wedding present and give them a good start in life with a really low house payment. I think it worked very well for them. Anna and Andy lived in theirs for a few years and then upgraded to a larger home. Deb got married in '05 and wound up selling her house as Scott got transferred to Roswell, New Mexico. That gave them a substantial down payment and they bought a nice house down there. Scott had gotten a good job with the Bureau of Land Management.

GRANDKIDS ON THE WAY

The next thing that happened with those kids was GRANDCHILDREN and it changed all of our lives.

Debbie and Scott would have a total of 5 children. Mary, Alexander, Sophia, Isabella and then we got a latecomer as our little Peter was born in 2021. Deb and Scott are homeschooling the kids and they are turning out just way awesome. What a wonderful family. Everybody that knows them, loves them.

Anna and Andy had 2 kids. Gabriel was born in 2006 and then Katie was born in 2007. As of this writing, they are both doing quite well in high school. Gabe is looking forward to his college years. Sad to say though, Andy and Anna separated and then divorced. Anna's precious artwork had been discontinued due to pain in her hands and arms and that is sad because she had such a talent. She is now running an exotic bird rescue out of her home. She loves it and is doing very well.

**John Scott and Deborah Wallen
Brenna**

**Andy and Anna Wallen
Sloan**

Abby Holthusen—Grandchild #1

Grace Holthusen– Grandchild #2

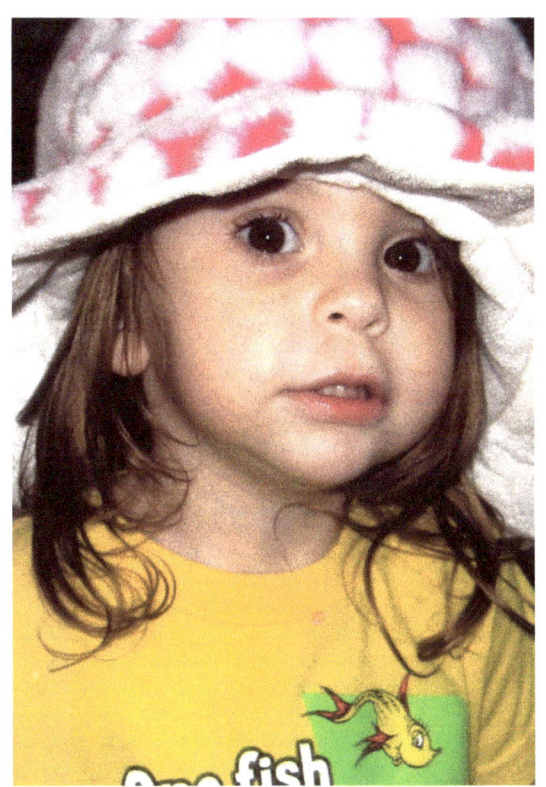

Mary Brenna– Grandchild #3

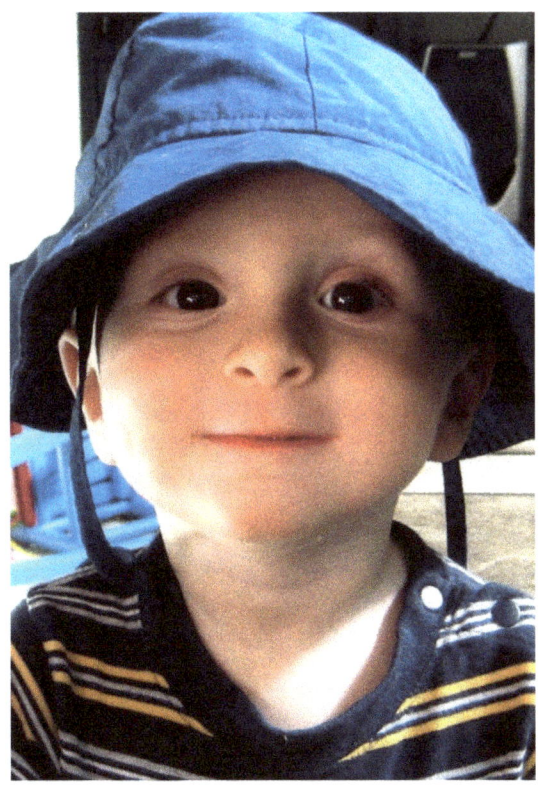

Alexander Brenna– Grandchild #5

Sophia Brenna – Grandchild #7

Isabella Brenna – Grandchild #8

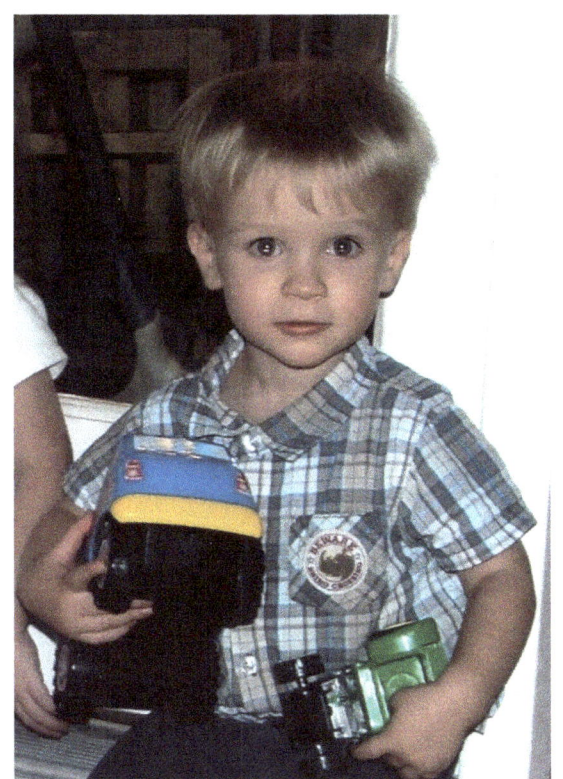 

Gabriel Sloan– Grandchild #4

Kaitlyn Sloan– Grandchild #6

Peter Brenna – Grandchild #9

Mary, Alex, Sophia, and Izzy sure love their sweet baby brother.

Left to Right: Abby Holthusen, Jeff Wallen, Julie Smith, and Grace Holthusen.

Left to Right: Peter, Sophia, Alex, Mary, Isabella, Scott, and Deb. Brenna.

Left to Right: Gabe, Andy, Katie, and Anna Sloan.

LOSING MOM, DAD REMARRYING

The early years of this century were tragic for all the Wallen families. In 2002 my Mom passed away. She was 90 years old. Mom was the most loved person I have ever known. Such a warm person and I doubt she ever said a bad word about anyone. She has been deeply missed. Dad was so torn up over losing her. He became very lonely even with all the kids and grandkids around him. I still remember all the really hard work Mom did for our family when we were young. I think a good bit of my own work ethic came from her. She taught us all a kind and gentle heart.

Dad met Wanda through the Dominic Wallen family in early 2003. They soon became friends and then became infatuated with each other. Wanda had been doing some babysitting for Dominic. She soon became Dad's angel. They were married later that year, and she took care of him until his passing in 2006. We all embraced her and were all very thankful for the way she took such good care of him. Mom and Dad were laid to rest in Tucson and Wanda has moved back to Kentucky. Wanda took Dad's passing really hard and is still missing him.

OUR NEW HOUSE

In 2001 I happened to see a for sale sign on 2 ½ acres of land off Iris Road. I had been looking for a possible place to build a nice house for Mary and me and the kids. That lot had a lot of potential and had a great view of the Rio Grande Valley and the Sandia Mountains. It had just come on the market. I told Mary about it that night and we went out to take a look. The lot had a slope with a drop of maybe 50 foot towards the city lights. The view was great from the lot, and we decided to make an offer. t was accepted, so we had our building lot. I wanted to build something big enough so the kids, who were both now in college, would have a nice place. The house on Twisted Juniper was nice but I wanted something really nice with some land to work with. So, I spent some time just sitting on the lot dreaming up ideas and then started to do the drawing.

The lot had a gully down the center, and I used it to our advantage. We would build a house with the lower level partly in ground. The whole back side would look like a two story and the upper level would be at ground level. Mary and I worked on the plans for several weeks and finally gave them to my drafting department for final drawings. Gary McEldowney helped me stake it out and we were ready to go.

The morning that the excavator folks were starting to dig the hole, Mary and I came out to oversee the project a bit and maybe take a picture or two. When we got to the lot, the guys there told us that a plane had just hit the World Trade Center Towers in New York City. When we got back home, we turned the TV on just in time to see the second plane hit the second tower. It was September 11th, 2001. Our happy day turned to being pretty sad.

The total square footage of the house was to be approximately 5,400 square feet, with a 3-car garage. I did a lot of the work on the house, as time would permit, and we moved in in April of 2002. It has been a great place for us, but has now, in the year 2024, become a bit large for just Mary and me.

Shortly after we were settled in I added a three-car garage down in the corner of the property and then in '04 we added a nice 40 foot indoor swimming pool. I love both of those buildings. The pool has been so good for me, as I get to work out in the water three or four times a week. I also got to teach seven of the grandies how to swim.

MOVING THE BIG COMPANY FORWARD

Bob Hopper stayed on running the framing company for me after Don and Julie left back to Arizona, but my relationship with him never really got back to what it was. We were down to only seven framing crews by the time Don went back and we did pick a few crews back up again, but without me out there drumming up work it just didn't go as well as it had. One of the problems was that builders like Centex didn't want a framing company that was also a builder doing their work.

We were doing well in the building company. I came up with enough building lots and land to develop several subdivisions. We were also buying developed lots from AMREP. It would work out over the coming years so we could be hitting around 200 closings a year. That was a lot of houses for this ole country boy. God is good and I must have had his help to keep that much land out front.

I also took our sales manager and my general manager over to Phoenix a few times to explore new floor plans. We also did the National Home Builders annual convention in Vegas to find new products. We were able to come up with new designs for some really nice model houses. They were selling well for us.

I decided on a plan to make changes to our floor plans if the home buyer had requests for changes. That was something no other builder did. It required a good bit of paperwork, and my field superintendents really had to stay on top of every house and our subs and suppliers had to do a lot of extra estimating. They all worked very well with us. I even set up our own drafting department. We had two guys on staff, and they kept us out of trouble.

STAFF MEETINGS

Once a week we had a staff meeting. It consisted of all the department heads. We all sat at a rather large table, and it would be my time to listen and make decisions, or check out new ideas. I also allowed the staff to override me, at times, if I had said no on some suggestion or idea, depending on what was involved. That allowed every employee to express things without worrying about backlash.

Once a week we also had a sales meeting with all the sales employees and the manager. At that meeting they would all report their sales for the week. It would also give them an opportunity to talk about any ideas that were on their minds. I learned a lot from my staff and always tried to listen as closely as possible.

Once a month we would have a finance meeting. This would tell me how we did for the month, and we could look for problems and give a forecast of the money needs for the next 30 days. We could pretty well forecast how many closings would be ahead for the next month. This really helped me with keeping up and having no shortages. We were making close to $50,000.00 on every closing and our payroll was running close to $200,000.00 every 2 weeks. I never once missed a payday with all the employees. Our debt ceiling stood at 50 million dollars with all the land development and house construction loans. Wallen Builders' income was staggering to me at times, and we paid our guys very well. It really showed in their performance. I always thought that the better you treat a guy, the more he will give back. It works.

CASINO PROMOTION, WOW

One day I received an interesting call from our local ABC television station, Channel 7. The Sandia Indian Pueblo had just completed their new huge casino along I-25. It included a big hotel along with a first-class golf course. The golf course itself was the second best rated in the state. It was beautiful. So, the casino and the TV station wanted to have a meeting with me. It turned out really exciting for us all. The TV station was going to put up a free spot on the news, once a week. They would come out and film me explaining the different phases of construction as a house was being built, from start to finish. I had a 4-minute spot every Thursday on the 6 and 10 o'clock news. Wallen Builders would really be highlighted. I then would have to give the house away, on the 11th week, at the casino, live on TV. Also, during those 10 weeks there would be a televised slot machine tournament. They all had to wear a Wallen Builders t-shirt, and the weekly winner would be in the final contest for the house. The casino would also be putting up over $200,000.00 in cash and gifts, like pool tables, jacuzzi tubs and $25,000.00 checks. I didn't even have to think about it. I said I was in. These folks knew my work and reputation and so I was chosen.

I called in all of my suppliers and subcontractors and asked each for a contribution from their products and labor. Everybody seemed excited about it. I would be naming them all in my broadcast. So, it would be good for them as well. We all knew it would really put our name out there and increase our work load by a good bit.

I built a one-inch scale model of the house we would be building as the giveaway. I built a beautiful stand to set it on and we put it on display in the middle of the casino where everybody could see it. The model looked great! They roped it off for safety reasons and so folks couldn't touch it.

Wow, did we ever have a fun time with the promotion. I explained the whole construction process on the air and was at each of the slot tournaments, which were broadcast live each week. It was a blast, there was just a lot of excitement. At the end of the 10 weeks, we had 10 tournament winners and, on the 11th week, the TV station gave us almost 10 minutes of news time for the final giveaway.

I had a display made with 10 little doors and each door had a separate lock. There were 10 keys. Behind each little door was a card with a prize shown on it. That night, that big casino was totally filled with people and everyone was excited for the winners of 10 large prizes. Chanel 7 had the largest viewing audience that they had ever had and that's what they were after. Their ratings had been low and that is why they wanted to do this promotion. So they came out a winner. The keys were drawn live on TV and the winner of the house was an older lady that had lost her husband but really didn't need the home. I think she gave it to her son.

The casino was very happy with their part of the deal, as they got a lot of people in their doors to see the new place and their business really picked up. Those ten weeks kept them really packed in.

As for Wallen Builders, all the staff were really excited to watch it all happen and our sales probably at least doubled. It really put our new little company on the map. Those 11 weeks of free advertisement were just what we needed. The whole city of Albuquerque was excited about it. It was a little different for me because everywhere I went people would say, "Hey didn't I see you on TV?" That was a little fun for me, but I was very happy for my company and all the people that worked with me. We sure hit a home run with that deal. It paid off for years to come. It turned out to be cheap advertising for Wallen Builders. A lot of folks were really interested in watching the house being built from week to week. We had a lot of visitors at the job site that wanted to see it in person. It sure got our name around and that is what got us to the point that we were building 200 houses a year.

Model at the Casino

GIVING BACK TO RIO RANCHO

As the company was growing, so did our responsibility to Rio Rancho. We did one promotion where we gave $500.00 to the city library for every house sold and closed for that month. I believe it was June. It turned out really well. It was not a sales promotion. It was mainly for the city. I believe we delivered a check for around $9,000.00 to the library that fall. It was to be used for audio books and they were very happy.

A few years later, the city was building a large new library and that got us excited. Rio Rancho was a new city, just a few years old and to be building a new library was pretty special. I got together with my office staff, and we put together a plan to help. After talking it over, we came up with the idea of helping supply books after the building was completed. We decided to build a house in Rio Rancho and get all the subs and suppliers to contribute to our cause of helping the library. It worked out great. By the time that building was complete, we had our house built and sold and all the profit was presented to the library. It was somewhere around $90,000.00 that Wallen Builders and all the subs and suppliers had contributed. We all had a good feeling about what we did, and all the city folks were sure happy toward us and our sub-contractors. I loved helping our community.

I believe it was in 2003 that we got word that the local battered woman shelter (Haven House) in Rio Rancho was in real need for a storage garage. Lots of folks wanted to donate items such as furniture, clothing and household items. They had to turn it all away because there was no place to store it. Christiana, who ran my finance department for me, was sitting on their board of directors at that time. She came to our staff meeting one day and told us of their situation and suggested that we do something to help them. I went out and took a look at it and decided that we sure could help them. So, I started in on the donation thing again. I went right down to the city and got them to give us a free building permit.

We ended up building them a 50 by 24-foot storage garage. Nice cement floor and all. It had a 16-foot garage door. The building came out really nice and we were all very happy to help. I think everything was donated for the project except Wallen Builders had to pay about $5,000.00 and Haven House had a nice $50,000.00 building. We were happy for them.

We were also front and center in the community with things like contributing a good bit at the Mayor's Ball each year. We always bought a full table and bid a lot on the auction items. The money donated at these events was always distributed to charities in town and much appreciated.

There was one other event that we always gave a lot to. It was called "Seats and Eats". It was an event put on through our local Chamber of Commerce. It always turned out to be a really big business community party. There would be maybe 25 wooden chairs that were handed out to some of the artist folks and they would be painted and decorated in all sorts of fashion. Some would be totally ugly and some really cool. The local artists that painted pictures and did other artwork would also donate their work. My daughter Anna did a painting one year, and I believe it was auctioned off for around $600.00 dollars.

Then there would be a silent auction with a load of things donated by the business folks. It would all come together with a big party and the chairs and artwork would be live auctioned away. Mary and I still have about six of those chairs here at home. All of the proceeds would go to the school system for classroom needs.

I would always decide how much we were going to donate, "spend," at the party, usually close to $10,000.00 dollars. We would have a great time bidding with it against other business folks.

There was always a great community spirit in Rio Rancho. The majority of the business owners always seemed to chip in when an event would benefit the city in some way. We all pretty much knew each other and liked working together. One guy that really stood out in those days was Don Chalmers. Don came to Rio Rancho from Oklahoma and started a Ford Sales Company. Within a few years he built it into one of the largest Ford dealerships in the south west. He was an awesome guy to know and be around. He gave a lot to the community, and it got so bad for him with requests for donations that he actually set up a committee with his staff to recommend who to donate to. I really admired Don, and I had the privilege of going to South Dakota on a four day pheasant hunt in the fall of 2006 with him. What a really great time that was. Don was involved with a lot of things in our little town. He was chairman of the Rio Rancho Chamber of Commerce in 2002.

CHAMBER CHAIRMAN

I was on the board of directors for the Chamber of Commerce

a number of years and in 2005 I was elected chairman. That was a very good experience for me. My goal as Chairman was to bring all of the entities of the city together for all of our common goals. Each entity had always gone to the State Legislature for money, each year, and it usually didn't work so well. This included the Fire Department, the Police Department, the School Superintendent, the Mayor, and City Manager. Over months of meetings, we put together a plan for funding requests depending on the real needs of each entity. A package deal was put together to present to the legislature and wow, it worked great! We pretty much got what we wanted. There were no over demands. It worked so well that I think the Chamber is still facilitating the group and our State Reps still love it. I think I had made a difference. Our local Chamber of Commerce was no longer a social club.

It was great being in the Chamber. It gave me a chance to get to know a lot of the business folks here in Rio Rancho. As Chamber members we all tried to use and honor member businesses as much as possible. As I remember buying our paint and all the door hardware locally helped out the Ace's Hardware store.

MOVING TO THE AMREP BUILDING

After several years in that old Armory building, we moved the business, once again, over to the five story AMREP Building. We took up the whole second floor of that building plus a little of the first floor. We were moving and grooving. We spent two years in that building.

THE NEW OFFICE BUILDING

I had purchased two acres of commercial property off of Southern Blvd., on 21st St. That was in 2001. My plans were to build our own office building there. I did the initial floor plan layout, and my drafting department drew the full set. It was 10,300 square feet and I wanted every office to have an outside window. So to do that we had to have a courtyard in the center of the building.

The courtyard was set up with all tropical plants and a nice patio table in the middle. Folks could eat their lunch in there or just go in there to chill out if need be. The plants were great, and I had a little waterfall in there. It was a cool room.

We had a nice kitchen in that building, as well and one large room for a classroom. The whole building was pretty plush and the employees just loved it. There was a large parking lot, and it was tree lined on two sides. It was a beautiful building and I was quite proud of it. I built it with all cash, no mortgage. I planned for it to be part of my retirement income.

Our New Building

BIG DEBT

We had a nice nest egg by the time AMREP shut down their building department and I had been putting aside everything I could into savings for retirement. But that money was quickly used up when we started the big building company. It was scary for Mary and me because it actually was a pretty risky thing to do. If I didn't make the home building part take off and grow, I could have lost everything. Those years from 1998 to 2007 put us in super debt. We wound up with a debt ceiling of 50 million dollars with the banks and we were constantly bumping that ceiling. Yikes! But that meant that we had a healthy business going. None of that debt was from operating expenses. It was all from home construction loans and land development. We had 80 or 90 houses under construction at any one time. And lots of dirt to buy and subdivisions to build. If the bottom had fallen out of the building industry as it did back in the early '80s, I would have probably gone down the tubes again. I do feel that God guided me in a lot of my decisions.

Those years from '98 into '06 went by really fast. It was just a lot of work, and I couldn't believe the money we were making. It was great. I knew I would have a good retirement. I was in my early sixties and felt at some point soon, I would want out. I had given over 40 years to the industry. Some of those years we had built over 200 houses a year. Our profit margins were awesome. The banks were really happy with us. Everything was good as gold. We had land and subdivisions all over Rio Rancho. We even built houses on some of the ½ acre lots with gravel roads on the west outskirts of town. We did very well there. We grew a reputation as the best quality home builder around and the best to work with. I am still proud of it. All of our employees were the folks that made it that way.

THINKING ABOUT SELLING

About the middle of 2005, as I was keeping an eye on developments in the country, I started getting a little uneasy about things. Our sales were still strong and we had a heavy backlog of over a hundred houses to get started. I just had an uneasy feeling. There were too many investors buying up new houses. They would sit on them for six months, or so, and then put them back on the market to sell again. They were making good money doing that as the price of housing was going up so fast.

At this point, I was getting calls from some of the really big builders in the country inquiring as to whether I might be interested in selling Wallen Builders. I talked to a few of them, and one sounded really good. After talking by phone a few times, they flew out here to spend a little time with me. They wanted to really look us over and after I was convinced that they were for real, I let them go over some of our books. Several weeks later they flew out and had an offer ready to buy the company. I was really interested at that point.

The offer was for 13 million. They wanted me to stay on working for the next 3 years. They were going to give me four million cash and the last nine million would be coming to me out of the profits over the next 3 years. I would also have little say as to which subs to use, the type of models we built and sold, and on and on with changes. I would have no control over how the employees would be treated and who would be staying on as employees. I also would have to fly back east once a month for meetings.

I thought it over for several months and I met with them again, but it would just hurt to see what I had built as a company get destroyed. I turned their offer down. It would have been a great safeguard should the bottom fall out again and the industry crash. I just couldn't see the company that I had built over all these years get mauled over by the big boys. We had a lot of really great employees. They would have all been hurt by it.

It was comforting to know that some of the national building companies were looking to expand, but to me, things were going a little too crazy in the country. Buyers could finance 110% of their mortgage for a house in some cases. Tons of investors were buying up anything they could get hold of, then reselling and prices were really going up fast. We had shortages in lumber and other supplies. Then sales started to really slow down. Not many people were concerned about sales because everybody had so many home sales in backlog. I was getting pretty concerned. I was getting too old to ever have to start over again.

A GOOD OFFER

Larry Filner, who had been our CPA ever since our early days shake up with the IRS told me, one day, that he had an old friend that he thought would be interested in buying Wallen Builders. And he might want to partner up with his buddy. That sounded great to me, so we invited the guy out for a visit. Eric Wallace was the guy's name and we had a great visit. Larry already knew what our books would show and knew how well the company was doing. So, Eric was sold on the idea. We just had to work it all out.

They wanted to give me 3 million cash out of the company and that left 5.5 million of my money still in the company of which they would pay me out over the next two years. The office building would stay mine and they would rent it on a five year lease at $15,000.00 thousand a month. Plus $15,000.00 a month on the notes on the money I was leaving in there. It sounded like a good deal to me. Eric also had an investor buddy that would put two million back into the company. This was going into 2007. I was ready to retire.

At that point we had about 180 houses under construction and another 85 under contract to get started. There were also three sub-divisions that they would receive, plus some odd lots around the city. We had a lot of land. I pretty much just wanted all that debt taken off me, someone else to pick it up, and enough money for a great retirement for Mary and I.

So, I kicked it around some and they kicked it around some and we did a contract on it. Wow! If this goes through, I would be retired! I felt a little unsure of leaving that much money in the company, but with the way things had been going, I felt sure that everything would work as planned.

SELLING THE COMPANY

It took the attorneys over a month to get all the closing docks ready and the money in the right places. All the debt that went along with the company, and that included all of the subs and suppliers, had to be transferred to them and all of the Wallen land holdings and model homes had to be transferred. Tons of lawyer work. Citizens

Bank was the only one that refused to transfer their loan from me to the new owners. That worked out great for me though.

So, all the docs were finally ready and the closing date was set. On the 30th day of April 2007, I sold the company and became a retired contractor, with plenty of money to retire on. It had taken a whole day to get all the paperwork signed. We were signing off and they were signing on.

START OF THE CRASH

Then came the bad news. Intel, our really large computer factory, here in Rio Rancho, announced a 1,000-man layoff. I think I went into shock. From that point on, the housing industry went downhill. Wallen Builders had a lot of buyers backing out of contracts, closings slowed way down, and it got to a point where the company couldn't hardly give a house away. The Obama Administration all but shut down the housing industry by a ton of new restrictions on banks. Builders were crashing all over the place. Several of my good friends lost their businesses.

The new owners kept the business going for about 18 months. They kept up their payments to me until the very end. Sales had stopped and they had run out of money to stay afloat. There were houses sitting unfinished and some buyers got hurt. I guess I took the biggest hit as I lost 2 million of post-tax money and 3.5 million in pretax money. That hurt really bad, but I counted my blessings because it could have been me going under. I don't know if I would have made it through or not.

GETTING SOME OF THE MONEY BACK

One good thing was the bank that would not sign the debt on a subdivision over to the buyers came after me and wanted I think, $500,000.00. I paid it off right away and then sold the lots to DR Horton for $900,000.00. So I made out really well on that transaction.

The next year, we took our huge losses to the IRS and got almost a million back as a loss carry back. That helped a lot.

The framing company was winding down before I sold the building company and when we shut it down, I had over $400,000.00 in that company, enough in there to build our new Lake House. That worked out really well for me. I have thought a few times that if Don had taken the framing over, he would have been out of business in '07 as housing came to a halt. That would have been really bad for him and Julie.

BUILDING THE NEW LAKE HOUSE

So, by early '07, the lake house had fallen into very bad shape. That old trailer house was rotting away. The roof leaked all over and the siding was falling off in areas. If we went down there for two days, I would have to work on things at least one of the two days. Not very good. In about 1999, I built a garage for all the water toys. It is 34 by 48 foot and that was nice but the house, yuck.

So, Mary and I took the drawing board down there in early '07 and sat down and we drew plans for a nice six bedroom house. Like at home, it would be half in ground with a lower walk out. It wound up being 4,600 sq. ft. in size and we added a nice sized two car garage on the front. We basically designed it to fit the lot, and it turned out to be one of the nicest places I have ever built.

The Great Room

With all of our selections of colors and material it is just really comfy there. It has two master bedrooms on the main level. It also has a bunk house room downstairs. That room has two sets of bunk beds and a queen size bed in it. That's where the grand kids just love to stay. Like the old place, we have had just a lot of fun at that house. We've had 3 family reunions down there and they have all been a blast.

There are only about 45 houses in our little subdivision at the lake. Only a few houses have permanent residences. In the cooler times of the year there are very few people around. That makes it very quiet in our neighborhood. It now gets a little lonely there sometimes as the kids have grown up and with all the grandkids, they are always so busy that they don't come down much.

Our place sits on a hill about 100 feet above the water and we have a wonderful view. That lake rises and falls between 30 and 50 feet each year and sometimes it gets pretty low but we have gotten used to it.

The damn for that lake was built in 1912, the year my mom was born, and the water has been backed up and used by the farmers downstream ever since. Mainly the chili farmers. When that lake is full and at the spill way, it reaches 44 miles upstream. It was like that in 1997 when we bought our place there.

Now in 2024 we have a nice Chaparral, open bow, 26 foot boat. We have two jet skis and a ½ ton four-wheel drive pickup with about 10,000 miles on it that stays down there. We also have 2 ATV's with very little use on them. Lots of fun stuff. I wish we used it all a lot more.

Aerial View

INVESTING

In 2008, we had a good bit of money in the bank and it was just sitting there, earning a low interest rate. I wanted to put it somewhere it would make decent money for us and we wouldn't have to worry about inflation or problems with the stock market. The housing market, at that time, was at an all-time low and there was a lot of repossession going on. Those houses that were bought for $250,000.00

were now going for $135,000.00 - $150,000.00. It was a perfect time to buy houses and most of them had been completely refurbished.

Julie lived in Gilbert, Arizona and we went over there to investigate. It was great and we decided to buy there. It turned out that we got seven homes and all of them were ready as rentals. We hired a good property manager and were soon in business there.

We did the same thing here in New Mexico. We wound up with eight houses here. Some really good friends of ours are property managers, so we are in business here with rentals as well. The good thing about owning houses is that their value goes up if inflation goes up and they also go up if the market demands it. The ones in Arizona have doubled in value since we bought them. It has not been as good here in Rio Rancho, but they are up maybe 50 - 60 percent here.

SELLING THE OFFICE BUILDING

I put that big, beautiful office building in Rio Rancho up for sale and I got what I wanted for it. I wanted $1,000,000.00 for it. I wanted to carry a land contract note on it for $700,000.00 after a $300,000.00 down payment. There was a $19,000 a year property tax on it and that was a little rough to carry. I had tried to lease it out but that didn't work. So, we sold it. That made me a little sad but it was good for us as it gave us additional income from the note.

In 2020, the guy that bought that building decided to pay it off as he could get a much better interest rate from the bank than what he was paying us. So once again, I wound up with a large sum of cash. At this point the cost of housing was out of sight. There was no way that we could buy houses in Arizona or New Mexico and make a decent rental profit on them.

Chesaning, Michigan, my old hometown, had been in a state of depression for the last 30 or so years. Then in 2017, the marijuana laws were changed in Michigan and soon a large company moved into town and started setting up shop. They bought all of the old large buildings in town, like the old dairy and the Farmer Pete's meat packing plants. These places had been closed up for a lot of years.

Soon they were hiring folks left and right and the town sprang back to life. They were growing marijuana and manufacturing lots of products from it, such as gummy bear marijuana cubes. It was great for the town. The money started pouring in. Roads were being repaired, infrastructure was being updated and stores in the main part of town were opening up again. It was great.

With all of that in mind. We took our money from the office building, added some to it and went house hunting in the Chesaning area. We wound up with seven houses in that area of which 4 of 'em were duplexes.

So, we have invested heavily in real estate for our retirement. It has been really good for us. Everything is under the control of property managers. It is working out nicely for Mary and me. Mary is keeping track of the business end of it here. She doesn't care for it a lot, but she does a wonderful job with it. She says it keeps her mind young and sharp. It is a good bit of work for her.

BACK TO THE PHILIPPINES

Anabelle and Garry

In about December of 2011 I received a sort of a strange message on Facebook Messenger. It was from a gal in the Philippines who wanted to know if I was the Garry Wallen that was stationed at Clark Field in the PI in 1965. I responded that, "Yes, I was." Her name was Doris Olivan and she was relation to Anabelle Olivan. She said that Anabelle was the daughter of Terry. Anabelle, at that time, was afraid to contact me for fear that I would reject her on the spot. So I made contact with Anabelle. Terry had found me on Facebook because of a picture that my son had posted. Terry told Anabelle that I was her father. After thinking out the date of her birth and the time that Terry and I had been on the beach in the Philippines, the numbers matched just right, and I felt that I in fact did have a daughter over there. So, I told Mary about it. Mary sort of got a chuckle out of it and responded with, "I wonder if you have any other kids over there."

At that point I really did need to know for sure and Mary and I made plans to fly over to the Philippine Islands. Anna went with us as she wanted to meet her new sister. The meeting went very well, and we really enjoyed our visit. Anabelle had just wanted to find her daddy and wanted nothing further, only to know. I was pleased and we had a good visit. We flew up to Manila with Anabelle and we went back to the old Clark Air Base, which was, by then, run and maintained by the Filipino's. It was very exciting for me to go back to such a place, from my younger years. We also toured the town of Angeles City where I had spent many days partying. It brought back a lot. I had found my old barracks where I lived there and the old building that housed the hydraulic shop that I worked in so long ago. Anabelle was thrilled as well. Anna and Anabelle hit it off very well. So, on parting we decided to do a DNA test just to make sure, but we felt confident it was real.

We did the DNA test. Anabelle sent hers through the mail and I sent it in. The test came back negative, and we were all shocked. We then found out that you could not trust the PI government to be honest with her side of the test. We then sent Anna over to the PI again to take the DNA sample and bring it back. We sent it in again feeling sure it would come back a plus, but it didn't. Terry still maintained that it was me. Annabelle was very disappointed, but the test results had to be true. We had tested twice. It appeared that Miss Terry had gone out on the town shortly after we got back from the beach. Yikes. We still talk to Anabelle online every so often. She is a wonderful girl.

TOYS

I got into flying radio-controlled airplanes and have enjoyed it a lot. I even bought 2 acres, out of town a little ways, and built a nice 400 foot runway. I deeded it over to our flying club in 2008. That little airport has had a lot of use over the years. I have slowed down some with my flying, but the gang just keeps on going.

In 2017, I bought a 1959 Edsel convertible. It needed a lot of work to get it shaped up, but I had a great time doing it and it is now a great car. It is so much fun driving it.

Then, in 2019, I went looking for a 50's car that I could do a complete restoration on. I found a 1953 Packard that hadn't been run for about the last 30 years or so. It had been sitting in the desert for the last 10 years by this guy's wrecky old trailer house. He sold it to me and that presented me with a ton of work. I put a lot more money into it than what it was worth. I did a 100 percent restoration on the car, and it is absolutely a beautiful car now. I love it. I would never do it again, but I really enjoyed restoring that one.

TO SUM IT ALL UP

Well, to sum it all up a bit: Building the Framing Company and the Wallen Builders Company was really rewarding for me. I helped a lot of folks build their careers and I enjoyed knowing so many people. It was so worthwhile and very rewarding for Mary and me. It has given us a really good retirement and we have taken advantage of it. I think we have been on 19 different Cruise Ships and maybe 35 different Islands in the Caribbean Sea, including South America and Panama. We love cruising. We've done a lot of travel in our retirement, seeing a lot of this country and we have been to the English Isles. As of this writing we are planning on doing a cruise around New Zealand, Tasmania, and Australia. It's a two-week trip. We've done a lot of traveling.

I've done a lot of building and flying radio-controlled airplanes; we built the Lake house and try to get there often; I've rebuilt several cars; I've done a lot of hunting; and Mary and I are doing our best to stay healthy. I really try hard to exercise every day. I love my swimming pool. Mary and I both stay close to God, and we spend as much time as we can with the grandkids. They are so busy now and growing so fast.

MY BOOK, MY LIFE

One of the reasons I wrote this book of my life was to analyze and try to figure out the reasons that my businesses were successful when I was fairly well uneducated.

First, I think you have to listen to what God really has to say to you if you are a God fearin' person. Studying and knowing your business well is a big thing. It is best if you employ folks that know more than you do and listen to them. Another big one is treating all of your employees with respect and making them feel that they are important to you no matter how small their job is. Everyone watches your motives and actions. You give them a feeling of really caring for them and they will give you 110 percent. If they feel that it is their company as well as yours, they will want to make it work.

So, for anyone reading this book I would like to suggest that you try this sometime. When you are talking with someone, try to let them know that you are really listening and trying to understand. It's fun to watch folks' reaction when you show that much caring. That sounds silly, doesn't it? If you are dealing with customers to make your living, treat them with the utmost respect and they will tell the whole world. If you treat them crappy, they will also tell the whole world. Do the math, it works.

Most of what I have written here seems to be on an up note as if all has been great forever. I left out some of the downer things for a reason. Things you maybe don't need to know and things that I maybe don't want to remember. There has been downer times but basically I feel that I have had a "Wonderful Life". Janet and I were just so mismatched, and we were both hurt deeply. We had, and still have, two wonderful children and they were a Godsend to us. Julie has given us two really great granddaughters. We all love them dearly.

Mary and I have had very few bad or rough times. She has been the love of my life and a true partner in all that we have done. We started out as really good friends and we are still really good friends. We have a great love for each other, our kids and our grand kids. Life has been really good since Mary and I met. Almost everything has been truly positive between and for us. We have kept God in our lives.

A big part of my success, I feel, is having a wife that stood behind me in almost all that I did with the business. She helped me in so many ways. Ya just can't beat having a partner in business and in life the way Mary has been for me.

I hope that this book will be around for generations to come. I know how much something like this would mean to me if my grandfather or even older folks had written their life history down.

OUR BIG LOSES

As age takes its toll on friends and family, really sad things can start to happen. The following has been some really hard times in my and Mary's life.

We lost Mary's Dad in 1987 to pulmonary embolism. We were so sad, and it was not expected. Her dad was such a hard-working, wonderful man. He ran that 100-acre dairy farm, and he loved his family dearly. Harold lost his wife Frances in 1960 and was left with the five kids to raise. He did a wonderful job. Harold got remarried in 1963. His new wife, Virginia, was a wonderful addition to the family.

My brother Edward passed away in 1997 from lung cancer. He has been really missed by his kids and all of the family. Eddie was really hard working, and I think he gave all of his kids a good work ethic. Ed and Janet got divorced and it is still strange that they both died within a year of each other.

Then in 2002 We lost my Mom, Pauline. Her passing is still hard on this family. I don't think Mom ever met a person she didn't like, and she had so much love for our whole family. Her passing even after 20 years is hard to take. Mom always had a lot of faith in me. I loved her so dearly.

In 2005 we lost such a very sweet lady when Mary's stepmom passed away. She died of cancer. She was a great and endearing lady. We all loved her dearly. Virginia had a hard act to follow becoming a stepmom. She did a wonderful job raising Mary and her siblings.

Dad lived another 4 years after Mom passed. He passed away in 2006. They were such a wonderful loving couple. I think they did an awesome job in raising all of us kids. They are happily in heaven together. Dad taught me so much and was always there when I needed him. He helped me get started in the building business. He meant so much to the family. I think we all learned a great deal from him.

We lost Sister Elaine in 2012. Everybody really loved Lainer. She had a bit of a rough life but always seemed to be happy. Her passing was especially hard on my brother Richard. They had such a good relationship. Elaine was always very close to God.

Gary McEldowney

In the year 2010, I lost my life long best friend, Gary McEldowney, he and I drew for the Elk hunt in 2010. It was to start the day after Thanksgiving. About the first of October I stopped in at his house for a beer and a visit. He had just gotten two mules and wanted to show them to me. We were gonna take the mules on our upcoming Elk hut. That was gonna be a blast. We had a nice talk about the coming hunt. We had been on lots of hunts together and we were excited for this one. The next Monday Gary wound up in the hospital. When they opened him up they found he was full of cancer. Mac passed away the day after Thanksgiving. That would have been the first day of our Elk hunt that year. It's been 14 years now and I still miss him a lot.

My other lifelong best buddy, from about the 3rd grade, Leon Kulhanek passed away in 2014. Leon and I had a great time all the way through school, especially our teen years. We were almost inseparable in all that we did. We had lots of fun chasing girls and just hanging out together. We spent many times camping together in Colorado, fishing. Then there were those trailer park trips to Florida. We always did so many cool things together. Leon, you left us way too early. We miss you terribly.

I think the biggest shock was when I got a call from my son Jeff. He called to tell me that my son in law, Don, suddenly took a heart attack and passed away. It was the day before Valentines Day in 2013. That was totally a horrible thing for Julie and all the rest of us. There were no words to say except to tell Julie, I love you. Don's poor little daughters were such a mess. Don and his Girls were very close. Julie is still hanging very close to him even after 10 years. I guess I will never forget that day either.

This is the year 2024. I started writing this book about 12 years ago in 2012. I am gonna turn 82 this fall, and I hope I can get maybe another 10 years out of this old body. I need to be here for Mary and all the kids. Mary and I have had such a wonderful life together. She helped me a lot in building the companies and is still there for me. Mary handles all of the business things now. She has been such a great mother to our girls. She is our mainstay. She is the matriarch in this family and will always be very much looked up to. She has been at 100 percent for all of us, forever. Oh, and she has been a lot of fun, and she laughs at my silly jokes!

When my days are done on this earth, I hope to again be with all those folks that have gone before me, and with our mighty God.

I hope this book will make it into the hands of any of the folks that wish to know me better. I feel that I have led a pretty full and good life. Hopefully I have made a difference in this world, even if only a small one. It is amazing how often you can touch other people's lives. Life has been good.

-Garry Wallen

A Little Fun with Garry and Dick Wallen

TO BE AN AMERICAN

I DO NOT CHOOSE TO BE A COMMON MAN. IT IS MY RIGHT TO BE UNCOMMON. I SEEK OPPORTUNITY TO DEVELOP WHATEVER TALENTS GOD GAVE ME--- NOT SECURITY. I DO NOT WISH TO BE A KEPT CITIZEN. HUMBLED AND DULLED BY HAVING THE STATE LOOK AFTER ME. I WANT TO TAKE THE CALCULATED RISK; TO DREAM AND TO BUILD, TO FAIL AND TO SUCCEED. I REFUSE TO BARTER INCENTIVE FOR A DOLE. I PREFER THE CHALLENGES OF LIFE TO THE GUARANTEED EXISTENCE; THE THRILL OF FULFILLMENT TO THE STALE CALM OF UTOPIA. I WILL NOT TRADE FREEDOM FOR BENEFICENCE NOR MY DIGNITY FOR A HANDOUT. I WILL NEVER COWER BEFORE ANY EARTHLY MASTER NOR BEND TO ANY THREAT. IT IS MY HERITAGE TO STAND ERECT, PROUD AND UNAFRAID; TO THINK AND ACT MYSELF, ENJOY THE BENEFIT OF MY CREATIONS AND TO FACE THE WORLD BOLDLY AND SAY--- THIS WITH GODS HELP, I HAVE DONE.

ALL THIS IS WHAT IT MEANS TO BE A TRUE AMERICAN.

-"An American's Creede." By: Dean Alfange C.1950s

Pictures

Bill Wallen Family Photo
Left to Right— Marcy, Art, Grandma Anna, Grandpa Bill, Francis (Curly), George, Agness (Tooty), Edward (Dad)

Grandpa Bill and Grandma Anna with some of the Grandkids

Garry and Janet Korf Wallen with children Julie and Jeff

Julie and Jeff with their Grandma Korf

260

Mom and Dad's 60th Wedding Anniversary
Brothers—Garry , Ed Jr. (L), Richard (R)
Sisters—Mary, Beverly (L), Elaine, Char (R)
Dad and Mom—Edward Sr. and Pauline Wallen

Mom and Dad's 90th Birthdays
Pauline Nietling Wallen and Edward Wallen

2019 Reunion
Wallen Siblings
Left to Right— Beverly, Richard, Garry, Mary, and Char

Visit with Grandparents
Left—Harold and Virginia Grater (Mary's parents) holding Deb
Right—Mom and Dad, Edward and Pauline Wallen holding Anna

We've had a good life and lots of fun together.

Abby, Jane (Janet's Sister), Julie, Grace, Janet

Julie and Jeff with their Mom, Janet

Don Holthusen with His Girls, Abby and Grace

**The Holthusen Family
Don and Julie with Girls, Abby and Grace**

Julie's College Graduation

Still Best Buds.

Julie with Abby and Grace

Don and Julie

Jeff Wallen with Patch

Jeff with Dad Garry

Jeff with Dad Garry, and Grandpa Ed

Garry, Mary, Anna, Deb

Garry and Mary Wallen Family Photo
Garry and Mary with Andrew and Anna Sloan, Gabe and Katie (Left), and Scott and Deborah Brenna, Mary, Alex, Sophia, and Izzy (on Grandma's lap) (Right)

Left to Right—Sophia, Izzy, Alex, and Mary Brenna

Brenna Family— Peter, held by Scott, Alex, Deborah, Mary, Sophia, and Izzy

Andy and Anna with Gabe and Katie

Sloan Family Picture– Left to Right Gabe, Andy, Katie, and Anna

Garry's 80th Birthday Party with the Scott and Deborah Brenna, Julie Holthusen, and Jeff Wallen families.

Julie and Jeff with Dad, Garry

Garry, with Jeff, Julie and Deborah

Garry and Mary Wallen—43 years and counting.

Index

Foreword	1
Introduction	2
Pictures:	
Great Grandparents	5
Mom and Dad	6
The Early Years	**7**
Pictures:	
Baby Garry	8
Toddlers Carol and Garry	9
Siblings (young)	10
Grandpa Bill Wallen	12
The Merle Cook Farm	**17**
Pictures:	
Ed Wallen's Painting of the Farm	18
Cook Farmhouse with the Cooks	18
Wallen Family, Siblings with Mom	21
Starting School	**21**
Holidays	**24**
Picture:	
Ed Wallen and His Three Boys	27
Mealtime	**27**
Farming	**28**
Outdoor Movies	**31**
Pranks	**32**
Making Merle Mad	**33**
Spooky Times	**36**
Bad Dreams	**36**
The Move to the Green House	**37**
Picture:	
The Green House	38
Large Garden	**38**
Nasty Cow	**39**
Our Creek	**40**
The Walnut Tree	**40**

Maple Syrup	41
Art's Firewood	41
Wrecking Jerry's Truck	42
First Job	42
Failing Seventh Grade	43
Odd Jobs	43
First Car	44
Fun with Cousins	45
Picture:	
Curly and Andy	45
First TV and Piano	47
Richard and I and the Explosion	47
Over the Roof	48
Bedroom Moves	49
Sneaky Brother	49
Winter Strawberries	49
Highschool Days	50
Picture:	
Teen Garry	50
Being Afraid of Girls	51
Picture:	
Our Local Movie House	53
Bad Cop	54
In Trouble and Fun	54
Pictures:	
Leon and Dick Gerding	55
The Good Guy Brooks Gerding	56
My Teenage Cars	56
Pictures:	
'56 Ford	58
'57 Chevy	59
DUI	59
Chesaning	60
Animals at the Green House	61

Mom Expecting **64**
    Pictures:
        Garry Holding Char and his '53 Chevy 65
        Family Picture with Char 66
The Trailor Factory and Sign Painting **66**
Teenage Fun **68**
Leon and the Twins **69**
Going Steady **70**
The Air Force Days **72**
    Pictures:
        Airman Garry 72
        Garry in his Air Force Uniform 73
The First 30-Day Leave **74**
Travis Air Force Base **75**
Wedding Bells **77**
    Picture:
        Garry and Janet 78
        Wallen Sibling Wedding Pictures 79-80
Changes at Home **81**
    Picture:
        Gary Mac and Garry, USAF 81
Off to the Philippines **82**
The Pink Elephant Bar **84**
The Dirty Dozen **85**
Trip to the Ocean **87**
Cleaning Base and Back to the States **88**
Time to Get Serious **89**
Lots of Work Ahead **89**
Building Our First House **90**
    Picture:
        House Dye Rd. 94
Moving into Our First Home **94**
Moving Along **96**
Starting Our Little Family **97**

Julies is Here – Yippie 98
    Pictures:
        Julie, Toddler 98
        Julie, Teen 98

Our Second Home 99

Mom and Dad Move to Arizona 99

Mac Scott Court House 100
    Picture:
        Julie on House Steps 100

Fishing Trip to Canada 102

Fun in the Yard 103

Snowmobile Wreck 104

Bad Knee 105

Back to the Buick and Quitting 106

Janet was an Angel 107

Jeff is on the Way 107

Lots of Work After Buick 108

Personal Troubles 109

Jeff is Here 110
    Pictures:
        Jeff, Toddler 110
        Jeff, Teen 111

John Groves and Rentals 112

Marriage Encounter 112

Not Going Too Well 114

Getting Involved with the HBA 114

The PPV 116
    Picture:
        Garry with Kids in the PPV 116

HBA Troubles for Janet 117

Building the Third House 118
    Pictures:
        Westly Dr. House 118
        Jeff and Julie 120

Christmas Time 1976 121
Building My Little Company 121
Helping at the HBA 122
Pregnant Fish 123
Christmas in '77 124
Forced Time Together Was Good 124
Off to Mom and Dad's and the Convention 126
Homeowner Warranty Program 128
Not Looking Good 129
Industry Slow Down 130
The H.O.W. Program 131
Builder of the Year Award 132
A New Model for 1980 133
1981 Vegas Convention 133
Falling in Love 134
We Crashed Sort Of 136
    Picture:
        At the Head Table 137
Parade of Homes Model 137
Moving Out from Home 138
To Sum It All Up 139
Failing Business 140
Protest to Washington 142
Trying to Move Forward 143
Mary's Divorce Final 143
Our Final Parties 143
Rough Times 145
The Right Decision 146
Pregnant 148
Wedding Plans 148
Julie and Jeff 149
Our Wedding 150
    Picture:
    Garry and Mary Wallen 151
    Garry and Mary with Mom and Dad Grater 151

Honey Mooning	152
Honeymoon's Over	159
Back in Flushing	159
A Little House to Move Into	160
Deb Came Early	162
Pictures:	
Deb, Baby	162
Deb, Teen	162
Out of Money	163
Long Hospital Stay	164
Moving West	164
Short Visit to Tucson	167
Our First Trip into the Desert	168
Getting My First Work	169
Picture:	
Loretta Staircase	169
My First Framing Job in NM	171
Visit to Michigan	172
Building the Company	173
Jessie Had to Go	174
Sammy Dog	174
Anna's Arrival	175
Pictures:	
Anna, Baby	175
Anna, Teen	176
Getting a Truck	176
No More Smoking	177
Growing	177
AMREP Framing	178
Spooks at Home	180
Moving Back to Rio Rancho	180
Julie's First Car	181
The Tucson Express	182
Expanding the Company	183
Losing Mary's Dad	185

Camping	186
The Birds	186
Finally Our Own House	188
Picture:	
Before the Remodel	188
The Aniellos	189
A New Plan for Wallen Builders	190
Remodeling and Being Happy	191
AMREP and Big Changes	192
Expanding the Company	192
More House Additions	193
Picture:	
After the Remodel	193
Yard Work and Horseshoes	194
The Upset Doctor and My Foot	196
Moving to a Rented Office	197
Growing Even More	197
Hunting	198
Julie Moving West	206
Pictures:	
Graduation	206
Wedding	207
Jeff Moving West	208
Picture:	
Graduation	208
Taxes and Cruisin'	209
Kids Making It a Go	210
First Spec House in NM	210
No More Pub	211
Moving the Office Again	211
Our Little Church	212
Jeff to Oregon	212
All Hispanic Crews	214
Big, Big Change Ahead	214

The Lake House and Boating **217**
    Picture:
    Lake House 217

Don and the Framing Company **219**

Office Move Again **220**

Ruined Relationship **221**
    Picture:
    Julie's Baby Shower 222

Deb High School to College **222**
    Pictures:
    Graduation 222
    Leon and Diane Kulhanek 223

Anna Highschool to College **223**
    Picture:
    Graduation 223

Grandkids on the Way **224**
    Pictures:
    Deb and Anna Weddings 225
    Grandkids 226-230
        Family Pictures 231

Losing Mom, Dad Remarrying **232**

Our New House **233**
    Pictures:
    New House Under Construction 233
    New House Finished 234

Moving the Big Company Forward **235**

Staff Meetings **235**

Casino Promotion, Wow **236**
    Picture:
    Model at the Casino 238

Giving Back to Rio Rancho **238**

Chamber Chairman **240**

Moving to the AMREP Building **241**

The New Office Building 241
    Pictures:
    The New Office　　242

Big Debt 243
Thinking About Selling 243
A Good Offer 245
Selling the Company 245
Start of the Crash 246
Getting Some Money Back 246
Building the New Lake House 247
    Pictures:
        The Great Room 247
        Aerial View 248

Investing 248
Selling the Office Building 249
Back to the Philippines 250
    Picture:
        Garry and Anabelle... 250

Toys 251
To Sum It All Up 252
My Book, My Life 253
Our Big Losses 254
    Picture:
        Gary Mac 255
        A Little Fun with Garry and Dick Walen 256

To Be an American 257
Pictures 258-274

www.ingramcontent.com/pod-product-compliance
Lightning Source LLC
Chambersburg PA
CBHW041241240426
43668CB00025B/2457